PARENT-CHILD REUNIFICATION

A Guide to Legal and Forensic Strategies

STANLEY S. CLAWAR

ABA
AMERICANBARASSOCIATION
Family Law Section

Cover design by Amanda Fry/ABA Design

All poems authored by Stanley Clawar

Printed in the United States of America.

26 25 5 4 3

Library of Congress Cataloging-in-Publication Data

Names: Clawar, Stanley S., author. | American Bar Association. Section of Family Law, sponsoring body.
Title: Parent-child reunification / Stanley S. Clawar.
Description: Chicago : American Bar Association, 2020. | Includes bibliographical references and index. | Summary: "Parent/Child reunification after divorce or other legal matters"— Provided by publisher.
Identifiers: LCCN 2020007316 (print) | LCCN 2020007317 (ebook) | ISBN 9781641056045 (paperback) | ISBN 9781641056052 (epub)
Subjects: LCSH: Parent and child (Law)—United States. | Children of divorced parents—Legal status, laws, etc.—United States. | Family reunification—Law and legislation—United States. | Family reunification—Psychological aspects—United States. | Forensic child psychology—United States.
Classification: LCC KF547 .C57 2020 (print) | LCC KF547 (ebook) | DDC 346.7301/73—dc23
LC record available at https://lccn.loc.gov/2020007316
LC ebook record available at https://lccn.loc.gov/2020007317

Dedication

To my good but departed friend Lynne Z. Gold-Bikin. Lynne served many functions for the American Bar Association, including chair of Family Law Section, Board of Governors, and more.

Lynne was a mentor to me as a young, beginning, and naïve forensic guy. Her guidance and mentoring helped greatly—especially when cross examination came due. She loved her family, her chosen field, the ABA, her clients, the law, and her many students—judges, lawyers, therapists, and college legal wannabees. Lynne taught for me as a professor in my forensic studies program. Every student loved and respected her—even when she pushed them to the wall to support their opinions. "Case precedent, principle, application, counterargument," she said, tirelessly.

Lynne wanted to see this book and I apologize for its tardiness, but she was always forgiving. Thanks Lynne—you are gone—but never forgotten. Your legacy lives on for all who knew you and your books, articles, appearances, presentations, and trials.

To my wife, Brynne, a true partner in the business of caring and helping families. She is a therapist, writer (coauthor of *Children Held Hostage*—an ABA Family Law Book), artist, colleague, and most of all, my life buddy. Thanks for your support, love, and ideas that made this project stay humane.

To my children, Debra and Deena, who in their adult years, support their father in ways too numerous to mention. Thanks for your love and for living a life that makes a parent proud.

Table of Contents

Chapter 11 Guidelines for Judges (and Masters) 215

Chapter 12 How GALs Can Help in the Reunification Process 235

Appendices are available for download at http://ambar.org/PCR

Diagrams, Charts, Tables, and Lists

Acknowledgments

This volume owes a great debt to David Noah Kraut. David is my forensic analyst, and provided many functions in helping this book come to fruition. To name just a few, he was instrumental in case reviews, data organization, formatting of the text and visuals, and bibliography structuring. David also served as a sounding board on many ideas that needed debate before finding resolution. His sheer patience with me as I drafted and redrafted the book deserves a medal. My thanks to David is beyond words. I salute you.

Acknowledgments

[illegible]

About the Author

Dr. Stanley S. Clawar is professor emeritus at Rosemont College, and previous chair of the clinical sociology/sociological practice, forensic sociology/criminology, and deaf studies programs. He also served as director of graduate studies in forensic sociology. He is presently adjunct professor of social work at Neumann University (where he teaches social mediation and dispute resolution). Dr. Clawar is director of Walden Counseling and Therapy Center in Bryn Mawr, PA. He is a certified clinical sociologist, diplomate in sex therapy, a sex educator, and a family mediator.

Dr. Clawar is the author of dozens of popular and scholarly articles that have appeared in numerous journals. The American Bar Association has published many of his articles over the years. He is also the coauthor of *Children Held Hostage: Identifying Brainwashed Children, Presenting a Case, and Crafting Solutions* (2nd ed.), published by the American Bar Association Family Law Section in 2013.

Dr. Clawar has been the recipient of many awards, including the National Endowment for the Humanities Award for College Teachers. He has served as scholar-in-residence for the United Jewish Appeal. He has appeared regularly on radio and television shows and gives lectures throughout the United States. He gives presentations to local, state, and national bar associations (for their CLEs). He has served as an educational and clinical consultant to hospitals and state agencies as well as to various industries performing leadership and management training. Dr. Clawar has been an evaluator, witness, therapist, mediator, friend of the court, and consultant on approximately 2,500 cases involving domestic relations issues. Children and their families are sent to his clinic from around the country for help.

About the Author

Chapter 1

Reunification: What Is It, What Is It Not, and What Does It Involve?

"What are we trying to do, what are we trying to achieve, what are we trying to prevent?"

– Henry Kissinger[1]

One of the biggest and most salient issues before the family courts and family law specialists (not to mention general practitioners who handle family matters) today is the need to repair damaged relationships that have occurred between a parent and a child. Some of the damage, or what I am calling Broken Bonds, may actually have occurred as a result of a family dissolution/divorce and associated tensions and conflicts. Judges and guardians as well as therapists, attorneys, and parents are often presented with a conundrum. Is it possible to effectively repair a damaged relationship of varying degrees and types in the face of litigation, acrimony, and embitterment? In many cases, serial re-bonding attempts may already have been attempted and failed or only partially succeeded. A relatively new term before the family courts is "Reunification Therapy" or "Reunification Counseling."[2]

A view has developed that children who are distanced from, and maybe even hostile to, a parent are virtually always the result of what is now referred to as Parental Alienation. This is not true, although Parental Alienation may

1. Peggy Noonan, *The Missing Order in American Politics,* WSJ | Opinion (May 9, 2019, 7:14 PM), https://www.wsj.com/articles/the-missing-order-in-american-politics-11557443675.

2. Even though the terms "therapist" and "counselor" are used interchangeably today, historically, a therapeutic process generally meant deeper layers of analysis and treatment. The term "counselor" has been employed to represent briefer forms of intervention with less analytical dimensions. In the rest of the book, we will use the term "Reunification Therapist" to apply to both options.

be a component, or the major component, in many cases of Broken Bonds.[3] In many cases presented for Reunification Therapy, alienation was not originally extant. However, some parental behaviors may devolve into alienating behaviors as conflicts and disagreements between parents increase. This can be as simple as one parent being angry at the other for either real or perceived misgivings and attempting to punish (consciously or otherwise) the other parent by undermining their relationship with the child.

In alienation cases, the parents are usually given one of two labels: Either the "target parent" or the "aligned parent." The target parent is the parent who is being alienated and of whom the child has developed a negative view. The aligned parent is the parent with whom the child has sided with against the target parent. There are exceptions to this pattern. For example, a third party could be the alienator (grandparent, paramour, professional, etc.). In many Reunification Therapy cases, these terms do not always apply because alienation may not be the (exclusive) basis of the parent-child breach. Thus, I would propose giving each parent a new label to better fit their status in these cases. The parent that has Broken Bonds with their child and is seeking to (re)establish the bond, I call the "seeking parent" or the "unbonded parent." The parent with whom the child has stronger bonds, I refer to as the "connected parent" or the "bonded parent."

The frustration levels of judges, parents, and, not to mention, children can be relatively high as various procedures are applied in order to reconnect a parent and child. Attorneys often find themselves in the position of having to agree to Reunification Therapy on behalf of their clients without having clear guidelines in terms of goals, plans, methods, timelines, and defined measurable outcomes. All of these important concerns will be addressed accordingly in later chapters of this book.

What Makes Reunification Different?

Reunification is a special type of intervention that is not, per se, psychotherapy (clinical); it is not family therapy, nor is it any other type of the presently practiced (forensic) therapeutic interventions. This is important to know because many therapists who come from different schools of thought and methodologies are applying their particular brand of therapy to this social and legal dilemma—usually without much success.

3. For a detailed analysis of programming and brainwashing of children, see Stanley S. Clawar & Brynne V. Rivlin, Children Held Hostage: Identifying Brainwashed Children, Presenting a Case, and Crafting Solutions (2d ed.) (2013), published by the ABA Section of Family Law.

Some Therapies (and Counseling) Practiced in the United States

There are hundreds of different social, psychological, and psychiatric therapies presently available in the United States. Following are just a select few:

- Adlerian Therapy
- Affective-Experimental Family Therapy
- Anger Management Therapy
- Animal-Assisted Therapy
- Art Therapy
- Attachment-Based Family Therapy (ABFT)
- Bowenian Family Therapy
- Client-Centered Psychotherapy
- Cognitive Analytic Therapy
- Cognitive Behavioral (Family) Therapy (CBT)
- Compassion Focused Therapy (CFT)
- Conflict Resolution Counseling
- Confrontation Therapy
- Co-parenting Counseling
- Dialectic Behavior Therapy
- Divorce Counseling
- Drug Intervention/ Rehabilitation/Post-Rehabilitation Therapies
- Emotionally Focused Therapy (EFT)
- Existential Therapy
- Family Systems Therapy/ Structured Family Therapy
- Focus Acceptance and Commitment Therapy (FACT)
- Forensic Counseling/ Therapy
- Freudian Psychotherapy
- Functional Analytic Psychotherapy (FAP)
- Gestalt Therapy
- Grief Counseling
- Holistic Therapy
- Imago Therapy
- Insight Therapy
- Intensive Short-Term Dynamic Psychotherapy
- Internal Family Systems Therapy (IFS)
- Marriage and Family Therapy (MFT)
- Mediation Counseling
- Milan Systematic Family Therapy
- Milieu Therapy
- Mindfulness Therapy
- Multimodal Therapy
- Parent Management Training/Coaching
- Pastoral Counseling
- Play Therapy
- Practical Application of Intimate Relationship Skills (PAIRS)
- Rational Emotive Behavior Therapy (REBT)
- Relational-Cultural Therapy
- Relaxation Therapy
- Role Play Counseling
- Sex Therapy/Counseling
- Somatic Therapy
- Strategic Family Therapy
- Stress Reduction Therapy
- Traditional Psychotherapy
- Trauma Therapy
- Twelve-Step Programs
- Values Clarification Therapy
- Wilderness Therapy

Because there are hundreds of therapies being practiced today, it needs to be specifically stated that virtually *none of them are the correct singular tool* for a reunification goal.

Differences between Other Forms of Therapy/ Counseling and Reunification

The question of the differences between Reunification Therapy and other types of therapies arises in about 60 percent of cases. Following is a listing of some differences between Reunification and other forms of therapy/ counseling.

Factor	Other Therapies/Counseling	Reunification Therapy
Length of time	Not usually determinant	Differentiates short and long term, but should be as brief as possible
Referral sources	Varied from self to other professionals/institutions	Often legal related Occasionally self and other professionals/GAL
Focus/goals	Individual and/or family/couple Simple to complex goals	Bonding between parent and child Clear goal: re-bonding
Treatment plan	Interventions matched to presenting problems (Often not done, but should be.)	Interventions matched to parent-child bonding problems Plan must be done (usually progressively)
Confidentiality	Usually exclusively between client/ patient and treating professional	Rarely present Specified at onset Obligations also to the court, GALs, and others
Reporting obligations	Limited, if any, by client/ professional contract	Often directed by the court, mediators, GALs, or others as well as to whom the information is reported
Metrics	Supposed to be present Often not articulated exactly	Should always be identified Short-term and long-term differential
Parties to the therapy	Limited unless otherwise specified Often a closed relationship	Often others Usually identified prior to the initiation of therapy
Legal involvement	None unless progress reports to probation or other agencies are requested/required	Often clear and named

Other professionals involved	None to one or few	Some to many—GALs, therapists, evaluators, etc.
Likelihood of previous interventions	None to one (sometimes more)	Likely none to many
Theories and methods	Based on school of thought/ training (mostly talk therapies; usually no radical interventions)	Evolving field—many nontraditional methods employed Sometimes radical interventions proposed; however, caution must be exercised here
Risk assessment for proposed interventions	Not necessarily done (but should be)	Should be done Helps to create safety/backup plans
Ground rules for participation	May or may not be necessarily stated	Always stated and verify they are understood
Signed releases	Few, if any (except for HIPAA)	A few to many clarifying what, how, and when things will be done
Basis for termination	Self-termination capacity or therapist recommended	Court or therapist determined Possible GAL input when goals are reached

So, What Is Reunification?

Reunification is different from all of the therapies just listed. It is a *goal-oriented process,* (usually) with specifically identified parties. It is often operating within a legal framework and generally driven by a court order for a parent (the seeking parent) and his or her child(ren) to (re)establish their social-emotional bonds. *It is the process, techniques, methods, and theories that are employed to repair, reconnect, rebuild, heal, normalize, and/or stabilize a relationship between a parent and child that has become damaged, distant, absent, and/or alienated.* GALs, attorneys, child advocates, other clinicians, and various family members may be involved in the process. In order to perform this function, it is crucial that the therapist have forensic knowledge and the skill sets articulated in Chapter 8 of this book ("Skill Sets and Qualities to Look for in Selecting Reunification Experts" on page 149).

Finally, we should differentiate bonding and re-bonding. Bonding, or *unification,* is when a parent and child *never bonded* or unified in the first place. Separation at birth or early on in the child's infancy is an example of such a case. Long-term alienation (even during a marriage) is a second example. *Re-bonding,* or *reunification,* is when a relationship between parent and child is damaged and/or severed at some point *after they were originally unified* to some degree and type. *The reunification is bringing parent and child back together* into a more coherent, caring, and functional relationship.

What Does Reunification Involve?

All of the following modalities are employed to facilitate improved communication, feelings, acceptance, shared time, activities, understandings, and, ultimately, a normalization of the parent-child relationship. It is a process to create or recreate family role engagement. It is reestablishing family cultural connections by rebuilding roles (such as fatherhood or motherhood) that have been impaired or even severed. It is based on the premise that these roles, if reestablished, will benefit the child in their present and future developments. The interventions and activities listed here are just a few that can be implemented in different sequences—*all toward the goal of mending damaged parent-child bonds*. Professional discretion is a key element in picking the right modality at the right time. The Reunification Therapist or Counselor can self-correct if one modality is not appropriate at a particular time. Keeping track of exactly which interventions are performed is important. Some will work better toward short-term goals, whereas others can be utilized for longer-term goals. Flexibility of application shows the child that the Reunification Therapist is not "out of tricks" and is not frustrated with them (as some parents and children are adept at developing frustration in the other parent and/or the Reunification Therapist).

Selected Examples of Reunification Activities and Techniques

- Articulation of therapist's roles and goals
  - Court-ordered role
  - Ground rules for all parties
  - "Middle man" role of therapist
  - Differentiation of reunification from more traditional therapies
- Coaching of parties (includes dos and don'ts)
- Teaching parents and children new scripts based on re-affiliation language
  - For old issues
  - For new issues
  - Proper behaviors and language guidelines both in and out of sessions
- Role playing and reverse role playing sessions
- Memory games (to reactivate and/or correct historical recollections/distortions)
- Guided emotional presentations
  - Parent(s)
  - Child

- Challenge session (also called "bubble busting")
  - Oppositional defiant child session (This issue is discussed on page 40.)
- Collaboration meetings (such as with both parents). Use of articulated agenda—with and without child present
- External activities (with and without the therapist present)
  - Shopping
  - Lunch/dinner
  - Park/playground
  - Movie
  - Visits with the extended family
  - Etc.
- Assisted session
  - GAL-assisted session
  - Relative assisted session (grandparents, siblings, etc.)
  - Targeted reintegration with extended family member(s)
  - Sibling(s) included
- Involvement of the other parent (with child)
  - Guided interaction with specific goals
- Resource sharing session
  - Parental knowledge/ideas
  - Common interests or hobbies
  - Educational assistance where indicated
    - Parental or therapeutic assistance
- Education on "what is a healthy social relationship" (See section on parenting on pages 167–168.)
  - For child
  - For parents
- Skype, FaceTime, or other alternative contact methods
  - With therapist
  - Without therapist
  - Coaching on utilization and possible problem scenarios
- Problem-solving session
- Question and answer session
- Project session
- Progress assessment session
  - Update on child's life
  - Update on parent's life
  - Update on relationship
- Story sharing session
  - Similar scenario discussions
  - Recollection comparison session

- Sharing videos/photos
  - Sharing family photos
  - Sharing family videos
  - Watching educational films related to family issues and functioning
- Child empowerment analysis and classification
  - Degree and type of empowerment
  - Which decisions are they (the child) making? (explicit/implicit)
  - Which decisions are parental and co-parental?
  - Which decisions are collaborative (parent and child)?
  - Which decisions are judicial/GAL/therapeutically based?
- Letter-writing session
- Alternative topic(s) session
- Resetting of agenda session with child and parent
- Concerns session
  - Parent(s)
  - Child
  - All together
- Music expression session
- Personal goals of child session
  - Peer relations
  - School
  - Future
  - Etc.
- Hobbies and interests delineation
- Maturity session
  - Defining maturity
  - Matching behaviors to maturity model
- Ventilation session
  - Anger
  - Frustration
  - Positive emotive time
  - When feelings are a positive versus a dysfunctional guide to action
- Understandings
  - Motive explanation session
    - "Why does my father/mother keep doing this to us?"
  - Child protective of a parent who doesn't have broken bonds
  - (Another) distortion clarification session
  - Co-parental common ground session
  - Parent-child common ground session
  - Historical flashbacks/corrections session (also see memory games)

  - o Child's perspectives
    - o Child's (continued) understanding of legalities/reunification therapy, goals, and progress
    - o Child's perspectives, beliefs, and understandings[4]
- Developing continuity plan for future
- Social contract for termination
  - o List for continued functional behaviors
  - o (Possible) checkup session (date, time, and place)
  - o Reporting of progress to appropriate parties

These are only some approaches employed in reunification. Some are quite different from "regular therapy." The choice of topic and sequence is up to the professional in terms of customization (no two cases are exactly the same). Even where there are some similarities to other therapies, the *Reunification Therapist sets and keeps the focus on bonding or re-bonding.*

Agenda for Initial Meeting with Parents[5]

It's important for all Reunification Therapy work to at least have a tentative agenda for each meeting. This flows out of the treatment plan and the social histories of the parent-child relationship. This is generally done with the seeking parent, but both parents can be (and usually are) utilized in gathering information. The initial meeting should include:

- Understandings of the present court order/legal documentation.
- The parent's perspective on the past (parent-child) relationship, quality, and contact.
- How they ended up in the present situation with less and/or damaged contact.
- What professional and nonprofessional attempts have been made prior to the present Reunification Therapy? Past records relevancy and availability?
- Their opinions on what has either helped or hindered their social bonding with the child.
- Their understanding of Reunification Therapy and providing them with the information on how it differs from other therapies.

4. See Appendix A for Child Inventory of Parent's Characteristics (p. 245).
5. A child meeting may also be advisable if it is adapted to their age and cognitive/emotional capacities.

- Listening to any specific concerns or anxieties they may have about the Reunification Therapy and responding to them.
- Any topics or approaches that they (the parents) would say are problematic or "off base" at the beginning.
- Their range of tolerance for different interventions that might be suggested/implemented.
- Any differentiation they have between short-term and long-term goals.
- Explaining their active participation in developing and implementing a (flexible) treatment plan.
- Educating them on the role that metrics has in actually being able to assess progress in specific and more global terms.
- With whom the sessions and progress will be shared.
- The nonconfidentiality feature of Reunification Therapy.
- Other topics as they arise for moving forward.
- Confirming that all professional releases are signed.

When meeting with the already-connected parent, a lot of the agenda items are similar. One difference is that it is important to emphasize the parent's degree of verbal, gestural, and physical cooperation, as this is very important to the potential success, or lack thereof. This professional encounter may be seen as somewhat unusual because the connected or bonded parent often feels (and could have been told) that they are not a key ingredient of the reunification process. In fact, many court orders and attorney agreements do not even include any mention of the connected parent. They may be given directives to "cooperate" with no guidelines as to what this term actually means. *It is the job of the Reunification Therapist to objectify terms like "support," "cooperation," "assistance," and any other synonym that relates to facilitating the process.* When this is presented, parents often say that they did not realize they would have to (or may not want to) be in such a (support) role. Hearing statements like, "I thought it was between Alice and her mother" or "Why am I involved in this when the problem is between my son and his father?"

Also, it is important to let the presently connected parent know that checkups with them by phone, e-mail, text, or in person may also be required and are helpful to the process.

It should be explained that if more time is allocated by the therapist to the parent seeking better bonds, that in and of itself is not evidence of bias, although some parents may (freely) claim this. This issue of "bias" should be explained and understood up front. If the Reunification Therapist is ordered to, asked to, or agrees to work on re-bonding, the therapist is actually, by assignment, perceived as "biased" in a way. The goal (and process) is to rebuild an important social bond. This does not mean that the therapist is obligated to execute on negatives presented by a parent or child ("I don't want to talk to him" or "This will never work"). *The Reunification Expert will listen and utilize all information in a discretionary way to meet a predetermined goal. If that's bias, so be it.* Bias needs to be differentiated from a clear mission.

The connected parent can be trained to keep his or her own log of the child's commentary and behaviors that reflect the metric progress items. Teaching them how to identify specific behaviors ("I'd like to call dad tonight") or the presence of certain feelings ("I liked being with mom this weekend. She didn't ask me any questions about court") can be contributory to the knowledge base of the Reunification Therapist so that he or she can continue with the treatment plan or modify it accordingly.

In general, *both the seeking and the connected parent are going to go through an educative process* in the early contact with the Reunification Therapist. What Reunification Therapy is, how it is different from other therapies, what the specifics of execution are, and how the parents can act cooperatively to ensure its success are all laid out in the early sessions, and continue to be reinforced throughout the process. Rewarding (acknowledging) the parents for their cooperation, observations, and support is also part of the reinforcement that the Reunification Therapist consistently provides. Obviously, there has to be *a corrective process* if a parent missteps. An example of this is a mother who agreed not to discuss any legalities directly with the children that arose while in session with the father (some parents are capable of co-joint sessions and some are not). Upon going home, she violated her agreement and had some in-depth discussions with her children that had socio-legal implications. The Reunification Therapist used this information to help her see the impact of continuing to draw the children into the "ping pong ball" role. She promised a self-correction and admitted that she had "slipped," but just needed to "check something out that came up in the session with the father." Reunification Therapy experts cannot be frustrated by this sometimes *up and down dimension* of rebuilding bonds, as it is very common and requires *patience and consistency.*

Figure 1.1 on page 13 visually represents the various areas in which a parent and child may become unified (linked/connected) for the first time or reunified (re-bonded/reconnected) after a gap occurred in time and meaningful contact. Reunification can take place on many social-psychological levels; from the individual level with himself/herself (micro) all the way to the societal levels (macro).

Disadvantages of the Nonbonded Parent

- Often out of marital or couple's home
- Lost time—wants more
- Lost authority
- Sees children only at selected (limited) times

- Comes to be viewed as an "outsider"
- Anger and resentment build up
- Custodial parent has undue or high levels of influence
- Viewed as antagonist due to court action and demands for more time
- Asking or begging for contact results in a perception of weakness
- Often afraid to behave like a real parent
- Other parent can generate past stories (real and otherwise) to use as ammunition for continued distance

Common Areas of Parent-Child Conflict[6]

Following are some of the common topics that arise in parent-child conflicts:

- Peer selection
- School performance (including homework)
- Dress and body adornment
- College selection
- Travel
- Sexual activity
- Drug use/abuse
- Cyber use/abuse
- Romantic relationships
- Family involvement/disengagement (including extended family)
- Sibling conflicts
- Sleep/activity schedule
- Planning
- Language use
- Spending/economics
- Loyalty
- Affection or lack thereof
- Helping the family
- Behaving responsibly
- Curfew
- Diet
- Physical activity levels
- Control themes
- Love credibility
- Legal conflicts
- Financial matters

6. These are often the themes where the seeking parent has lost impact and connections.

- Contact frequency and types
- Religious differences

These and other topics may have legitimacy or are part of the conflict patterns that are not well grounded in social reality. The latter occurs when a child asserts "You've never loved me," and the history is replete with social data to confirm the opposite.

Figure 1.1 shows the levels in which reunification can occur. Reunification is therefore a multilevel process from an individual child (Level I) coming to grips with false or inaccurate beliefs (my mother abandoned the family) all the way up to integrating more effectively with society (Level VI). A successful bonding experience not only (re)connects a child with a parent (Level III) but may also bring divisive parents together (Level II) over common goals for their child. Healing a breach with a parent frequently improves sibling relations (Level IV).

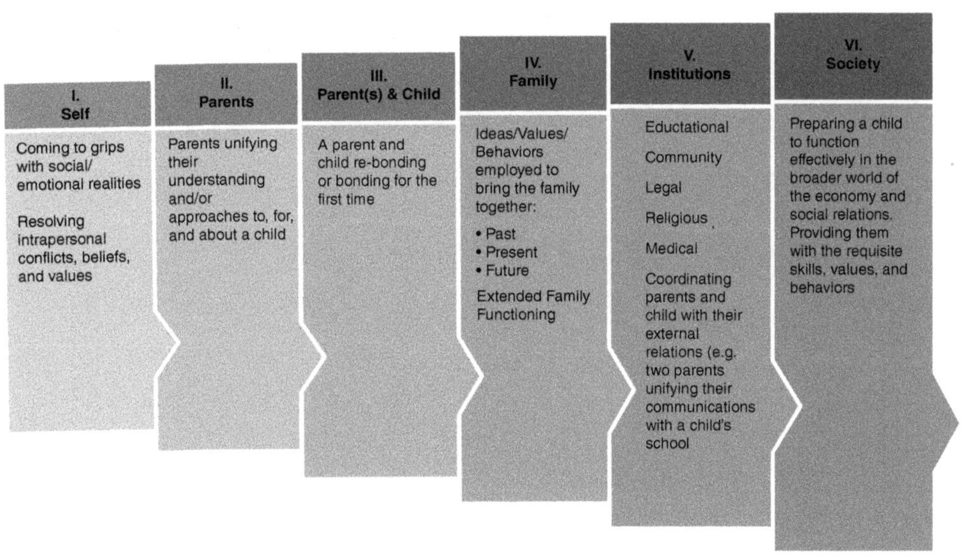

Figure 1.1 Levels on Which Unification and Reunification Can Occur[7]

Finally, re-bonding usually spins off into stronger connections to the institutions (educational, religious, etc.) in which the child is already functioning or will be soon.

7. Re-bonding impacts on all six levels of individual, family, and community functions.

Chapter 2

Sources of Referral for Reunification Endeavors

"Knowing where you came from can help you know where you are going."

– Stanley S. Clawar

There are many different sources from which reunification requests, agreements, or orders can emanate. Each source may have its own concerns, goals, and motives for recommending this professional process. Following are some of the more common sources and how they might impact on undertaking reunification and even on the potential outcomes.

Judges (A Court Order)

The most common source is an order from a judge or court mediator/conciliator who directs certain parties into a reunification process. The role of the judge in terms of articulating an exact order is one of the most important considerations for a Reunification Therapist. For a full discussion of the guidelines for judges, see Chapter 12, "The Resistance Factor and the Legal System," in *Children Held Hostage: Identifying Brainwashed Children, Presenting a Case, and Crafting Solutions*, an ABA Family Law Section publication.[1] In summary form, there are a number of elements that help a reunification expert be successful in terms of the judicial guidelines and backup to the re-bonding efforts. It helps if judges:

- Issue a timely ruling (and not let a case drag on)
- Set time limits on the process and identifying the expected outcome; keeping the focus on the issue of rebuilding the relationship rather than just "therapy"

1. Stanley S. Clawar & Brynne V. Rivlin, Children Held Hostage: Identifying Brainwashed Children, Presenting a Case, and Crafting Solutions (2d ed. 2013).

- Explain the order not only to the parents but also to the children
- Create a follow-up schedule to measure compliance of the parties and the professional
- Articulate the exact judicial expectations (such as "The father will have private overnight time with his children every Wednesday evening from 4 p.m. until school starts on Thursday at 7:30 a.m.")
- Set clear legal protection for the professionals involved
- Explain to the parents conditions that constitute noncompliance
- Develop and present a list of penalties for noncompliance
- Identify and reprimand surrogate parties who are possibly interfering with a parent-child relationship (such as stepparents or paramours)
- Avoid the use of general terms like "therapy" and "counseling" (but say exactly what is to happen in the professional setting)
- Appoint skilled forensic counselors/therapists who understand the relationship between legalities and various therapies
- Appoint a monitor to oversee the case (such as a GAL) and refine reports to the court on a specific time frame

When and how the judge wishes to be informed is important, too. If a trained forensic therapist is not available, the judge can order "oversight" training and guidance for a local therapist by an outside expert. Skype and Facetime can be used by experts not in the locale to help the local professional.

For more on the judicial side, see Chapter 11, "Guidelines for Judges (and Masters)," starting on page 215.

Attorneys

In an attempt to comply with an order, help a client, settle a case, or simply activate an ethical concern, it is common for an attorney to make a recommendation for reunification. Attorneys also have to manage some difficult clients who may not have made favorable appearances in court in regards to their claims for legal and/or physical custody.[2] Attorneys have many questions (and should) on the therapist's experience, training, reputation, ethics, methods and processes, reporting obligations, timelines, and other socio-legal considerations. Forensic therapists are used to this kind of questioning and many make it clear to their clients/patients that they will share various

2. For more information on the "difficult client," see the article "You and Your Client" by Stanley S. Clawar. S. S. Clawar, You & Your Clients: A Guide to Client Management Skills for a More Successful Practice (2d ed. 1996).

information with the attorneys—not only in the beginning but throughout the process. Reunification Therapists who are experienced also know that interfacing with attorneys, if done correctly, can actually facilitate the ultimate goals of re-bonding between a parent and child. *Keeping attorneys in the dark will usually exacerbate already existing problems.*

Again, attorneys can be very instrumental in helping the process as they may be one of the few people their clients trust.

Chapter 10, "Guidelines for Attorneys," starting on page 203, goes into more detail about attorneys and the reunification process.

GAL

Guardian ad litem (GAL) professionals are increasingly being appointed/recommended to serve various functions. They can *oversee* a judge's order to make sure it is properly executed. They can serve as *translator* among the various parties (parents, children, professionals, and the courts). They can *advocate*, when necessary, on behalf of the child(ren). It is important to identify upfront their specific functions so there is no confusion on the part of all the various parties involved in the reunification effort. It is also important to know the history of the GAL, as some have served purely as child advocates, whereas others have served as liaisons in the re-bonding process. It is crucial for all parties to know that the *GAL has the ear of the court* at any time that is necessary.

For more details on a GAL's duties and obligations, see Chapter 12 in this book entitled "How GALs Can Help in the Reunification Process," on page 235.

Mediators/Conciliators/Co-parenting Officials/ Masters[3]

Many mediators will refer their cases to Reunification Therapists. Some mediators and associated professionals that operate within the court system may have judicial or quasi-judicial authority. Others have only the power of recommendation. Some mediators will use reunification in conjunction with their own efforts to help parents settle differences, whereas others refer the case out when they feel that mediation has run its course. In some states,

3. For additional information on masters, see Chapter 11, "Guidelines for Judges (and Masters)."

mediators have the power to demand additional (mediation) sessions and serious efforts on the part of the parents; in other states or locales, they may only exercise their influence to meet a few times, and if they are not successful, that ends the mediation.

Mediators can have useful information on parental agreements, impasses, and styles of communication. Some have also seen the children and can provide important information to the Reunification Therapist.

Arbitrators

Some family law cases end up in arbitration whereby a professional has the authority to make decisions in certain areas of family life. They may not have the power to change a custody order, but they could have the power to make a change in school, the nature of parental communication, or the selection of particular medical personnel. Some arbitrators have the right to report their findings (especially in regard to parental cooperation) back to the court, either directly or indirectly through GALs or attorneys. They work hard to get the parents into an agreement mode, but, if that doesn't happen, they can issue a binding decision. In a recent case, two parents fought for four months over a doctor. Finally the arbitrator (who was also mediating) said, "We're done with this. You'll use Dr. Sidney."

Voluntary Selection (Self-Referral)

Some parents have voluntarily sought Reunification Therapy in an attempt to improve a child's relationship with one or both parents. This particular type of self-referral often has the highest rates of success, because both parents are usually committed (to varying degrees) to the rebuilding of relationships. Some parents will turn toward Reunification Therapy after having been through extensive mediation, arbitration, litigation, and/or private attempts to settle things. For some, "it's a court of last resort." This could put (extensive) pressure on the reunification professional. I have heard many times, "You're our last hope." This is not something professionals like to hear, but certainly they have to respond to it in a realistic and ethical fashion. Children surrounded by two parents on the same page (on key issues) often accommodate faster to recommendations and positive changes. However, even parents who agree on Reunification Therapy may have differences to be considered. Sometimes, the child is the outlier in the case, not the parent(s).

Agencies

Some social agencies may seek the services of a Reunification Therapist in order to build bridges between a child and a parent who may have been separated for longer or shorter periods of time. Agency work often involves work related to the health, security, and safety of the child. So, they may be seeking more targeted information as their role is often one of oversight and safety/wellbeing foci.[4] These professionals may have charge of a child who has been removed from an environment where there has been abuse, criminality, drug involvement, abandonment, unhealthy living conditions, or a combination of these. They may seek an opinion from a Reunification Therapist on the viability of reunification. This can be to assess the possibility of its undertaking, the conditions of contact, and a focused risk assessment. In a recent case, it was clear the children needed significant healing time from abuse that transpired in the maternal environment. The children needed no contact until, and if, all treating professionals thought the children's personal and mental health risks were manageable or nonexistent. This proved to take longer than expected, because once the children entered into in-depth treatment, even more problematic histories came to light (as they often do).

Professional Referral

Therapists of various types are sources of referral for Reunification Therapy. This can occur without actual contact with the legal system. Some notice that a child is disconnected from a parent for various reasons but do not think that they have the level and type of expertise to effectuate reconciliation. At times, a child will already be in therapy for other reasons and a Reunification Therapist is directed to perform reunification for their patient. This usually necessitates mutual access and sharing of case-related information. This enables each of them to accomplish their independent but interrelated goals. Of course, in all of these cases of professional interface, appropriate releases need to be activated. Different states have different requirements regarding the age at which children can or must give specific permission to professionals who wish to share their case information.

4. Safety issues are usually the primary concern of social agencies. For more on this, see the Ohio CPS Manual on Reunification Assessment (n.d.). Retrieved from http://emanuals.jfs.ohio.gov/FamChild/CPSWM/Policy/Reunification-Assessment.stm.

Additionally, other professionals, such as teachers, principals, coaches, and medical doctors, can serve as referral bases. It should be clarified as to whether these sources request or require progress assessments. For example, school counselors often form relationships with children whereby they discover that part of a child's problem may be a breach that they have with a sibling, a grandparent, or a parent.

Various sources of referral will likely increase as more of the public and professionals alike come to understand that reunification is a separate field in social and mental health services.

Finally, pastors, priests, ministers, imams, and rabbis not infrequently discover that there has been a loss of a meaningful relationship, even in the adult years. One case comes to mind of two sisters who were in their seventies and had lost their sibling relationship. Once their mother had died (who was instrumental in keeping them separated), they were interested in reconnecting but didn't know how. This is a good case to make the point that reunification can occur across ages and circumstances.

Child Referral

This is a special condition type of referral. It happens on occasion—a child requests "deunification," possibly from both parents. I've encountered children who, in the course of Reunification Therapy or other forensic services, have requested help in *"getting out of the middle of two fighting parents."* Some have asked for help in living with a grandparent or family whom they selected as a surrogate type family. One 12-year-old girl said, "It's nice to be in a home where people are nice to each other." A 15-year-old boy said, "I'm just trying to grow up and they won't let me." An eight-year-old boy (quite mature for his age) and I had a conversation about his parents' fighting:

Therapist: Tell me how you'd make your family better.
Boy: Stop the fighting.
Therapist: How often do they fight?
Boy: Everyday . . .
Therapist: What do you do when your parents fight?
Boy: Try to get them to stop. Sometimes I have to take one of them in another room and tell them to calm down. I can't stand it anymore. Sometimes I think what it would be like with no parent fighting. Oh well, I guess that's not going to happen. Maybe I could live with Grandmom for a while.

Who Wants What?

Who sent the case in?
It could create a push for a different spin;

The judge who has to focus on the law
But that's really not all;

The Guardian who has a goal
That the child's experience results in a minimal toll;

And then there is the lawyer who represents
A client who may not always be content;

Of course, there is always the clinician
Who wants to know how it's finishin';

The parent who wants success post haste
Puts pressure on time not to waste;

So many masters to serve
Make it hard not to issue a curve;

There could even be a parent who'd like to see it fail
Having even been warned by the court they could see some jail;

Meeting all their needs
Ain't an easy task, which all will concede.

Summary of Referral Sources

All sources of referral contain crucial information about the type of chasm that has occurred, how long it has been in existence, past efforts to build bridges, and other information that can be useful in the efforts to relink parents and children. Reunification Therapists will always seek as much background history as they can get, even though the specific sessions they hold are not necessarily focused on history as much as regular therapies or counseling efforts may be. There is a saying that *"the only new things are histories not known."* Although this doesn't apply completely to Reunification Therapy, it is very important to gather social, medical, educational, therapeutic, familial, legal, and other histories. A recent case exemplifies this important rule: a therapist embarked on extensive and immediate contact sessions between a father and his son. She did not know that the child was previously diagnosed with severe ADHD. In general, the child had trouble with focus and concentration, which led the therapist to interpret the child's behavior as one of resistance and hostility. She also targeted the father as "insensitive." He got this label because he was actually taught to repeat things due to his son's memory retention problems. Neither interpretation would likely have been made had the therapist gathered the relevant social-emotional and educational histories.

Also, different sources of referral have different expectations once they issue the referral. Some sources may have no need for further information or contact (such as another professional who has finished their services). However, other sources, such as judges and social agencies, may have a high *NTK* (*Need to Know*). Because traditional confidentiality does not (usually) apply to this type of forensic therapy, the therapist must still be very clear about what information gets shared back to the source(s) of the referral. As part of the introductory session with parties, Reunification Therapists should make this clear.

Honoring the needs and desires of different sources of referral is one of the complexities of forensic practice in the area of Reunification Therapy. Of course, Forensic Therapists may be serving many masters. This means that even though a referral comes from one source, information may need to flow to multiple sources. So, a judge may write a court order but also appoint a GAL who, in turn, may end up recommending a private therapist for a particular child or parent. In this sense, it increases the informational flow obligations geometrically. What, when, and how this communication process happens is important to be shared with all of the relevant parties. These demands can take significant extra time away from the core practice of meeting with the people in order to solve their immediate social problems between parent and child. Professionals need to make sure they apprise all parties if there are additional professional fees in servicing these varied constituencies and communication obligations. (This should be part of and made clear in the fee contract issued prior to initiating any services.)

It would help particular cases if each source of referral would supply as much relevant information as possible rather than the therapist getting into accidental discoveries of really important data during the course of rebuilding the relationship(s). So, if five counselors have failed before or had partial success, it would be good to know that (and why they failed or partially succeeded). If a child has threatened suicide, it would be important to know that and have that information confirmed by a psychiatrist. If a parent has been cited for contempt three times for noncompliance, it would be good to know that. All major and other minor case specifics can be utilized to guide the method, content, and speed of a reunification process. From the therapist's point of view, it's helpful to know that one of the parents has sued two of the last three therapists.

This work can be so highly charged. The usual scenario is that one of the parents is supportive and the other may not be, therefore having all of the relevant information is not only helpful but likely mandatory. Lawsuits against professionals and character assassinations have become so common that many forensic therapists have simply opted out of the field. This is why, elsewhere in this book, we have noted the *importance of protecting the reunification professional by the court* and even by other means (including special releases that professionals require the clients to sign). More reunification experts are refusing cases if they do not have court-ordered protections and/or their own indemnifications.

Chapter 3

Causal Considerations—Broken Bonds—How Did It Happen

"If it looks like a duck, walks like a duck, and quacks like a duck, it could be a hippopotamus."

– Stanley S. Clawar

The cause or explanation du jour for parent-child separation/breaches has become toxic parenting—also known as alienation, programming and brainwashing, learned hatred, or estrangement. It took many years for parental alienation to be accepted as a legitimate topic of discussion and decision by the courts. Now that it is here, it has entered into an "overkill zone." If in doubt, bring up alienation. However, it is not always alienation.

Surprisingly, there are approximately 26 other causes for broken bonds—either in addition or in exclusion to alienation. The following list itemizes these causal factors. Let's examine each of them briefly as they have relevance for reunification efforts and its possible success.

Selected Causes for Parent-Child Separation

- Foster care
- Parent-child enmeshment
- Relocation of one parent
- Personality/social style conflicts
- Military service situation
- Voluntary parental abandonment
- Adoption
- Professionally caused separation (case mismanagement problems)
- Parental rejection

- Loss of contact at birth
- Court-ordered PFA
- Misunderstandings
- Kidnapping (physical/ mental/social)
- Religious, racial, ethnic, and gender conflicts
- Adult incarceration
- Parental discipline
- Juvenile detention
- Child abuse
- One parent living with an unacceptable partner
- Child experiencing abuse/ aggression against their other (favored) parent
- Oppositional defiant behavior by a child/the hard to manage child
- Substance use and abuse
- Child runaways
- New adults in the child's life
- Munchausen by proxy (factitious disorder imposed on another)
- Immigrant children separated from parents

Understanding the causes of broken bonds can be very helpful, as it can be determinative for designing intervention treatment plans and improvements in parent-child relationships.

Foster Care

Many children lose contact with their parent or parents because they are or were placed into the foster care system. Some of the breaches that occur between a child and their birth parent are due to a (legal) decision that has identified their (birth) parent(s) as dysfunctional, enabling truancy, abusive, incapable of providing an acceptable environment, incapable of effective care, or other (more benign) reasons that limit the care by the (birth) parent(s). Some of these children may eventually reconnect with their (birth) parent(s) and some never do. Parents who are incarcerated may also leave their children in this absent parent social situation (see Adult Incarceration section later in the chapter).

Relocation of One Parent

Some parents exit a particular geographic area with the child left behind. This can be due to remarriage, employment demands and opportunities, or simply abandonment. Another scenario is where one parent relocates and takes the child with them. This may be a legally supported move permitted by the courts or it may be one of various forms of "kidnapping."[1] Also see Figure 3.1 on Kidnapping on page 37. Whatever the basis for relocation, the child may lose connectivity to one parent and their associated extended family. Some children have a relationship with the vacating parent and some have minimal to no contact with the parent who has left the area (of the child's main residence, school, peers, and neighborhood).

Military Service Situation

Some military service involves (extended) stays in foreign ports, which creates another basis for parent-child separation. There may be extended periods of time where a child is in absence of one their parents, or possibly both if both of them are in active service. If there is not a divorce during military service, these children may reconnect (relatively easily) with the absent parent, but will still have experienced significant loss of time, involvement, and relational fit. This scenario can be compounded if a divorce occurs while one of the parents is away and the parent remaining behind decides to also relocate. These veterans can return home to no spouse, no family, no home, and no child. They will need as much assistance as the child, or more, if they also have physical war injuries and/or PTSD-related problems. This is a multiple change experience for the child (and parents) and requires significant adjustment capacities and possible assistance.

Adoption

This is a very common social situation. Some children never see their birth parents, but the newer trend is to allow them to know and possibly develop a relationship with their birth parent(s) as well as their adoptive parents. Reunification skills may be applicable and helpful here. Scripting skills are useful in these cases for the birth parents as well as the adoptive parents. Also, preparation of the child is often done prior to actual birth parent contact. Some parents who have had complete or long periods of disengagement could benefit from role modeling by the reunification expert on parenting skills. These can be articulated as part of the treatment plan. They can include listening skills, accepting and channeling criticism, support for the

1. For more on kidnapping, see Stanley S. Clawar *Predicting the Abduction of Children: The Flight Risk Factors and What Can Be Done*, 26(4) Family Advocate (Spring 2004).

child's accomplishments and goals, ways to demonstrate effective caring, and learning about degrees and types of (re)immersion.

Parental Rejection

At times, parents reject contact with their own children for a myriad of reasons, including but not limited to:

- Their personalities and social styles clash.
- The child has done (either legal or non-legal related) hurtful things to the parent.
- A child has testified in court against that parent or a child sides in other ways with one parent in a custody conflict.
- A parent has gone off into a new relationship and wants no (familial) historical "baggage." This is one of the more socially and emotionally laden reconciliation scenarios. The personal childhood experience of rejection usually results in feelings of anger, sadness, hostility, and/or defensiveness on the child's part. These feelings must be navigated in the process of the re-bonding activities.
- The child has had (serial) addiction experiences (and/or problematic behaviors) and becomes unmanageable.

Court-Ordered Protection from Abuse (PFA)

Courts can and do order short-term and long-term breaks in the parent-child relationship for different reasons. This could be because claims of abuse are being investigated, as well as the fact that there has already been an adjudication of a dangerous or problematic parent. Some of these PFA's can last up to three years, and although they are structured to protect children, they also have a secondary or latent fallout (impact) of reinforcing or creating the physical and social-emotional gap between the parent and child. For some children, this brings about peace, safety, and comfort, but many still maintain a curiosity and need to reconnect with that (historically abusive) parent or a parent who permitted abuse in their living environment. Developing a careful parenting plan and/or other guidelines for reunification can and should be done, especially in these types of cases. An example of case conclusions, recommendations, observations, and planning follows.

Conclusions, Recommendations, Observations, and Parental Planning for Reunification

The family has been in disarray for years. The healing process is long and slow. Following are some general and specific conclusions, recommendations, and observations:

1. The children were all negatively impacted by some of the historical experiences they encountered under their mother's care.
2. Tammy remains the most severely impacted and is still under psychiatric treatment.
3. The father has tried, and succeeded in, creating a safe haven for the children.
4. The pending criminal litigation of the mother's brother hangs over all parties in negative ways.
5. The mother has made major progress in relooking at the children's traumatic experiences, reflecting on her role in regard to the home situation, and developing new found behaviors under professional guidance.
6. Regardless of their diverging vantage points, both mother and father had an excellent joint session that attempted to deal with some sensitive issues, with regard to the children's futures. This resulted in a separate, but highly detailed agreement.
7. The mother's offer to help the children with high school tuition related to monies, transportation, auto insurance, etc., is gracious.
8. The father needs to stop second guessing the mother's overtures.
9. The two children (Adam and Edward) have a strong and positive desire to continue the healing process with their mother.
10. Living with the mother on a more full-time basis will further assist them (Adam and Edward) in the healing process.
11. The conditions for living with the mother have been discussed and they include, but are not limited to:
    a. School selection
    b. Extracurricular activities
    c. Guidance for homework
    d. Regular contact with their father and siblings
    e. Job search and employment opportunities
    f. Summer activities
    g. Household chores
    h. Driving with strict conditions
    i. Selected child supervision

12. The mother is willing to discuss these aforementioned items (a through i) with the father.
13. The father should now reduce his rescue role, which was necessary in the past.
14. The other children (James, Joel, Ellen, and Tammy) need to have a further period of healing (under the father's guidance and with professional care). The mother can be brought in at an appropriate date (with professional discretion).
15. The children's key issues from (objective) professionals are concerns for their health, safety, and welfare due to the past negative experiences at their mother's. The treating professionals are clear on their opinion of the damage done to the children under the mother's care.
16. The mother accepts some of the children's accusations of what happened within her home.
17. The stepmother has been a positive/helpful force and should continue to use her influence to bridge family relationships (both internal and external to her household).
18. The future offers of financial help from the mother need to be set in a practical reality context—what she can do may vary over time.
19. The mother and father should consider continued social communication counseling/mediation.
20. Adam and Edward, if they do reside with their mother, should continue communication sessions with their father. The father needs to foster a better understanding of the many benefits of supporting the children's (Adam and Edward) desire to live with their mother; the boys are clear.
21. The father should understand that by resenting Adam and Edward for their desired residential change is only holding off the inevitable. He should strongly consider the resentment factor that would be present for the coming year if they continue residence with him.
22. The children should continue and/or begin in therapy with clear treatment plans including, but not limited to:
    a. Eliminating parentified behaviors where some of the siblings moved into parent-like roles with the others.
    b. Moving on—concentration on appropriate phase of life activities/normalizing their lives and expectations.
    c. Acknowledging their growth.
    d. Treatment for PTSD and possibly other diagnosis, as needed. This has previously been identified by professionals.
    e. Checking for any possible guilt factors.
    f. Continuing to help with suicidal ideation (where present) and other mental health issues.

g. Identifying any positive historical contributions of their mother prior to her brother's negative and possibly criminal behaviors.
h. Letting go of past negative feelings.
i. Strengthening sibling bonds.
j. Disengaging from mother/father legal issues.

23. Helping the father with new scripts as the children bring up contemporary and historical issues.
24. Creating a "Readiness Plan" for the mother to see the children in the future. The mother should consider obtaining forensic clinical guidance on the following issues:[2]
    a. Working on reasons why she may not have acknowledged her own limited culpability. Following are some possible reasons presented by the children and professionals:
        i. Denial
        ii. Need for control
        iii. Distorted reality—believes in her excellent parenting to the exclusion of any problems within her home
        iv. Other blaming
        v. Status reassertions ("I'm the Mother.")
        vi. Her need to "correct the record"
        vii. Damage to the other parent's image
        viii. Her "truth," that she was the best parent
        ix. Winning versus what is best for the children
        x. Exoneration from accusations
    b. Understanding the present social realities of the children and what they need at this point in their lives.
    c. Developing a dialogue that is non-accusatory with the children (for both parents). Mother has made good progress here.
    d. Understanding what the children mean by "a safe zone."
    e. How to reassure the children that her presence in different settings will not be disruptive.
    f. How to have "phase-in" communications that are progressively more direct. Initially using a professional setting, technology, and, then possibly more direct contact.
    g. Other suggestions for enhancing relational comfort proposed within the context of this report.
25. Due to reports by the children concerning violence in various forms, it is important that the children feel that any future contact is truly "in a safe zone." This fear has reduced over time and is not likely to be an issue as in the past, except for, possibly Tammy.

---

2. This aforementioned "Readiness Plan" will limit social/behavioral changes for her if they are absent.

26. Careful consideration should be given to the impacts of having the children go to court again. Any more involvement will likely have negative consequences. Although, Tammy would like to testify at the mother's brother's criminal trial.
27. As noted in the children's section, any premature re-engagement between Tammy and her mother runs the risk of regression in the personal, social, psychiatric, educational, and peer dimensions of her life. A re-contact plan should include multiple phases—with the first phase being a reassessment phase. This reassessment phase would need to be activated once item number 24 in this section is considered and executed. The key element of a reassessment phase for the re-bonding of the mother and Tammy is the daughter's health, safety, and welfare. In other words, a calculated risk assessment is to be the key part of the phase. The mother has appropriately acknowledged Tammy's needs and is willing to be fully cooperative.
28. Working out a "phase-in plan" for the four siblings (James, Joel, Ellen, and Tammy) and the mother is in their best interest. The exact time frame can be based on professional input and other mental health (social) indices of "readiness." (The mother's progress to date actually accelerates these aspects of a phase in.) The 13 aspects of this plan are noted here.
    a. Explaining the ground rules for the contact sessions between children and mother
    b. Deciding on the selection of individual versus small group sessions and explaining the rationale to the relevant parties
    c. Limiting the content of the first meeting to topics that are more likely to be successful (e.g., children's performance in school)
    d. Preparing the mother for appropriate dialogue (assisting her with actual scripting)
    e. Preparing the children socially and emotional
    f. Gauging the success of the early contact, on both sides
    g. Monitoring any possible concerns in continuing any contact
    h. Detailing and excluding content that is "out-of-bounds" on both sides
    i. Meeting with the guidance of a forensic specialist who has mediation and clinical experience
    j. Gradually expanding the content of the meetings as the children feel "safe"
    k. Setting realistic expectations for the meetings for all parties involved
    l. Educating the father on what he can do outside of the sessions (between children and mother) to assist and support the process of re-bonding for children and mother

m. More delineation of a four-phase plan can be supplied if so desired by Dr. Clawar

29. The four siblings (James, Joel, Ellen, and Tammy) are fearful that their present guardian, their father, will meet some negative fate. This is a common concern now that they have reconfigured the fact that their father is the major basis for the present "safe haven." The continued litigation has direct and indirect impact on the children; it negatively impacts their sense of security, their safe zone, and their ability to move forward in terms of their social development. They do however need some end points. Of course, this is only if the judge deems this appropriate to accomplish.
30. All future issues of medicine, education, travel, and so on should be shared with more open communication between the parents. This includes face-to-face interactions, e-mail correspondences, text message notification, Skype/FaceTime, and so on.
31. Both mother and father should limit the use of the children as conduits in the exchange of information, except in the cases of factual notifications (e.g., change in pick-up time or location) and related matters.
32. This report does not purport to present "ultimate truths." However, there is a consensus that there were real problems in regard to maternal care in the past. This report is a forensic summary undertaken, largely, for ethical and social clinical reasons—to devise information upon which to consider further contact between the children and their mother.
33. These professionals (including Dr. Clawar) find the children as credible.
34. The mother and father should enhance their efforts to learn how to present a united front on education, transportation, counseling, and other key issues pertaining to their children and their subsequent futures.
35. Given the children's advanced ages throughout the time of the counseling sessions at Walden and the briefing of this report, their opinions and decisions are deemed to have a rational basis; the children also convey an understanding for the substantial amount of weight these decision carry in terms of life choices and their subsequent consequences.

Parents who are accused but later adjudicated as "unfounded" or "falsely accused" present a special challenge. Some children (and the other parent) may have identified with the accusations (and still believe and support it) rather than the actual formal finding(s).

Kidnapping

There are three dimensions to kidnapping—physical, mental, and social. A general definitional perspective for kidnapping would be the exclusionary, proprietary, and/or restrictive control of a child in regard to their relationship with a parent. Kidnapping may take place in all different types of parent-child relationships. These include intact families, marital separations, and divorces. Of course, children can be kidnapped by a stranger for short or long periods of time. Reconciliation of a child and a parent under the latter condition may be less problematic for the parent-child bond; however, there will be trauma-based problems that still necessitate treatment.

Physical Aspects

Physical kidnapping involves the actual separation (of access) between the child and parent. Disallowing visitations is one example of physical control and separation. In some cases, the parent absconds to another location (near or far) in order to control the contact between the other (target) parent and child. Foreign flight is more challenging, as a country may not be part of the Hague Convention[3] or they do not honor it when asked to return the child. A case and point would be a middle-aged man who married in a northeastern city to a woman who had dual citizenship in the United States and Canada. As the marriage dissipated, they navigated many different custodial arrangements. The father was a highly engaged, functional parent who was fully involved in child rearing, religious ceremonies, extended family contacts, and educational endeavors. Progressively, the mother made it harder and harder for him to see the child, but he was able to get some enforcement from the local courts. At one point, she up and moved to Canada, which created both logistical and custodial problems. He made agreements in good faith assuming her sense of honor was similar, including relinquishing his rights to court orders that were issued in the United States. Once she was secure within the Canadian borders, she began to restrict access, engage in reported alienating dialogues with the child, file multiple allegations against the father (all of which came up "unfounded"), and entangle him within the Canadian court system. He visited the child multiple times per month, although these visits became more difficult. The mother was able to navigate her desired restrictions by involving various professionals whom he was required to see. Eventually, the child became almost completely alienated

3. The Hague Convention concerns civil aspects of international child abduction. It is a multilateral treaty that is supposed to provide an efficient method to return a child abducted by a parent from one member country to another. There are approximately 98 member countries that are cosigners to the convention.

and performed many of the classic attitudes and behaviors cited in this book as part of the Parent-Child Estrangement Inventory. So, in effect, the child was successfully physically kidnapped with a large overlay of social-psychological damage to the paternal-daughter relationship. Many of the conditions set up for custodial influence and contact were violated and no sanctions were ever issued to the mother. This scenario was played out over a number of years.

There are ways parents can have new school records, birth certificates, and other documents forged as part of various underground movements. Kidnapping on a more local level occurred in the well-publicized Travitsky case from Whitehall Township in Pennsylvania. The mother had absconded with the children "into Lehigh County" for approximately "four years." The children were discovered as a result of the father appearing on a Philadelphia television show dealing with kidnapped children. In an unusual twist, a new evaluator was appointed in the case who argued that the children were so severely alienated that they could not be returned to the father and have a successful relationship with him.

In an article in *The Morning Call*, the children "begged during the ride to the courthouse not to be returned to their father, although he has not mistreated them."[4] The case is full of many of the characteristics of an extremely high conflict divorce—one parent having proprietary views of the children, limiting access to the other parent, programming and brainwashing of the children, long drawn-out court battles and contempt citations, physical and other forms of kidnapping, and custodial claims and counterclaims.

Mental Aspects

Mental kidnapping usually includes some forms of programming and brainwashing. The purpose of these processes is to distort the perceptions, beliefs, and behaviors of the child in regard to the other (target) parent.[5] Many techniques are employed to inculcate distorted beliefs and ideas about the target parent. This process may induce thoughts that the other parent destroyed the marriage, that they are amoral, teaching the child that the parent doesn't really care or love the child, that the child is unsafe, and teaching them that a target parent loves a stepchild more than they love them. These are just a few examples. Children who have been so unduly influenced can come to believe in ideas and occurrences that are not (totally) true and/or never even took place. This latter phenomenon is actually *memory creation*. For a more

4. Dan Fricker, *Father Gets Unlimited Rights to Visit Kids Taken by Mother*, The Morning Call (Jan. 22, 1986. Retrieved from https://www.mcall.com/news/mc-xpm-1986-01-22-2515611-story.html.

5. For a detailed analysis of this phenomenon, see S. S. Clawar & B. V. Rivlin, Children Held Hostage: Identifying Brainwashed Children, Presenting a Case, and Crafting Solutions (2d ed. 2013).

elaborate discussion of this phenomenon, see Chapter 4, "Alienation," on page 67 of this book.

Social Aspects

Social kidnapping usually includes the control of interactional access that can result in significant parent-child separation. Controlling social access to grandparents, neighbors, friends of the family, and a whole host of other social networks can be a powerful tool in child control. Many children in divorce experience restrictions on their ability to see their grandparents who may have been (positively) involved in their entire lives. This control of social access to ancestry can be experienced as a significant loss. It also disallows for the positive input that the older generation could have on the child's future. Some children are told, "This isn't your family anymore." Sometimes stories are made up to demonize particular social relationships that were historically positive in the child's life.

All forms of kidnapping involve some type of isolation, just as all other forms of abuse usually involve (or at least attempted) isolation on the physical, social, or psychological levels.

Figure 3.1 shows an example of the escalation pattern that typically occurs in kidnapping cases (often accompanied by alienation type activities).

Adult Incarceration

Large numbers of children in America lose contact with a parent due to imprisonment of a parent. The percentage of children in America who have a parent in jail for a short or long period of time is approximately 7 percent. Currently, about 1 out of 28 children have a parent in jail.[6] In some communities incarceration is quite common, so the sense of parent-child separation is more understood and accepted as a (problematic) feature of life. For many of these children, the only regular contact they can and do have with that parent is on visiting days. Of course, the child loses the regular patterns of love, guidance, and support that that parent may have been able to provide. These children may also come to see prison as a normative aspect of life because that's all they ever knew ("I see dad once a month on Sunday"). Also, the child grows up in a social milieu where "family" is defined by the single-parent model. After release, the child (and parent) may need

6. https://www.prisonfellowship.org/resources/training-resources/family/ministry-basics/faqs-about-children-of-prisoners/#children_with_parent_in_prison.

Kidnapping
(Mental, Social, and/or Physical

↑

Extended Litigation (If This Fails, Then...)

↑

Report Target Parent to Police, Tax, and Other Agencies

↑

Filing for, and/or Supporting Charges of Child Abuse

↑

Manipulating Forensic/Therapeutic Evaluations

↑

Legal Action to "Protect the Children" and "Give Them a Voice"

↑

Limiting Information about the Children's Life or Giving Misinformation

↑

Telling Doctors, Teachers, and Others about the "Mal-intent" of the Other Parent

↑

Making Up Stories about Why the Children Are Not Available to Target Parent

↑

Allowing Children to Be Party to Conversations and Other Conflicts between Parents

↑

Encouraging Physical and Emotional Disagreement from Target Parent

↑

Telling the Kids "The Truth" about Child Support and Other Socio-Legal Issues

↑

Negative Comments on the Role of a New Man or Woman in the Target Parent's Life

↑

Redefining History of the Family and/or Marriage

↑

Questioning Character or Behavior of Target Parent

↑

Occasional Negative Comments about Target Parent

Figure 3.1 Behavioral Escalation Pattern of Programming and Brainwashing Parents

Source: Modified from S. S. Clawar & B. V. Rivlin, *Children Held Hostage: Identifying Brainwashed Children, Presenting a Case, and Crafting Solutions* (2d ed., American Bar Association 2013).

help in re-bonding or just bonding (unifying) for the first time. Performing some preparatory work on this prior to release is suggested for both parent and child; it can help their relationship as they (re)develop a regular healthy parent-child contact pattern.[7]

Juvenile Detention

Children who commit various violations of the law may be sent to different forms of juvenile detention for short or long periods of time. Some may even be tried and convicted as an adult, with associated punishments. The ages for being tried as a juvenile versus adult also vary state by state—ranging from ages 15 to 18 (New York and North Carolina try a juvenile as an adult at 16 whereas the District of Columbia it's 17 years of age. Some states even specify a minimum age, for example, North Carolina will not try anyone under six years of age as they "cannot be responsible for their behavior").[8] Detention times are around 15 days on average but can either be shorter or longer depending on the case. Serial offenders exist who may be in and out of the system (the so-called revolving door). Although parents may maintain contact through visitation, the break in the continuity of regular parent-child relationships can be significant. There are racial, gender, social class, and ethnic differentials in regard to juvenile detention adjudications. Some of the findings are:[9]

- Females are the fastest growing population.
- Females are less likely to be detained than males.
- Racial minority youths are overrepresented and treated differently than their white peers.
- Racial minority youths are more likely to be detained than their white peers.
- African American youths have the highest rate of legal involvements compared to other racial groups. They make up 16 percent of all youth in the general population, but 30 percent of juvenile court referrals, 38 percent of youth in residential placement, and 58 percent of youth admitted to state adult prison. However, African Americans in total are only about 13 percent of the general U.S. population.

7. For a study on maternal incarceration and its effects on the children, please see Marguerite D. Downing, *Barriers to Reunification for Incarcerated Parents—A Judicial Perspective*, 50 Fam. Ct. Rev., no. 1, 2012 at 71–76.

8. National Research Council and Institute of Medicine, *Juvenile Crime, Juvenile Justice*, Washington, DC: The Nat'l Academies Press (2001), https://doi.org/10.17226/9747.

9. https://youth.gov/youth-topics/juvenile-justice/youth-involved-juvenile-justice-system.

A hidden but significant population is children who went to prison as teens—sentenced to life (often without parole). The Supreme Court has ruled this is cruel and unusual punishment. Many have been released into a society of incalculable social, economic, technical, political, educational, and cultural changes. As one lifer released said, "'Reentry' can't begin to describe the challenges of returning to the outside world."[10] Fortunately, many cities have formed reentry coalitions to help with their preferred term, "transition." These individuals left society, family, and community as children and are therefore reunifying on all the levels illustrated in Figure 1.1 on page 13.

One Parent Living with an Unacceptable or Problematic Partner

Family lawyers see many cases where children flee a particular home and Children and Youth Services (CYS) or similar organizations are brought in due to claims of child abuse. In these cases, the parent's partner may be guilty of coercion, abusive language, and/or physical or sexual abuse of the child and/or their parent. Children in these circumstances often witness partner violence, alcoholism, criminal activities, and a host of other social problems. I have had a number of cases where these dysfunctional environments finally surfaced and "the secret is out." Once this happens and a social and/or legal intervention is necessitated, the child may become separated from that parent for safety and general welfare reasons. Even though the separation is often presented in terms of the safety of the child(ren), nevertheless, it still results in a separation between parent and child. Even if the child is now safer, more comfortable, and living in a healthier environment, they are still without one of their parents (who may also have been victimized).

Helping the parent who had this dysfunctional home to develop a healthier lifestyle and mindset is often the focus of forensic counselors in order for them to be able to reconnect the child(ren) with the parent from whom they were separated. So, the child ends up in a lose-lose situation. If they stay in the home with many social problems, they will often develop social and mental health deficits, or worse. If they leave, and do experience a healthier environment, they still are absent a mother or father.

In this context, a case comes to mind where a girl was reportedly sexually abused by the mother's paramour. Even though it is many years later, she is still suffering from mental health issues, including PTSD and associated night terrors, depression, and other social-psychological problems.

10. Abd'Allah Lateef, *Life After Prison "Reentry" Can't Begin to Describe the Challenges of Returning to the Outside World*, Philadelphia Inquirer, June 16, 2019, at C1–C3.

These resulted from her actual experience with the mother's paramour, but they also resulted from the loss of her mother. They have not reconnected to this date, partially due to residual anger at her mother, but also at the recommendation of her regular therapist. Parents who have lost a child due to these circumstances frequently become more motivated to work on a constructive game plan for reuniting. They often hope that this will result in them mending the parent-child relationship.

Oppositionally Defiant Child Behaviors, or The Hard to Manage Child[11]

Children with this disorder or behavioral pattern have a number of characteristics. They often lose their tempers, are easily annoyed, and are frequently angry and resentful. These behaviors and attitudes can be focused on various authority figures. Managing these children can be trying, at best. Their defiance can result in conflicts within the family, their schools, their peers, and, ultimately, with the law. Sometimes, they get bounced from one parent to the other (if they are divorced or separated), have trial periods of living with a grandparent, or in other cases, a friend of the family may offer to take them in. If they end up in detention, drug rehab, or jail, they have an even more serious basis for being separated from their parent(s).

Reintegration with one or both of their parents may necessitate special forensic therapy, ground rules, and other aspects of careful planning. If untreated, these behaviors can and often do escalate beyond the family's ability to provide parental guidance and discipline.

The difficulty in treating these children is that they tend to be "other blamers." Other blamers have a very low rate of positive behavioral change. As noted elsewhere, behavioral science tells us that this is largely because unless one is willing to accept some responsibility for their behaviors and seek/accept criticism, the potential for (meaningful and long-lasting) change is minimized.[12] Additionally, anger is their dominant emotion and this emotion can be largely antisocial. Consequently, people in (all) aspects of the child's life may seek to distance themselves due to burnout or pure self-defense. You will often hear parents of these children say things like, "I feel guilty because I don't like to be around my own child," "I don't understand where all of the anger is coming from as all I've tried to do is be a good

11. See Appendix B for Child Incompatibility Quiz (page 247).
12. Therefore, helping these children to accept some responsibility is often a starting point.

parent," "If I just ask a simple question, it can often escalate into an outburst," "I worry that his anger will continue to hurt him/her in all areas of life," "Sometimes I'm just afraid of my own kid," "My son's approach to life is 'my way or the highway.'"

In our culture, we often focus on what adults, especially parents, do to and with their children (that is problematic). However, we must not ignore that children can have (somewhat) independent personalities, social styles, and character traits. Children can be loving, kind, supportive, sensitive, understanding, and collaborative. They also can be mean, aggressive, hurtful, oppositional, defiant, antisocial, or any blend of these qualities. What has been called in the social science literature "the difficult child" is a fact known to many families. These may be children who have received proper (appropriate) guidance, caring, love, therapy, instruction, and healthy forms of communication. However, they may still elicit some of the aforementioned negative attitudinal and behavioral qualities. *Knowing that a child has been "hard to manage" prior to any reunification attempts is very important.* It's helpful knowledge to a judge, a GAL, an attorney, a teacher, or any other (professional) with whom they may come into contact. I have worked with these children, some of whom fit into the preceding description of oppositionally defiant children, and have become over-empowered. These children can point their fingers in my face and tell me of my incapacities, stupidities, and other "qualities" before even getting to know me. I have had these types of children tell me why all therapies will fail and how they will specifically contribute to their presently anticipated failure. Their social styles and behavioral patterns cannot only be rigid but the negative energy they put into attacking relationships is inordinate. These are the children who will tell the Reunification Therapist that they (the therapist) have already taken a side on some issues or are for a parent before any meaningful discussion even occurs. They tend to perceive negativity, attacks, challenges, competition, and, in general, are extremely defensive. How much of this negativity is a result of marital separation or divorce issues needs to be determined.

In these cases, assistance to the parent is as central as what's being offered to the child. These children present a great challenge to a reunification process. A fair number of the failures that I've heard about from other interventionists are due to this impeding factor.

Table 3.1 demonstrates the validity (or lack thereof) of an oppositional child's accusations against a parent. On the left-hand side is the child's accusation. On the right-hand side is social data that largely contradict their accusations, which may be strongly held. In other words, their assessment of social reality is flawed. This data can be used as a reference point for designing interventions.

Table 3.1 Social Reality Chart

Child's Accusations		Social Reality—Father's Involvement (Counter-Information)
Mom has never told me she loves me.	vs.	Tells her that her father loves her, too Encourages the other children to be gracious to her Comes to most of her events and games Connects her with extended family who love her and tell her the same Tells her kids she loves them all the time, "I love you." Especially at night. As recently as July 20, 2016, the daughter has reportedly issued "I love you Mom" statements. This shows her real feelings and confusion. Boosts her when she's down Shows her daughter respect—even in sessions where daughter was "disrespectful"
My mom's world revolves around her and only her.	vs.	Reinforces daughter's positive assets when opportune Gives talks to boost daughter's self-esteem Gives up personal things so daughter can have possessions she likes Sets her paid professional work aside to be with her Gives her daughter advice that has nothing to do with herself Sets special time aside for her above and beyond other children and husband, at times Spoken with the other children to stop saying the daughter isn't smart or capable—she protects her Was there for her in hundreds of capacities since she was born Has been entirely focused on the daughter both before and after the present breech to the exclusion of her own needs (in order to be re-engaged with her daughter)
My mother is a control freak.	vs.	Guidance provided by the mother is regular and functional Mother can be authoritative at times Mother seeks to set appropriate boundaries for behaviors Sanctions are issued or suggested (when appropriate)[1] Tells her daughter how to do better in different sectors of her life "Wants to know where I am and who I'm with all the time"—this is actually quite reasonable in today's world of drugs, violence, and other potential dangers Involvement in therapeutics, school, and extracurricular activities on a regular basis is functional
Why should I have to listen her?	vs.	The father supported contact (to some degree) She used to listen to her mother when they lived in the same marital home—to some degree The court ordered regular contact and sleepovers The Reunification Therapist explained the importance of regular contact and respectful behavior The mother asserted her legitimate parental role, to little avail The limited contact that has taken place was largely positive The parents agreed to Reunification Therapy Historically, she was also frequently oppositional, to some degree

Mom only does for herself, she hasn't contributed to the family at all.	vs.	Researches school situations, doctors, and other important needs Totally family centered Coaches children's teams—often to award-winning status Beautiful home Provides therapy for all of the family Employed one of the older children to learn how to be a professional Bought new home for father and children (during a divorce) New cell phone Provides paid chores to children Backs up the other parent when needed Provides tutoring herself and by others There in crises when needed New cars for everyone when they come of age Involved with school teachers regularly Provides access to the best medical care Private bedroom for daughter Talks about her children with pride New sports equipment Protects children from each other if they fight Takes the family on varied vacations Drives daughter to her events

1. Some older sanctions are no longer even employed.

Child Runaways

Children flee their family homes for many reasons. During the average year in the United States, approximately 1.6 to 2.8 million children run away.[13] Some of the reasons for running away include, but are not limited to, domestic abuse, sexual abuse, mental and/or social health problems, lack of supervision and guidance, being driven out by a parent's paramour, being drawn into a drug and/or gang culture, Internet seduction, being induced to leave by an adolescent or adult paramour, or family conflicts.

Fortunately, many children return quickly, but others are gone for longer periods of time or even permanently. Running away is likely a symptom of other social, personal, and family problems that would need to be addressed, usually prior to or in collaboration with any reunification possibility. Some children do this fleeing behavior on a serial basis as the preferred mechanism of coping with personal and social problems. The assistance of a skilled GAL is often helpful in these cases.

Munchausen by Proxy

The newer diagnostic term is "Factitious Disorder Imposed on Another." This disorder is about falsifying and/or inducing medical/psychological/physical

13. https://www.1800runaway.org/runaway-statistics/third-party-statistics.

symptoms, diseases, and/or injuries onto a child. The child who is experiencing this disorder feels legitimately ill, impaired, or injured. Children may take on the symptoms and behaviors of various types of maladies that have been induced by a particular parent. This behavior may result in separation from many types of social interaction, including the frequency and type of contact with the other (possibly healthier) parent. So, the child is separated because they "can't get out of bed" or "she's too sick to come to the phone" or "I have to keep her out of school because she is nauseous again" or "he can't go to the ballgame with you because I think he is about to have another migraine." These perpetually ill children often miss many days of school, extra and co-curricular activities, and parental contact.

Frequently, the parent who has induced these maladies presents themselves as the (only) one who truly understands and/or can help the child cope with their distress. This further separates them from the other parent and reinforces a survival-type bond between the inducing parent and the recipient child. Psychiatric assistance is (often) indicated in addition to any reunification interventions. *Separation anxiety for the child from the inducing parent is pro-forma and may be the main reason that is issued not to visit or be with their other (healthier) parent.*

Somewhat ironically, the non-inducing parent can come to be seen as the problem for even wanting a relationship with the child, and so they are labeled and vilified as "insensitive" and even possibly the cause of the child's problems.

Figure 3.2 gives a summary of the patterns in these dysfunctional relationships.

Parent-Child Enmeshment

This is a phenomenon where a parent and child are *overly integrated* (connected) in psycho-sociological terms. It may not involve the physical symptom-inducing pattern as with Munchausen by Proxy. However, the child's ability to function independently on an age-appropriate basis is hampered. This often can lead to submissive and clinging behaviors. Fear of separation from a particular parent is also common. In custody cases one often hears statements by the child such as, "I need to call mommy again" or "I really don't want to go down to the shore with you and Grandmom for the weekend—I'd rather stay home with mom (or dad)." An occasional special need for a parent contact is not enmeshment.

These children have difficulty making basic decisions that they should be able to at their given age. As a ten-year-old girl said when in the custody of her father, "I need to call mom about which hair ribbon to wear." She would call her mother about ten times per day; she'd do more if allowed.

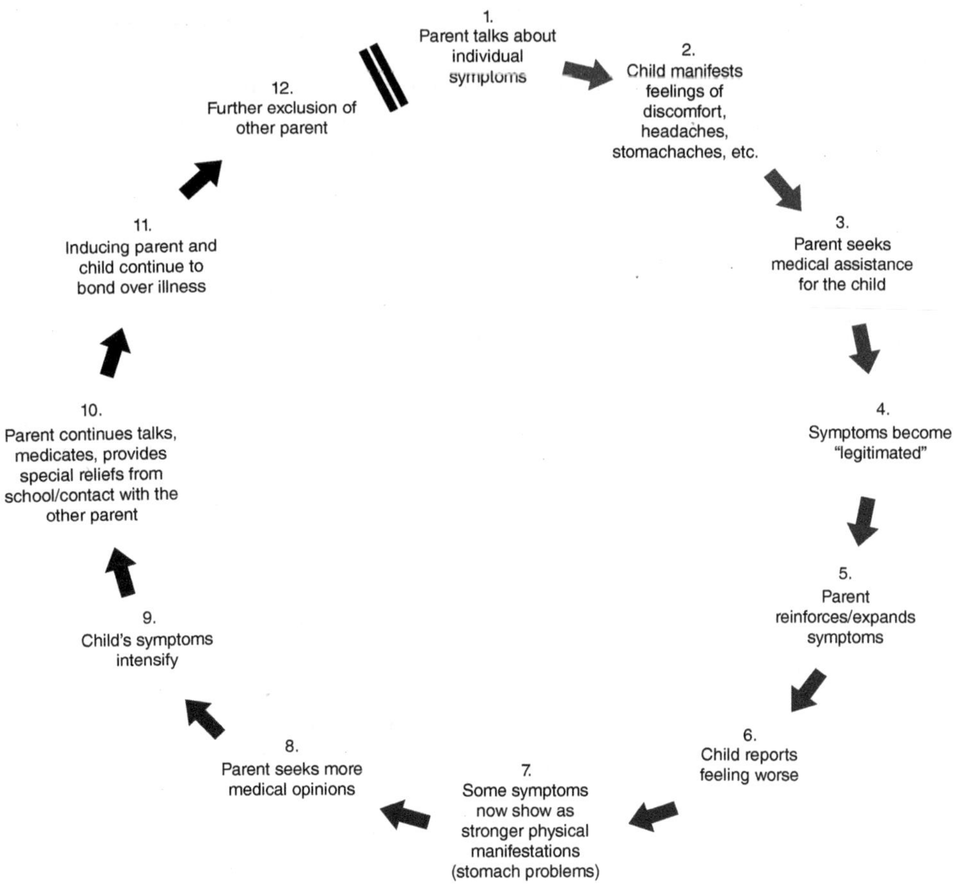

Figure 3.2 Model Cycle of Parentally Induced Child Illness

Separation anxiety is a constant companion for these children, as in the Munchausen child. This may not have been as noticeable when the family was intact because children were free to make as much contact as they desired with their respective parent.

These children seem to have difficulty in issuing an opinion of their own. And, if they do issue an opinion, they tend to seek high degrees of affirmation for what they are about to say. Fear of being alone is also a regular assertion. Wanting to go back to the custody of the other parent because the parent they are with is going out for a few hours to dinner is one possible indication of this enmeshment. The child may exhibit feelings of helplessness and a need to be taken care of by one of the (connected) parents. *They need contact reassurance.* Psychologists and psychiatrists refer to it as Dependent Personality Disorder (DPD). In more simple terms, it is a form of attachment that *disallows independent functioning and the development of multiple attachments*. It can be quite serious because as we grow, multiple attachments become a necessary social skill for functioning in the broader community and society. As a professor, I have heard many "jokes" about parents who offer to move into the dorm with their son or daughter. Some Human Resources Directors are reporting incidents of job applicants arriving with their parent(s) in tow or a parent calling to see if their child got the job.

Personality/Social Style Conflicts

In this culture, children are expected to develop their own independent social personality styles. As the components of these social personality styles become clear, they may run into conflict with the social personality characteristics of one or both of their parents. For example, peaceful and negotiating parents may be living with a child who enjoys social confrontation and challenge. Parents who often lie and cheat may be residing with a child who believes in truth, candor, honesty, and loyalty. Parents who can argue and then forgive and forget may have a child who fears arguments or disagreements and never forgets (especially negatives). Following are some examples of social personality types put into popular language. Some parent and child types match well (Pleasers versus Shy types) and some are bound for conflicts or misunderstandings (Know It Alls versus Analytical types). Brief advice is also shared on dealing with them. The type can be the child and/or parent.

Fourteen Social Personality Types (of Children and Parents)

Type	Key Characteristics and Behaviors
I. Pleasers	• Likes to make everyone happy, okay, or feel good. • Providing targeted praise to them is helpful. • Watch out for their over-soliciting of how they are doing. • Can be taken advantage of by others [including doing their (home)work for other children]. • Make good mentors/tutors.
II. Analytical	• Can over-scrutinize, at times. Investigative. • Can slow up a process or decision by overthinking. • Good at details. • Two subtypes: detail versus principle. • Best in certain types of jobs/roles that requires probing. • Can probe too much. • Often like challenges. • Good at checking others' work/progress. • Can be overly critical. Helping them to use this talent in a focused way is important. • May need to be told "This doesn't require analysis, just completion or acceptance" at times. • Loves to ask "why?"

Type	Key Characteristics and Behaviors
III. Passive Aggressive	• Attacks or challenges (indirectly). • Let them be heard. • Don't counter with aggressive commentary. • Don't argue. • Redirect conversations. • Don't let them attack individuals inappropriately. • They often like to think there are "secrets" afoot. • Cause others to stay distant or become angry in reaction. • They don't always know what they are angry about. • Teaching other modes of interaction is good (done best by role modeling).
IV. Schmoozers	• Can gossip and extend talk time. • Can distract others. • Highly social. • Feel cramped if they can't do a particular task. • Teach them productivity or relational impacts of their "over talking." • May rationalize their conversational wondering (with some truth). • Good in drawing out new members to a group. • Good at interaction requiring contact with those outside the family.
V. Worker Bees	• Good at task completion. • Can stay on track. • Good concentration. • Don't like distractions. • Good on deadlines and punctuality. • Annoyed with people who waste time. • Self-directed. • Often need to make them to take a break. • Goal oriented. • Don't appreciate Schmoozers or Time Wasters. • May need help to "chill" at times. • Can be very intense (and this can be confused with them being angry). • Likes to see results.
VI. Egocentric/ Narcissists	• Self-focused. • Takes credit (sometimes for work/tasks/activities of others). • Hard to see other points of view. • Put positive comments before criticism or they won't hear you. • Not great for team (collaborative) projects. • Tries to be "top dog." • Likes to be complimented in front of others (groups). • Needs to learn to share limelight. • Not always good at task management. • Makes sessions all about them. • Weak empathic skills.

Type	Key Characteristics and Behaviors
VII. Know-It-Alls	• Believe no one is better or knows more (it may be true). • Can make good "teachers" (with limits). • Likes to demonstrate their knowledge. • Impatient with slow learners. • Teaching them tolerance is important. • Body language can be off putting—watch your own with them. • Can be assertive and scare "shy" types away. • Can spend too much time letting others know how much they know. • Can't understand why "others don't get it" (including professionals).
VIII. Controller	• Possessive of information, relationships, and/or "property." • Needs praise with detail. • They rationalize their control in positive-sounding terms. • Can be good on detail(ing) tasks. • They have tight relational boundary issues (who is "in" and who is "out"). • Teach them appropriate domains of influence. • They misread conversation/behaviors as control elements. • Tend to push others away when the latter reach their limit of "being controlled."
IX. Constant Complainers	• Always finds the negative in people or situations. • May need ventilation time. • Teach them to "cap it" or limit negatives. • Set time limits on some dialogue. • Teach them solution language. • Watch impact on family—it can be divisive. • Often called "negative thinkers." • Others may want to stay away from them. • They wonder why they don't have friends.
X. Other Blamers/ Victim Role	• Everyone else is the problem. • They believe in their justifications. • They shift conversations/don't take responsibility. • Difficult to change/poor at accepting criticism (even constructive criticism). • Make poor team (family) members. • They are time intensive. • Employ fact-based dialogue with them. • Needs reaffirmation that your commentary is not personal. • Channel dialogue to their specific behaviors. • They tend to repeat same mistakes over and over. • Difficult as clients/patients. • They tend to "over-read" and misread body language. • Don't look frustrated with them; they will usually reflect this back.

Type	Key Characteristics and Behaviors
XI. Shy	• Withdrawn, private, low-interaction types. • Some are innately this way—estimated 10 percent of the population. • Prefer working alone. • Don't push them too hard into social relationships. • Acknowledge their value (rather than that they are shy, which for them may be equal to a liability). • Don't personalize commentary too much. • Allow space—physical and social-psychological. • Best with 1 on 1 or small group interactions. • They have a hard time in initial professional meetings. So be patient. • Create a comfort factor prior to raising deeper relational issues.
XII. Suspicious Style	• What's behind the issue or the dialogue? • Easily hurt. • Looks for problems or issues. • Never be defensive or offensive with them. • Caution in dealing with them, but don't show anxiety. • Fact-based commentary is best. • Don't argue—it's often a trap that goes nowhere. • Reality perceptions—you can compare their views with reality. Use a no challenge tone when speaking. • Explain their questions calmly and factually. • Seek clarification of their views/opinions. • Limit any judgmental commentary.
XIII. Gossipers	• Three styles: 1. Just performing ventilation. 2. Politically based (power aspects or goals). 3. Seeking social stimulation and connections. • Family issues versus personal content—they often confuse them. • Negative gossip can damage a relationship ("Mom said . . . Dad's got a new girlfriend.") • Incidental (one off) type comments usually not a problem. Don't make it bigger than it is. • If they are challenged, do it with explaining the (relational) impact of what they say.
XIV. Emotional/ Expressive	• They think and speak in affective (emotional) terms and language. Most of their language has an emotional dimension "It's scary." "I get sad when . . ." • Likely to say "you don't get it" if you speak in purely factual terms. They won't feel heard with just factual language. • Listen to key words ("I feel . . ." "It hurts me that . . ." "I'm upset") • Sees and feels the world in affective terms. • Factual language doesn't work as well as emotive language.

Unfortunately, these fundamental social-personality characteristics and social styles are often missed; this can complicate interpretations as to why one or both parents and child(ren) cannot get along. If they are used as general guidelines, they can be diagnostically and application-wise very useful. It's especially important to employ them prior to jumping to a more serious or clinical assessment and labels. As a 13-year-old girl said, "It's simple. My dad and I never understood each other. He's always pushing me into relationships and he doesn't get it. I'm just shy. If I see him more, he'll do the same." After getting her father to agree to lessen the push on relationships, she agreed to reinitiate more regular contact.

Some parent-child linkages are damaged when you have two control types. Some children create relational separation by simply spending less time with a particular parent. They may self-isolate, spend more time at friends' homes, and in other ways, disengage. In a sense of frustration and possible loss, some parents may intensify their attempt to connect. This results in a vicious cycle of pursuit and avoidance and then possible conflict. A common cycle of parent-child disconnection is illustrated in Figure 3.3.

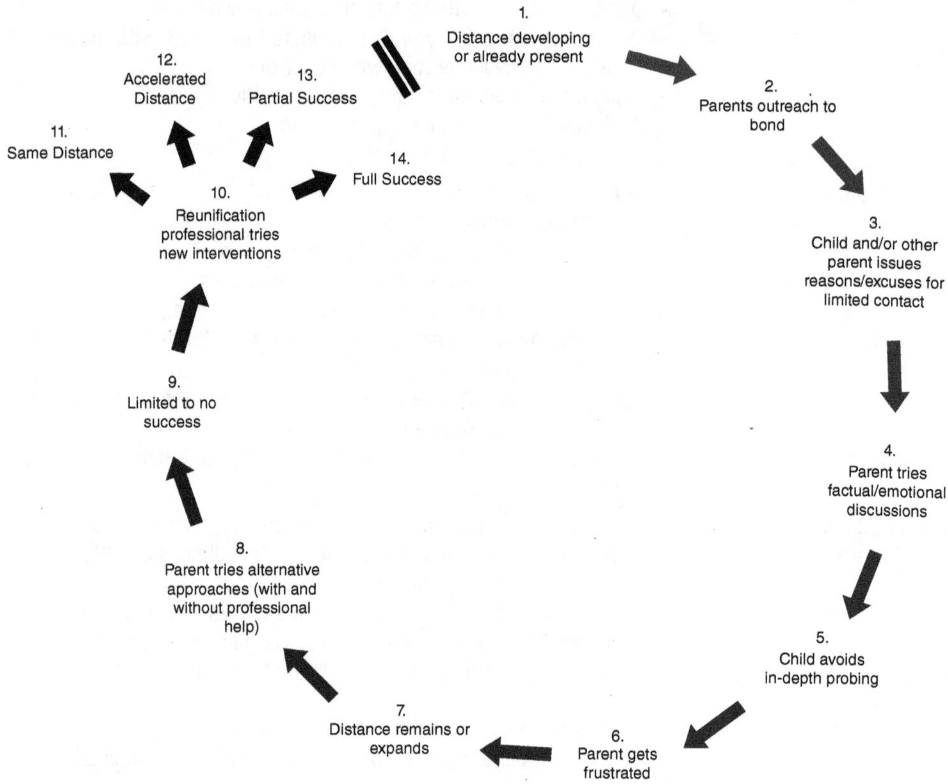

Figure 3.3 Cycle of Parent-Child Disconnection

Personality and social style differences can become so intense in their behavioral manifestations that they may have the capacity to create stress and, as noted, the desire to disengage. Worker bees don't usually fit with lazy individuals. Narcissists don't usually fit with charitable types. Know-it-alls don't usually fit with people who seek continuous inquiry. Constant complainers don't usually fit with solution-oriented people. Other blamers don't usually fit with people who take responsibility. Control types don't usually fit with people who let things pass through. Shy people don't usually fit with (crowd) pleasers. Emotionally expressive people don't usually fit with people of limited affect or purely analytical types. These and many more differences don't necessarily have to lead to a parent-child separation, but they can. They are most often overlooked in family law issues, including custody assessments, alienation studies, and reunification efforts; overlooking them may lead to false conclusions as to the source of parent-child differences and separation. Social patterns and styles impact greatly on the levels and types of interaction that people seek and are happy with. This is another reason why customizing Reunification Therapy is crucial to its potential success. Knowing the parents' and child's key characteristics serves as building blocks/approaches and helps to side-step mistakes due to differences in social/personal styles.

Voluntary Parental Abandonment

Some parents simply leave their children for a whole host of reasons. Personality/social conflicts, lack of funds to continue a custody battle, commitment to a new family, pressures to leave the life of the child, sabotage by others to their attempted relationship, residential relocation due to job or personal desire, inability to be competitive with a stepparent, character assassinations that have been effective, and other factors can all be causative in regard to the ultimate action of parental abandonment. Some parents have said the following to me:

- Due to their desire to not cause further stress to the children: "This litigation is hurting us all. I've been advised to walk away."
- They were disengaging from the legal (conflict) arena (due to financials, time, and other reasons).
- In the context of forensic therapy/custody evaluations, they were recognizing that they will (or may) lose contact with their child(ren), anyway.

Ironically, in some of these cases, the child(ren) who had pushed to be with the bonded parent (sometimes ten years later) have said, "Why did you stop fighting for me—I guess you didn't really love me." This is a damned if you do, damned if you don't type of dilemma for the parent seeking reunification.

In any event, the child often loses out on the benefits of continued parental interaction and love. Later in life, many of these children will likely struggle with issues related to real and/or perceived abandonment, relational continuity, trust, empathy, social skills, issues of love, and other social-emotional deficits and problems. The author has seen this, and the performed literature is building in this area. When the children become adults, they usually do have these personal and social issues.

Professionally Caused Separation (Case Mismanagement Problems)

Unfortunately, not all professional interventions and support systems are operating as they should. Some professionals may actually facilitate distancing between a parent and child due to lack of adequate knowledge and/or skills, no or inadequate treatment plan, no or weak metrics, bias (conscious and unconscious), and creating triangulation(s) (pitting various family members against each other).

Reunification/reconciliation/reconnecting of people who have been separated for various reasons and periods of time are really a special type of forensic activity. It requires special knowledge and skills that include but are not limited to:

- Setting and keeping to a treatment plan.
- Sharing a treatment plan so that divergent parties can collaborate around it.
- Being able to clearly explain the content, process, and goals of Reunification Therapy (as differentiated from other types of therapies and counseling).
- Knowing how the legal process works (due process).
- Knowing the lawyers' code of ethics.
- Being able to read legal documents.
- Taking, reading, and understanding social histories.
- Comfort and technical skills in crisis intervention.
- Knowing traditional and nontraditional methods of rebuilding relationships.
- Having a high frustration tolerance.
- Being able to stay objective under highly emotional conditions.
- Being able to depersonalize communications under conditions of challenge and/or attack.

- Designing and utilizing metrics.
- Ability to write clear memos and reports. This includes progress reports, evaluation reports, and homework sheets for family members.
- Being able to collaborate with diverse types of professionals from varied disciplines.
- Being able to delineate when reunification approaches are contraindicated.
- Abiding by professional ethics from their relevant professional societies.
- Being able to communicate progress to the clients, even if it's incremental.
- Utilizing all information for the best interests of all parties.
- Being up to date on the (scientific and popular) literature as befits this field of study.

These and other features of professional conduct, and many more, are central to the potential success of any reunification. Professionals who develop bias early in the case are worse than useless; they will likely accelerate already existing problems that are before them, let alone create new problems. Developing beliefs and opinions too early in a case can lead a professional and the client(s) down the wrong path. The person you think (or have been told) has been abused might actually be a perpetrator. The person who appears cooperative may externally seek to undermine the process. The child who seems strong and independent may, with time, prove to have been directed by an external party and be fairly fragile.

As already noted, because the specialty has become in high demand, therapists of all different backgrounds and training have flooded into this area of practice. Actually, it doesn't matter if the professional is a social worker, psychologist, psychiatrist, clinical sociologist, or marriage and family therapist. *What matters is their experience, knowledge, and their ability to connect with all ages and backgrounds, as well as their ability to create a forensic treatment plan that is customized to the relationship that they are charged with repairing.*

Reunification may have been attempted many times. I have had many cases where I am the fourth or fifth professional who was asked to mend the broken bonds. However, these cases often involve having to deal with the original causes as well as any possible problems that may have been introduced by previous professionals as well as the damage of time itself. Even if the previous professionals did not introduce new problems, the parties themselves often arrive with a sense of "here we go again." Sometimes, clients may turn and say, "You're our court of last resort. If you can't do it, nobody can." Unfortunately, this kind of grandiosity of expectations can actually hinder the re-bonding process. Trained therapists will try to bring these elevated client expectations back into some reality context, without dashing their hopes completely.

Sometimes, professionals will develop inappropriate alliances with clients. This often happens when the therapist loses their specific role as the therapist and moves into roles of advocacy, attorney-type advisory behaviors, or other roles for which they were not originally cast and/or trained to execute. As noted, precipitous judgments on the part of the professional that a client has been abused, victimized in various ways, or hurt by the other parent can add to the complexity of the case. I've had many of these cases where the "accused party" was not in fact (likely) guilty of anything, but now had a new social negative label that also had to be dealt with. As one midwestern therapist said to me, "I know the father was cheating and caused the divorce and the child has held onto that belief for dear life." Interestingly enough, when the forensic history of the case was reviewed and further researched, it appeared that the cheating party, throughout the marriage, was the mother. Additionally, the therapist in the case even told the children that their father cheated on their mother, which intensified the breach of parent-child relationship (triangulations). *So, again, professionals can compound already existing dilemmas by being precipitous and judgmental.* Sometimes the topics, issues, and problems hit too close to home and the professional has not learned to separate their personal issues from the client issues. Simply put, *if it's not personal, it's not personal, and if it's personal, it's still not personal.* This adage is very helpful for this kind of professional work. More professionals could use training and retraining in the application of this professional obligation and related demeanor.

Finally, there simply may not be adequate "chemistry" between the professional and client. This refers to the intangible fit that all parties feel when there is a working professional relationship. It could have to do with feelings of caring, being understood, being listened to, and, in other ways, having a connection between professional and client that facilitates a comfort factor for all parties. This might not occur in the first session(s) and so it might be necessary to give each other a reasonable period of time to see if this special sense between professional and client can exist or develop. Caution on this consideration is necessary because it is common in Reunification Therapy for "fit issues" to be present in the beginning or maybe even throughout the process. A "fit issue" is not necessarily a reason for termination of the reunification venture. Some parents will assert this as an obstructionist tactic (For more tactics or theories, see Chapter 7, "Nineteen Popular and Professional 'Theories' That Can Be Problematic to the Reunification Process" on page 137).

Loss of Contact at Birth

Children may lose connection with a parent early on in life for many reasons:

- A father/mother may be unknown and unidentified.
- A mother may give birth and move away or a father may move away shortly after birth.
- A parent may give up their rights or have them removed.
- At the time of birth, a father (or mother) may be incarcerated.
- A child may be adopted.
- A child may be put into foster care.
- Someone else may obtain custody or become the social parent (such as grandparents).

Parents can (re)surface later on in a child's development. The reunification process can be anything from a simple re-engagement by developing a common sense of historical understandings to a complicated process because of social-emotional, safety, welfare, and legal factors.

Misunderstandings

Surprisingly, this can be a very common (but simple) element in parent-child separations. Misunderstandings can occur due to whether a parent really loved the child, who caused a divorce, whether child support was really ever paid, that the development of a new blend of family members meant that a parent didn't care about their previously formed family or them. Misunderstandings can occur surrounding court actions whereby children come to feel that one of the parents is trying to hurt the other parent by litigation—when, in fact, they were really trying to reestablish a bond with their child. Misunderstandings about why a parent had to move away for a while and how that may have affected the parent-child contact are also common.

Misunderstandings can fuel anger, resentment, disengagement, confusion, and even guilt on the part of one or both of the parents and child. Clarifying the singular or mutual misunderstandings often results in enhancing the re-bonding potential. Getting these out on the table for examination and clarification is key to effective Reunification Therapy.

Religious, Racial, Ethnic, and Gender Conflicts

Religious, racial, ethnic, and gender conflicts are also common but can be difficult to resolve. Not infrequently a parent maintains or develops a religious commitment that is different than the one developed and held by a child while a couple was together. These can result in an (extreme) separation of a parent and a child even though these differences don't necessarily have to result in this consequence. I've had cases where a child maintains their Orthodox Jewish traditions with their mother only to have a father become more secular (or less orthodox). Ironically, in a number of these cases, the very religious foundation adhered to by the child was taught by the parent they now reject. In other cases, one parent tries to draw a child into their post-divorce religious preference, which may be different than the religious orientation that existed as an intact family. An example of this is a mother who consistently took the children, during a marital separation, to the church of her choice when the children had been raised for the first nine years of their life as Jewish children.

In other cases, children who are from mixed race families are frequently drawn into favoring one of the family's specific racial characteristics and identity. So children from marriages between Caucasians and African Americans can be drawn into either side of the family, which can result in *learned xenophobia* for the other side. So, a child who is black and white by background identifies as "black" in exclusion to the white ancestry. Of course, there can also be the reverse phenomenon. A case in point is siblings whose father was African American and whose mother was Caucasian. The children clearly came to identify (as the father was sidelined over years of litigation) as "white."

In terms of ethnic identification, there can be a strong pull on children to identify as Italian or Irish or Greek even though they are clearly a combination of different ethic/national identities.

The ability to create a sense of common ancestry can be a touchy situation but doable, especially if the Reunification Therapist has a high sense of comfort and knowledge with the various ancestries. They both can be "gifts." Conflicts and tensions can be resolved by developing a *scene of mutual appreciation and respect for both backgrounds*. This is easier said than done if one parent wants a singular identity. If the children identify as a racial or ethnic group different than the seeking parent, the goal for connectivity is further challenged.

Acceptance of gender issues is also increasing in this field of reunification practice. Parents who cannot accept that a child "comes out" as gay or transsexual may require new areas of knowledge and skill sets. Therapists who do not have training, experience, and/or certification in the field of human sexuality/sex education should approach these cases most cautiously and possibly enlist the help of someone who does. In one case, a mother would not accept her son who had come out as gay, but the father did. (The parent situation can be reversed too.) This then created a split in the marriage between husband and wife. So, reunification can actually be between a child and a parent, but, at times, it can also involve the need to reunify the adult partners or the family along selected areas of difference as a whole. In the case just cited, the father continued a relationship with his son, but the mother never did. She asserted that her religious beliefs could not allow (a sense of) acceptance of his "gayness." She also continued to believe that there are therapies that would "make him normal." It was explained to her that some states have even begun to outlaw these therapies because they have been found to have negative consequences in many cases. She also was apprised that the terms "normal" and "abnormal" are not employed any longer and that most professionals do not see homosexuality as aberrant or as a mental health disorder. This did not deter her from the continued rejection of her son. The son was pleased with his father's love and acceptance and remained distressed not only at his mother's position and rejection, but he worried about her because she stored this hostility and rejection; he further worried that she would ultimately become mentally ill. The metric in this case was initially parent acceptance and then became maternal acceptance; the latter failed to materialize. The positive metrics were enhanced self-acceptance and paternal linkage. Success can be partial but still be positive; here only one parent obtained the mended ways.

Transsexuality is another gender issue for a parent or a child, whether male to female or female to male. These transitions can include change in dress, speech qualities, facial and body hair, mannerisms, shaving of Adam's apples, genital reconstruction surgery, and hormonal therapies. Some partners stay with the trans partner and "work it through." However, some partners cannot adapt to the transformation and the relationship can end in separation or divorce. A breech in time and place (different residences) can occur, possibly including a parent and child becoming separated. Later on, there may come a time when the child(ren) and/or parent wish to reconnect. Having knowledge about how to respond to questions and statements such as, "How come daddy looks like a mommy?," "Mommy's voice is different," or "I don't understand why daddy is wearing dresses" are important and need to be addressed with clarity and respect.

Parental Discipline

It is frequently the case in separating and divorcing families that disciplinary styles, philosophies, and practices become or were previously divergent. This is also true in intact families as well. Children, partially because of social personality types and styles, may feel more of an alliance with one style of discipline than the other. One parent may be more focused on task completion (follow through), respect, household tasks, academic performance, and other aspects of child development versus the other parent who may be more focused on social and emotional well-being, stress issues, and peer affiliation. These parents can often end up in conflicts over what needs addressing (context) and how issues should be approached for a child. As one child (and hundreds of others) said, "All my dad cares about is meeting the rules and getting things done like you're supposed to." When asked about his mother, he said, "She's more sympathetic if I slip or don't get a piece of homework done. I can talk to her more about all different things cause she doesn't come down on my head." Another 16-year-old boy also made statements such as, "I'm not seeing my dad. I like things the way they are." By "things the way they are" he meant that there were less (and different) restrictions, guidelines, and responsibilities. These parental differences are common and can lead to a child driving a wedge between the parents even further. Reunification has some special ground rules in these kinds of family dynamics (see page 6 on Reunification Techniques and Activities). Actually, these parents were helped to see that their differences were complementary rather than contradictory. The Reunification Therapy shifted to some couple sessions more than just parent-child sessions.

Child Abuse

Child abuse comes in many forms (just like kidnapping)—physical, social, and emotional. New modalities are being developed to safely connect parents who may have behaved inappropriately, if not illegally, and where the child was actually victimized (as well as a parent who lost contact). Of course, in these cases, Reunification Therapists have to be extremely cautious so that they do not set up conditions that will facilitate any possible reenactment of past misdeeds.

Some children have "crossed over," meaning that they never want to have contact with those parents again because of experiences that have induced fear, anxiety, suicidal thoughts/actions, other types of self-harm, self-esteem depletion, and a whole host of other negative consequences. As one child said, "Just the thought of seeing him made me feel scared and like a bad person all over again." Abuse is on a continuum from infrequent to very frequent, in various forms and intensities. This variation, however, does not make the abuse any less significant. Reunification Therapists have to be able to have some definitional frameworks to be able to understand the reality that is in front of them. For example, a child recently (with some coaching from his father) reported that, "My stepfather pushes me." When further inquiries were made, the child reported that it was infrequent (a one-off incident) and suggested it was not that serious, but that he just didn't like it. Upon some further prodding from his father, the child "recalled" that on one occasion he (the child) fell down from the push. The father was, even if unwittingly, possibly facilitating a further breech between step-father and his son. (Also, the fact that the child was disobeying the stepfather and "getting in his face" came out in a later interview.) A custody case was ongoing and the father was likely trying to position the professional into a mandatory reporter status. Child abuse claims in divorce cases, especially high-conflict divorces, are relatively common compared to other socio-legal family situations. A significant number of these accusations come up as "unfounded."

A study from 1990 in which 9,000 divorces across 12 states were studied produced the following results:[14]

Abuse Allegations in Divorce Cases

- In 48 percent of cases, mothers accused fathers
- In 19 percent of cases, mothers accused stepfathers or others
- In 6 percent of cases, fathers accused mothers
- In 16 percent of cases, fathers accused stepfathers or others
- In 11 percent of cases, third parties accused fathers, mothers, or others

Out of all the cases in the study, 5 percent to 8 percent of the accusations were deemed intentionally false reports.

One case that exemplifies this is a father who had been accused of serially molesting his daughters. Each time he was exonerated only to be followed by another abuse accusation, facilitated by the mother. One of the suggestions that I made in this case was for him to install cameras in different locations within his home, as serial accusers usually continue that behavior. Sure enough, the mother re-accused the father of molesting the children again. The mother was asked for the day and approximate time when this alleged incident occurred. She issued the requested time and day information only to find out that the video camera, which had a timestamp, revealed that the father was at bedside reading storybooks to his daughters. All of the time before and after that was also accounted for. Unfortunately, children can actually "report" abuse when it didn't occur or they can expand a non-abusive incident to a bigger-than-life occurrence. This may not be the norm, but forensic experts must be aware of the possibility.[15]

In another case, a mother had filed 15 accusations—all came back "unfounded." Custody was finally shifted to the father, but it was too late—the father had committed suicide.

---

14. Editorial Staff (Ed.), *Child Sexual Abuse and Divorce* (July 20, 2016), https://www.divorcesource.com/blog/child-sexual-abuse-and-divorce.

15. False accusations can be operative in all types of social situations. See Alan Dershowitz, *I Want to Be Investigated by the FBI*, WSJ, Mar. 21, 2019. This is an accounting that occurred on the adult level.

Of course, there is actual child abuse and when this is present it will understandably, but severely, interfere with most aspects of reunification. Maybe the therapy shouldn't be done at all in certain cases.

The term "abuse" has different thresholds and meanings in different cultures. In some cultures, not spanking a child is considered a dereliction of parenting. In other cultures, child nudity, even into the teen years, is considered normal and healthy. A story comes to mind of a father, some years ago, who was waiting to have his pictures developed at a K-Mart (pre-cell phone era) when he found himself being approached by police. He was handcuffed and taken into custody as the clerk, who saw the pictures, called the police. The pictures showed his son bouncing on a bed in different positions and degrees of undress along with a buddy. This was identified as "pedophilia-type photography." This was used as incriminating information in the (family) court along with his practice of kissing his son on his mouth, squeezing his cheeks, and hugging him regularly and in a very robust fashion. It became my task to explain to the court that he was a first generation Italian male and that he had done nothing culturally inappropriate. Nudity, and pictures thereof; kissing on the lips; and extensive physical contact, including hugging, kissing, and patting children were all appropriate behaviors within segments of this first generation Italian family (ethnic) culture.

Figure 3.4 shows some differences in physical discipline by country.[16]

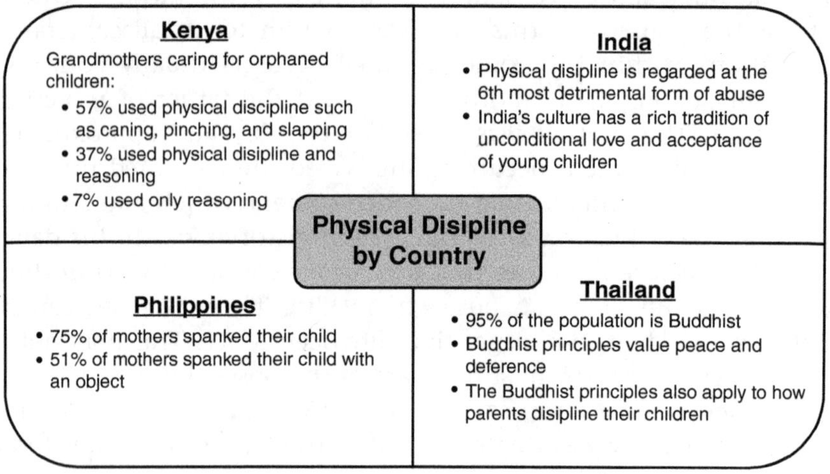

Figure 3.4 Physical Discipline by Country

16. Jennifer. E. Lansford et al. *Physical Discipline and Children's Adjustment: Cultural Normativeness as a Moderator*, 76(6) CHILD DEV. 1234–1246 (2005). Retrieved from https://www.ncbi.nlm.nih.gov/pmc/articles/PMC2766084.

So, real abuse is an impeding factor for reunification, but it must be clearly sorted out from abuse allegations that may either be unfounded and/or false. Cultural knowledge is imperative. If in doubt, check out behaviors with a cultural anthropologist or (clinical) sociologist who knows about cultural definitions; this would be a safe and judicious rule.

Child Experiencing Abuse/Aggression against Their Other Parent

Children can observe/witness various forms of aggression by one or both parents against each other. Reunification Therapists have many cases where a child has (legitimate) anger toward a parent (or both) because they have, in different ways, hurt their other parent (or it was so reported).

This grievance can result in anger and disengagements of long standing. Children can identify either with someone who was victimized or with the perpetrator. Rebuilding a relationship where a child believes (and it may be true) that a parent has physically, verbally, socially, economically, and/or emotionally hurt the other parent can present a very challenging assignment. A child questioned her father, "Are you still fighting with Angie (stepmom)?" If this is accompanied by the presence of parental drug use in any form, it gets even more complicated. I've had many children say to a parent, "Are you still drinking?" "Do you still take those little pills?" Of course, this is another impeding factor—the historical and/or contemporaneous use of (prescription or street) drugs.

The reunification becomes more difficult if the parent who has been victimized continues to talk about the experience and "keeps it alive" in very real (even verbal) terms. So, yesterday becomes today and today becomes a basis of fearing tomorrow. As another child said, "Why would I want to go to the movies with him? He's the person who hurt my mom and I will never forgive him for that." These cases have significantly higher hurdles and external parties, such as lawyers, GALs, judges, other therapists, and so on, need to set realistic expectations. In some of those cases, I have failed to create the reunification. I have had children say to me, "I can't wait to grow up and get bigger and stronger so I can beat the living hell out of my father (or mother). And I will!" In another case with this theme, I had a male child who was virtually at the age and strength to execute on his historical anger toward his father. He actually revealed that his "plan" was "to kill my father." It's something he said and thought about for years. He said, "I've just lived to settle the score." After trying many interventions, pleadings, and other approaches, it was clear that I was failing to deter him from what had become his main mission in life. Finally, I hit upon an idea (after developing a safety plan for his father) and I said to him, "What's the most important thing to you?" He answered quickly, "My mother. She's been my rock and has done everything in her life to take care of me." I said to him, "So does that mean that you wish to return her care and her love and her protection or do you just want to leave her on her own?" He looked back at me like I was an idiot and said the following, "That's kind of a stupid question doctor because, if you were listening, you would know how important she is to me." I said, "So that means that you kind of need to be around to take care of her in return for her dedication." He said, "Of course." I said, "How are you going to do this when you're in jail?" There was one of the longest periods of silence I had experienced in the therapy room at which point he simply cried—all 180 pounds of solid muscle—and said, "Okay. Okay. I get your point. I got it. I wasn't thinking of that kind of consequence. I was just thinking by my feelings." I said, "Go home and make your mother dinner. We'll talk next week." As he got up to leave, he threw his arms around me and hugged me and said, "Thanks doc. Thanks for everything." I said, "No, thank you for caring and trying to do the right thing. Take care of mom (which was one of his main missions in life). And remember, *feelings are not always the best guide to behaviors."*

Figure 3.5 diagrams a case example of one parent's negativity toward the other parent to which the child(ren) were subjected.

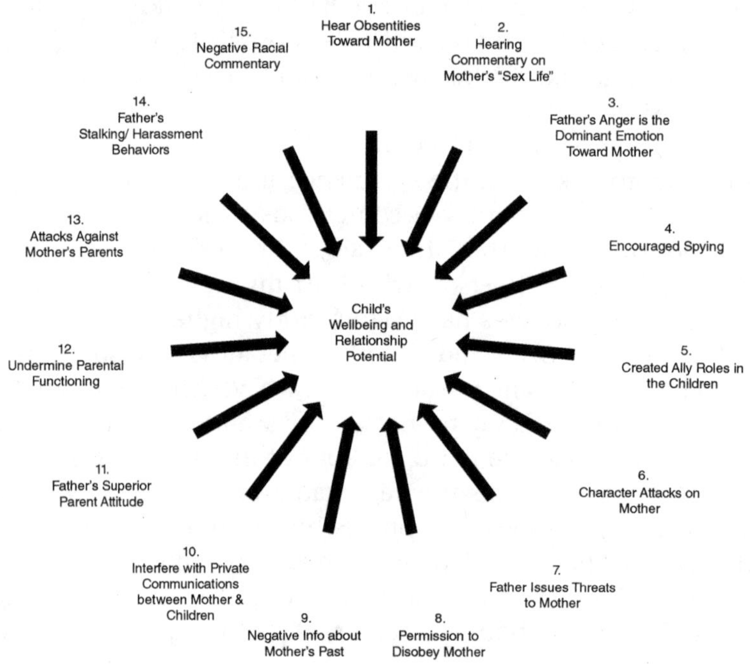

Figure 3.5 Factors Impacting on a Child's Well-Being and Relationship Potentials: A Case Example

Substance Use and Abuse

Substance use has been identified as a causative factor in many divorces. Substance use not only damages the parental relationship but also filters down to the children. It can lead to a parent being absent, abusive, aggressive, accusatory, neglectful, withdrawn, insensitive, noncommunicative, ill, having memory problems, negligent, and in other ways impact on a parent-child relationship. Some parents have driven drunk or high and this may be identified as problematic by the other parent, a professional, the child, or the court. Because the relapse rate is so high for addiction, a parent going into detox or rehab is not necessarily guaranteed sobriety. However, many parents have received professional assistance and continue to be successful in their sobriety. The problem in these cases is that the child(ren) or the other parent may remember them in their drug-induced state and may not want to interact with them in the present. However, the drug-related problems are not just on the adult side. *Many children, including preteens, have developed significant or evolving drug dependencies.* At times, these may not even have been identified prior to a reunification process. Cases are appearing now where children are going to secret vaping parties, pot gatherings, Adderall sharing, and partaking in every other kind of drug that is readily available. Adderall in schools and colleges is readily available. In fact, Adderall use is pandemic. Cocaine is now recreational for some children as well as heroin, which is becoming an increasing problem as it's easily accessible. Binge drinking has become an epidemic in high schools and colleges. Many of the clues that the children are becoming drug dependent may be missed by parents and professionals. Once they are identified, the need for drug treatment may take precedence over the reunification goal. Here are some of the things that are known about children and drug use:[17]

- "For all teens, more first time use of nicotine, marijuana, and alcohol occurred during the summer months of June and July than the rest of the year."
- "The earlier youth engage in any substance use, the more likely they are to develop a substance use disorder later in life."
- "The brain may not finish developing until age 25—and the prefrontal cortex, responsible for decision-making and moderating social behavior, is the last rejoin to mature, making teens uniquely vulnerable to impulsive decisions and higher-risk behavior."

Janet Hopson, in her article "Bad Mix for the Teen Brain,"[18] cites many of the dilemmas related to teen consumption of alcohol. "Heavy alcohol consumption may harm the developing brain, significantly impairing learning,

17. Katie Greeley, *High Time to Talk to Teens*, Philadelphia Inquirer, June 18, 2019, at 18.
18. Janet Hopson, *Bad Mix for the Teen Brain*, 24(3) Scientific American Mind 68–71 (2013).

memory, and thinking in young people."[19] She cites some very important statistics and medical findings that include the following:

1. About 10 percent of eighth graders, 18 percent of 10th graders, and 24 percent of high school seniors binge on alcohol; they consume a minimum of four or five drinks at a sitting at least once every two weeks.
2. High blood alcohol levels are toxic to organs, severely impair sensory and cognitive functions, and encourage habit formation or addiction.
3. Recent findings show that heavy alcohol consumption can also damage parts of the maturing brain, producing lasting deficits in learning and memory in young people."

"In the past decade, neuroscientists have revealed that the prefrontal cortex, which sits at the surface of the brain just behind the forehead, is relatively slow to reach maturity. This region is the seat of inhibitory control—the ability to stop oneself from acting impulsively—and of working memory, the mental scratch pad that enables a person to temporarily hold and manipulate information.[20]

The gist of the research just cited is that various types of drugs (especially alcohol, which is one of the most common) can have significant impact on teens' physical, social, and emotional functioning. Many tests have been performed on their intellectual, spatial relations, and social judgment capacities—all of which show problematic levels of functioning. *Working with these children who are actively involved in drug-related activities will prove problematic, at best.* Sometimes, it is the reunification expert who discovers social and emotional deficits that can then be traced to various levels and types of drug utilization. *I and many other Reunification Therapists have had children that needed to be referred to drug interventions prior to proceeding with reunification efforts.*

Again, when drug addiction is present for either parent or child during reunification efforts, it will almost always complicate the process and outcomes. In fact, some therapists and counselors operate by the common perspective that procedures and goals of therapy cannot proceed effectively as long as drug addiction is an outstanding issue. It needs to be treated prior to, or at least in addition to, any other regular treatment processes. In other words, *the presence of drugs increases the likelihood of minimal progress or complete failure.* However, some caution needs to be exercised, as one person's perception of "addiction" may be another person's view of "occasional" or

19. *Id.* at 68.
20. *Id.*

"recreational" use. Accusations of drinking and driving are not to be taken lightly as the possible consequences can be quite serious. The availability of prescription and street drugs in and around the house can also be a danger to both child and adult. Accusations of selling and/or distributing also need to be clarified. Today, and not infrequently, it is the child who has become a "user." Again, at times, this is discovered in the reunification process. The reunification expert has to use this discovery in accordance with their professional and personal ethics, but always for the maximum safety of the parties involved. Following are some of the common behaviors that are correlated with both adult and child addiction.

Common Emotions, Social Behaviors, and Attitudes Associated with Addiction

- Repetitive/ritualistic/cyclical behaviors
- (Self)destructive (socially, mentally, physically, medically, and spiritually) thoughts/actions
- Self-centered (narcissism)
- Socially damaging (isolationism) and selection of new and bad peers
- Deceptive (and self-deceptive)
- Anger (generating responses)
- Other blaming
- Perceptual distortions (reality testing issues)—loss of focus
- Maturity restricting ("freezes" social-emotional development)
- Anxiety producing
- Confusion producing
- Productivity limiting
- Poor peer selection (negative choices and involvement)
- Rigidity (in thinking and behaviors)
- Conflict generating
- Trust damaging
- Consistency damaging
- Depression inducing
- Manipulative thoughts and behaviors
- Mood fluctuations
- Deviant behavior producing
- Reactive (vs. proactive) behaviors
- Culturally reinforced (by peers, media, adults)
- Lying
- Stealing and other (pre)criminal behaviors

New Adults in the Child's Life

Bringing new adults into a child's life can modify or usurp a parent's role and interfere with the role of the parent seeking closer bonds. This is where children may come to see a mother's paramour as "dad" or a father's new wife as "mom." In same-sex adult relationships, the new partner can also be seen as a parental replacement, too. The distancing or broken bonds can be accelerated as the new adult is presented (by a parent) as (more or equally) legitimate and, thereby, nullifying the other (birth) parent's role as perfunctory. These children will say things like, "I already have a dad (or mom)." Of course, in healthy adult relationships, a child can have a number of adults who are not necessarily vying for ascendency or legitimacy. Teaching adults to share their respective assets with a child is part of Reunification Therapy.

Immigrant Children Separated from Their Parents

A radically increasing phenomenon is immigrant children being separated from their parents for varying amounts of time; some by circumstance, some by political policies, some by criminal cartels who use the children to create "fake families." Some children end up in sex slavery. In any event, these children undergo various and sundry traumas. This is so vast that these children need a special form of assistance to cope with their loss, living in strange facilities, and ending up on the streets or with strange families. Reunification work in these circumstances is a whole new specialty.

Chapter 4

Alienation

"I know my dad's a liar, cause my mom says so, and she never lies."

—14-year-old girl

"Mom broke up the family—she doesn't deserve to have children anymore."

—13-year-old boy

Alienation is one result of a programming/brainwashing process that often ends up with a child being estranged (acting like a stranger) from the target parent. The two separate, but related, aspects of this alienation process are programming and brainwashing.

> Programming is the formulation of a set or sets of directions based on a specific or general belief system directed toward another (child victim or target parent) in order to obtain some desired end/goal. The programming may be willful (conscious) or unintentional (unconscious). The set of directions, messages, and/or other themes contained within the programme may be used to influence the thoughts, perceptions, opinions, ideas, values, beliefs, attitudes, feelings, and/or behaviors of the victims.[1]

The second component is brainwashing, which "is the selection and application of particular techniques, procedures, and methods employed as a basis for inculcating the programme. The brainwashing is the applied dimension."[2] This distinction is important for reunification experts to understand, as it helps them sort out the values, beliefs, attitudes, and feelings (programming) that a parent has versus actual behaviors (brainwashing).

A program can be, "Your father was never there before, so I don't know why he's demanding time now." This is an articulation of a real or imagined belief. The brainwashing component is the verbal repetition, restricted

1. Stanley S. Clawar & Brynne V. Rivlin, Children Held Hostage: Identifying Brainwashed Children, Presenting a Case, and Crafting Solutions 12 (2d ed. 2013).

2. *Id.* at 13.

access, or constant challenge to the father's request for time and contact. This patterned behavior can result in the child being confused, angry, or actually repeating the (mother's) message. By absorbing the (reflective) anxiety of the mother, the child may manifest their own anxiety and fear of the father. Obviously, the roles can be reversed—the father being the source of this "learned hatred."

As we noted, alienation is often the cause du jour for activating reunification, even though it is only one of a couple dozen factors that can lead to the need for reunification efforts.

It is often assumed that alienation is the result of a parent inculcating negative attitudes and behaviors into a child. However, it is also possible that children can and do develop hostile, rejecting, and distancing feelings and behaviors due to real events that may have occurred. I call this *"self-induced alienation."*

For example, a child may figure out (without input from a parent) that financial hardships have resulted from the other parent not paying support. They may come across information that a parent had cheated during the marriage and blame that parent for the dissolution of the family. It is also possible that a parent has been largely absent and there is resentment and hostility because of that situation. A child may come to resent a parent who is hostile to their other parent. Children can become angry, hurt, aggrieved, sad, and/or confused on their own. They sometimes do not like the new family that has been formed by one of their parents and the resulting behavior is disengagement and possibly negative statements. It is also possible that the history between a parent and child involved poor communication and this became even worse once a separation or divorced occurred.

Therefore, not all alienation comes from an adult to a child (even if most does), as there may be real historical events and circumstances that have facilitated a child in developing and targeting one (or both) of their parents. As one child said to me when I inquired about why he didn't want to see his father, "It is revenge for his breaking up the family and always talking negatively about my mom. I developed these feelings on my own, even though everybody seems to want to blame my mother. In fact, she is always telling me to see my dad and I guess I should do it a bit because if I don't, I figured out she could get in trouble." Reunification Therapists, GALs, forensic evaluators, and others involved in these family dynamics can sometimes have difficulty in sorting out when a particular scenario is self-induced or when it is facilitated by one or both of the parents. Actually, it can be a blending of both inputs from adults as well as child-initiated behaviors.

Figure 4.1 reveals the sequence of a father's behaviors/attitudes impacting on the children and then impacting on the children's relationship with their mother.

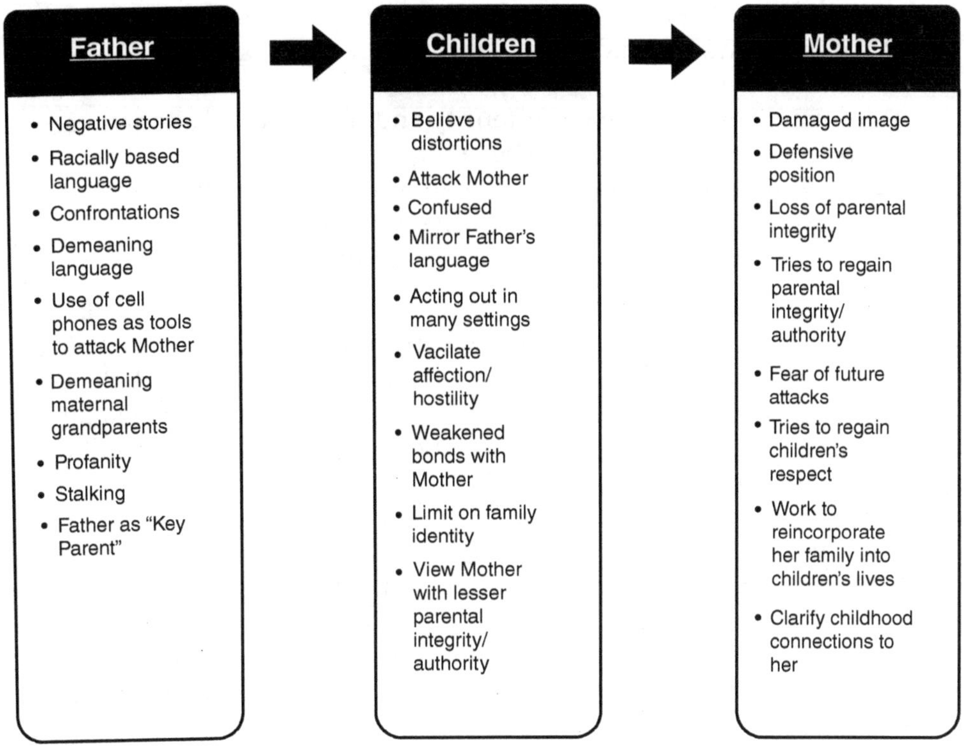

Figure 4.1 An Alienation Process: A Parent's Behaviors Impacting on the Children and Mother's Relationship

Things to Consider When Deciding Whether Alienation Is Present or Not—Detection Factors

Forensic Evaluation

Has alienation previously been identified in a forensic evaluation with specific metrics? If a forensic evaluation has already concluded that alienation is present, then

- It is important to delineate who reportedly did what to whom.
- What beliefs or behaviors were caused (induced) by the alienation process?

- Who was the perpetrator and who is/are the target(s)?
- What interventions have been recommended and possibly executed?
- Does the report identify the intensity and frequency of alienating behaviors and how they have been implemented?
- What ultimate impact did the alienation have on the parent-child bonding (words, feelings, values, behaviors, etc.)?
- Have other alternative explanations been ruled out?

In some cases, there may have been alienation, but it was not detected in previous evaluations. Also, the wrong person may have been identified as the perpetrator. In other cases, both parents may have performed alienating behaviors (called "cross alienation"). The ultimate concern for the Reunification Therapist is the impact on the quality of the parent-child bonding, as this is the main focus of their work.

Unfortunately, some evaluations conclude that alienation is present but do not have adequate data to issue such an opinion. In many cases, no systematic study of alienation was actually undertaken and yet a finding of alienation may appear. (This is common.) There are specific, objective measures of alienation that have been articulated in the social research literature, especially over the past 40 years. The Parent-Child Estrangement Inventory articulated later in this chapter (page 81) can be helpful in beginning to identify the presence versus absence of the phenomenon. Each item is abstracted from the clinical and research data. The term "estrangement" is employed as this is an idea articulated by parents who have been the recipient of an alienation process. "I feel like a stranger to my child." "They behave like they don't really know me." "Things they say and do are like it's not my child." The estrangement feeling can be mutual between parent and child.[3]

Historical Relational Inaccuracies

Children will often present historical information, events, circumstances, and particular memories that are inaccurate, inverted, distorted, or maybe even never occurred. By obtaining factual information from an understanding of the history of the case, Reunification Therapists can often sort out social reality from fancy. In fact, some Reunification Therapists often have a disadvantage in this area because they are not trained to, nor inclined to, do comprehensive social histories. It is somewhat a catch-22. If they do too much social history, they are using time that could be utilized in the re-bonding work. On

3. Some researchers are calling estrangement the unintentional aspect of alienation. This author uses the term "estrangement" as a result of programming and brainwashing. Additional definitions and discussions of estrangement can be found in Leslie Drozd, Michael Saini, & Nancy Olesen, Parenting Plan Evaluations (2d ed. 2016).

the other hand, *if they do not understand the factual social history, they will be operating at a significant disadvantage.* A child who says, "My father was never there for me" may, in fact, be inverting social history. With a better understanding of what really happened, the Reunification Therapist may realize that the father was not only there but, during much of the child's life, was actually the child's primary care parent. *So, distortions, false memories, inverting history, confabulation, and related problems with social reality regularly occur in cases where alienation is present.* Children can learn to believe that something has actually happened that did not (or the opposite) simply by being exposed to massive repetition with an emotional unpinning by an alienating parent.

All Good or All Bad Factor

It is not always true, but frequently it is the case that parents who present themselves as martyred and identify the other parent as tantamount to the devil are presenting a false reality. One of the clues that alienation may need further investigation is when a parent cannot think of one positive aspect of the other parent. When asked to name some of the positive qualities of the other parent, they may say, "I guess in their own way, they love Joey." It is unlikely that any one parent is the perfect model of care while the other parent is the devil incarnate. It can happen, but it's at least a possible red flag.

Facilitations to Disobey a Parent

Alienating parents often provide direct or indirect messages that a child does not have to respect, honor, be with, or listen to the target parent. They may also send messages that they do not have to love or accept the love of the target parent.

Induced Fear of the Other Parent

Many parents exaggerate or create fear or anxiety in the child in terms of the contact with the target parent that is seeking a better relationship. *Induced fear is experienced as tangible and real by the child.* Clinicians who operate by seeing the child individually may discover them issuing opinions without the social context of that feeling.

Secret Keeping

Alienating parents often set up a communication pattern whereby the child and they have special secrets from the target parent. "Don't tell mom this, but you and I know. . . ." Either child or parent can create the secret linkage, but a parent often sets it into motion.

Mirror Imaging (Clone or Puppet Behaviors and Attitudes)

Alienated children often appear as a direct reflection of the words, ideas, behaviors, and hostilities of the alienating parent. At times, it is hard to distinguish the two. They often think and behave as one. In fact, one or both of them will often say things like, "We are so much alike." This is above and beyond the regular and normal identification that children develop with (both of) their parents.

Scripted Views

Children who are alienated often speak in adult language; they issue legal terms, power phrases of the alienating parent, and, in other ways, issue a type of speech that is unusual for a child at that particular age. Sometimes simply asking them where they got the idea from will reveal the source. "My dad says mom is a liar." "Mom said dad has always run around, even in college." Scripted views often reveal historical information that a child could not know unless an adult told them. Commentaries about their parents' relationship before they were even born is not uncommon. Legal knowledge and terms are a good giveaway. Caution on this aspect, as some children at 12 years of age are reading and comprehending on the college level.

In summary, there are about 25 different ways (metrics) to detect if alienation is present. The preceding is just a short list. For a more detailed list, see Chapter 4 "Detection Factors" in *Children Held Hostage: Identifying Brainwashed Children, Presenting a Case, and Crafting Solutions*.[4]

Cases with alienation as a primary factor can range from very mild to severe. The more severe they are, the more involved and complicated the reunification intervention needs to be. Often testing out the degree and type of support that the alienating parent will issue is key. Unfortunately, progress can be made in the office only to have it undermined at home. Developing a series of support questions is important in the treatment plan. For example, major progress was made in the office (meeting with, talking to, sharing positive history, and promises for parent and child to see each other outside of the office) only to have the child reject the actual contact outside of the office when an overture or opportunity presented itself. Investigating this revealed that the mother said to the child, "Well, it's your decision and I'll support you as I always have." This was after the mother agreed in the office to say, "Both mom and dad want you to renew your relationship." This is showing a "good face" in the professional setting and "bad behavior" (undermining) out of the office.

Figure 4.2 articulates the professional procedures necessary in alienation cases.

---

4. Clawar & Rivlin, *supra* note 1.

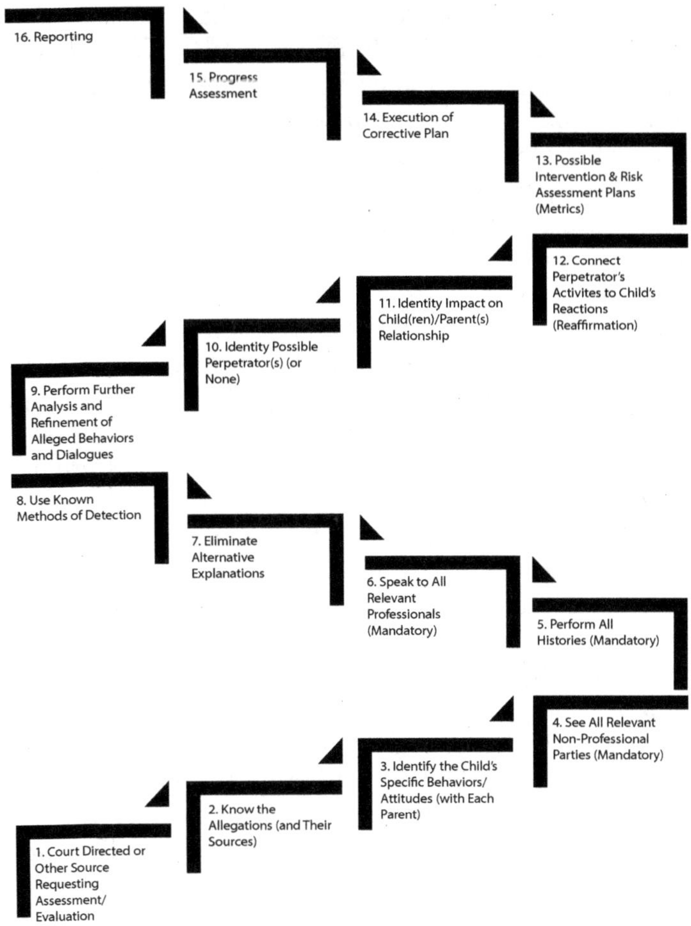

Figure 4.2 Sequence of Identifying Alienation and Possible Perpetrators: A Staircase

The New Science of Memory

The science of memory has been expanding significantly in the last 20 years. It is revolutionizing our understanding of issues that come up in divorce, marital conflicts, and reunification work. Questions arise like "Can a false memory be induced into a child?"; in other words, can they say something happened that never actually happened? The research answer is yes. Another question that arises is "Can a child's memory be deleted?" In terms of this latter issue, can they have a parent-child experience or set of experiences that occurred (sometimes with regularity), but the child has no recollection of these experiences? The answer is yes. More commonly in reunification work, a more pressing issue, especially when alienation is present, is whether "reality memory" can be restored.

Recent studies like those of Donald G. MacKay in "The Engine of Memory" (*Scientific American Mind* May/June 2014) help us understand that *"the memories that suffer the most are those we use infrequently." So a child who hasn't seen a parent for a month versus a year versus five years is likely to have more memory problems* of various types as they are not being stimulated by actual interaction with that parent. Interestingly enough, the new research is also suggesting that the role of the hippocampus helps us to "craft new memories to replace those that have become degraded over the years." This means that children can develop new memories of old events or new memories of present events that delete or modify past experiences.

A more common need for reunification professionals is *how to restore memories that actually are based on real life experiences.* For example, a mother who has spent the first five years of her life being the primary care parent for her daughter is confronted with the statement, "You were never there for me in the past, so why should I (a 12-year-old) be there for you?" By gathering objective evidence from relatives, photographs, diaries, and therapeutic histories, it became clear that the mother's description of the past did, in fact, occur. *Reactivating the child's memory to coordinate with historical reality* is a task that befalls reunification professionals. The more they know about physiological and biochemical aspects of memory, the more likely they will be able to *refurbish memory that comports with social reality.* We now know that some areas of the brain store memories for words, whereas other parts of the brain store memories for images, and other parts of the brain store memories for emotions. The different physical structures of the brain actually interact to create what we call "present memory." It's also interesting that for some children, memory triggers are different. I've had particular children respond to particular words (playground) whereas others responded to pictorial presentations (pictures of mother and daughter after a dance recital) and other children responded to emotionally labeled descriptions ("Remember how you felt the first time you went down the slide yourself and mom was there to catch you?").

A further curiosity in terms of memory is that the research shows that by engaging in actual social situations, memory may not only be protected for longer periods of time, but by *reactivating these social situations, a more accurate memory could be reactivated.* An example of the latter is a child who asserted that his father did little, if any of the family functions and get-togethers. Yet, when I took him and his father to a restaurant, he began to have a flooding of memories about them eating together in a great number of different places. This social situational analysis (contextual) is fodder for the argument that *recreating social arrangements as part of Reunification Therapy can be a very helpful tool.*

Given the *principle of recency,* we tend to recall things better and stronger that have occurred more recently. We can also understand why new family circumstances (father and stepmother or mother and stepfather) appear to a child as more powerful, more meaningful, and maybe more emotionally fulfilling. As the science of memory advances, it will continue to inform us even more of what Greg Miller refers to as "how our brains make memories."[5] Miller also sensitizes us to how "surprisingly inaccurate" memories can be. What are called *"misperceptions" are very common* and these possibilities must be respected in reunification work.

Finally, memories can also help us delete characteristics that make us or another look better than we really are. A glaring example of this is the child who remembers his father leaving the marital home in a huff as part of their parents announcing their impending divorce. Actually it was the mother who fled. This is an example of inversion and is also an aspect of memory, self-serving recollection. This is in preservation of our egos and self-status.

As is noted in the article titled *Honest Liars*,[6] "there is a human tendency to generate explanations for events." This means that we "can dream up completely plausible explanations. This is called 'choice blindness.'" There are circumstances where the brain can "no longer . . . reign in their fantasies." This is because part of the brain produces explanations for experiences and there is a separate

> control circuit in the VMPFC (ventromedial prefrontal cortex) and limbic system which tests the plausibility of these concoctions. *This dynamic between creativity and control is an important component of our thought process.* Both mechanisms occur unconsciously and usually occur in equilibrium. *In confabulating patients, however, the brain's supervisory circuits have gone haywire.* They are no longer able to reign in their fantasies.[7]

This is likely more pronounced in children and adolescents, because their brains are still in various stages of development (probably until their mid to late twenties, according to recent research in neurological development).

Social-emotional memories can be retrieved differently in different contexts (where and how it was acquired are factors). So, when I met with a parent and child at a playground, the dialogue that was stimulated was qualitatively different than in the professional setting. The mother said, "Ella, remember when we used to play on the swing set every Saturday?" Her daughter excitedly responded, "Yeah! And then we'd play on the slide!" This was after the daughter was unable to recall any memories in the office about going to the playground with her mother.

---

5. Megan Gambino, *Greg Miller on "Making Memories,"* Smithsonian, Apr. 20, 2010. Retrieved from https://www.smithsonianmag.com/science-nature/greg-miller-on-making-memories-21601824.

6. Maria-Dorothea Heidler, *Honest Liars*, 25(2) Sci. Am. Mind, 40–44 (2014). Retrieved from https://www.jstor.org.ezproxy.neumann.edu/stable/24946069.

7. *Id.* (emphasis added).

Going through a list of facts in the office (We did this and that . . .), which is common in various therapies, may bring minimal to no to negative to distorted memories. When meeting a father and daughter at a restaurant, the father asked his daughter, "Should I order for you?" His daughter, Cinda, said, "You used to do that, didn't you?" "Yes" said the father, "and I bet you still like the same thing. Want me to guess?" Cinda quickly retorted, "I bet you can't." When the waiter arrived, the father ordered for his daughter, "Chicken Parmigiana with extra sauce. A side salad with creamy Caesar dressing and no onions." Cinda stared at her father before finally saying to him, "Wow dad, how did you remember?" This was the first time that she had called her father "dad" in more than a year.

Contextual reactions of memory are not only about facts of particular events, but emotions associated with the event. *This means the professional office is only one setting for Reunification Therapy*—and maybe not the best for every re-bonding goal.

Memory inversions and distortions are harder to deal with. Some examples are:

- The mother cheated, but the father becomes the "cheater."
- The father yells at the mother, but the mother becomes the "screamer."
- The father pays support, but the mother "carries" the family.
- The mother takes us to court, but the dad is seen as limiting access to the children.

Helping to correct this, if that is part of the plan, can create secondary problems for the child. Loyalty issues are one such problem. If I let go of the mother/father being the victim, am I abandoning them? in some ways is a childhood dilemma. Reunification Therapy must, at times, deal with these deeper dilemmas.

Types and Aspects of Memory

There are many types and characteristics of memory. Following are some of the types and their special aspects and features that can impact on the reunification process.

- *Short-Term Memory*—things that are stored and retrieved from seconds to weeks. Sometimes called "working memory" (five to nine items).
- *Long-Term Memory*—things that can be stored and retrieved from months to years/decades. This can be further divided into components:

- *Declarative (Explicit) Memory*—facts, general knowledge, and personal experiences. This is then divided into semantic and episodic memories.
    - o *Semantic Memory*—deals with general factual matters and matters related to your world: multiplication, the concept of a book, and civil war information.
    - o *Episodic Memory*—personal experiences: first kiss, last meals eaten, first time you met your partner.
- *Procedural Memory*—a second subtype of long-term memory. It deals with sequences and tasks.
- *Sensory Memory*—an automatic type. Can degrade in seconds or less.
- *Adaptive Memory*—features that help with several needs: environmental, personal, social, and adaptations.
- *Primary Memory*—the feature that arouses specific memory. Any stimuli can prime or arouse certain memory types.
- *Rehearsal Factors*—memory that is reinforced (or created) by exposure to repetition.
- *Recognition Memory*—stimuli that facilitates recall. What you remember when you see a picture.
- *Recall Memory*—retrieved without exact stimuli.
- *Detail versus Global Memory*—ability to remember exact aspects versus a general sense of events.
- *Topographic Memory*—memory of places, directions, and settings.
- *Flashbulb Memory*—often episodic and emotionally changed memory. "I remember the time, place, words, and feelings when I heard you and mom were getting a divorce."
- *Retrospective Memory*—historical aspects of events, circumstances, communication. "You ran to your room every time Uncle Joe came here."
- *Prospective/Future Memory*—anticipation of future (based on past memories). "You'll probably feel badly for quite a while."
- *Paired Associate Learning*—associating words (dad/mom) with another fact or emotion (sad, scary, confused, etc.).
- *Cued Recall*—providing hints at information in the memory.
- *Color Memory*—the ability to recall or recognize individual or blended colors within a certain context.
- *Name Memory*—the ability to recognize or recall names of people, streets, objects, places, things, and so on.
- *People/Facial Memory*—the ability to recognize or recall particular individuals, such as extended family members, neighbors, and others.
- *Word Memory*—the ability to remember specific words or patterns of words.
- *Trauma Memory*—the ability to recall shocking or impactful events usually associated with emotions of fear and anxiety.

- *Object Memory*—the ability to recall or recognize objects such as houses, cars, clothing, toys, and so on.
- *Story Memory*—the recognition or recall of themes, details, and scenarios about a particular event or experience.
- *Sequential Memory*—recalling or recognizing the ordered steps of an event or circumstance.
- *Contextual Memory*—recall or recognition that involves the setting, place, and/or atmosphere of an event.
- *Elaborated Memory*—the recognition or recall whereby facts, emotions, details, and circumstances get inserted into an original memory.
- *Inverted Memory*—a process whereby an event or circumstance gets reversed (e.g., a father is hollering at a mother but the inverted memory becomes that the mother was hollering at the father).
- *Activity Memory*—the recall or recognition of movement patterns within a particular context (e.g., "We went from the movie to the ice cream parlor.").
- *Induced or Created Memory*—this is a memory, usually formed through repetition, that is created by one person and transferred to another (e.g., "Remember when dad crashed the car?" This memory became real, but did not happen because the father was out of town at the time.). **This is one of the most important memories to understand, especially when alienation may be present or suspected.**
- *Olfactory Memory*—particular smells or odors can be retrieved with or without the actual physical stimuli being present. These memories can also trigger flashbacks to events, peoples, and circumstances (e.g., "Dad, remember the smell of that house you were going to buy? It smelled like rotten eggs. We walked in and walked out.")
- *Auditory Memory*—the recognition or recall of particular sounds that are usually associated with certain places, settings, or events (e.g., "Mom, remember when we lived there? The train would go by every day at 8 in the morning").
- *Role Memory*—the recall or recognition or particular attitudes and behaviors attached to a status (position) (e.g., the role that a mother or father played during a separation).
- *Culture Memory*—this is the recall or recognition of elements of an ethnic, racial, national, or religious culture. This includes rituals, prayers, foods, beliefs, and other elements of culture (e.g., "I remember grandmom's meatballs with the Italian sauce").
- *Ritual Memory*—recalling or recognizing the sequence of family, religious, or educational patterned behaviors (e.g., "Every day when we went to school, we stood by our desks and said a prayer").

Cognitive neuroscience is an evolving discipline. So far, we know that *memories can be expanded, modified, distorted, blended, confused, inverted, deleted, suppressed, falsified, and/or created.* This statement should provide pause to any Reunification Therapist in accepting or rejecting information related to their mission of re-bonding.

A case in point recently was when a judge ordered a 14-year-old child to increase his time with his father. The judge was presented with forensic evidence that the child's recall of events, dialogue, and parental aggression was confused, inverted, and, in general, historically inaccurate. *With solid forensic evidence, the court can make more informed decisions* or, at least, enhance its understanding of various assertions and positions of children and adults. *The more emotionally charged an incident or recollection was (and is), the more caution needs to be exercised in accepting what is presented as exact recall.*

Therapists are not philosophers dealing with issues of ultimate truth. That does not mean that forensic social science can't be value additive. Some memories are susceptible to variations due to a myriad of factors. Knowing these factors is one of the foundations of Reunification Therapy. Given the great diversity of types of memories, it is important to exercise caution in collecting social-psychological data for all types of therapies and evaluations.

Some assertions are easier to determine than others—especially extreme statements like those in Chapter 5, "What Children May Say about Reunification." *Also, the longer a child has had no or limited contact (with a loving, caring, and functional parent) the more memory modifications, distortions, and rigidities can form.*

Speech patterns, repetition, social-emotional linkages, and challenges can all modify memory. So, *memory is not a box of events and emotions that are accurately available upon request.* Note, the new science of (faulty) witness recall in criminal cases as a case in point.

Also, *stress is one of the big modifiers of memory.* Divorce, separation, litigation, worries about the children, fear of loss (house, reputation, income, status, parenthood, etc.) are some of the highest stress times in a person's life. Children, too, live within these stress zones. Children, too, are part of, and recipients of, the entire divorce process.

Memory appears to be a stage-dependent process. There is an acquisition stage, which is about storage and retrieval, whereas the consolidation stage has to do with strengthening neural connections. Research tells us that memory is consolidated more while a person is asleep. However, memory (qualitatively) can change when memories are transferred to long-term storage.

The sleep deprivation of many children today (as well as adults) raises real questions about memory accuracy. *Damaged sleep equals damaged memory.*

So, *memories are actually constructed* given the preceding considerations. Some older, but valuable, studies[8] found that the very words used in questioning determined the answers given. For example, witnesses were asked if a car was "smashed or hit." If the word "smashed" was used, the subject claimed a car was moving faster versus when the word "hit" was being used. For family law, a question could be "Did your father stop the fight?," "Did your father grab your brother?," or "Did your dad have any reaction to the situation you described?" Different questions about the same event can result in significantly different answers depending on the way they are phrased or how the words were employed. Lawyers know this well when examining a witness.

Following is a Parent-Child Estrangement Inventory that can be useful for forensic evaluations of all types, including reunification work. The more items that are checked by a parent, the greater the probability that they are involved, in some fashion, in an alienation process. It is geared toward what is called the "targeted parent." It is also a good guideline for developing intervention approaches, as it signals attitudes and behaviors that the child may have experienced and/or their aligned parent may have undertaken. It further provides data on the perceptions of the seeking (or less bonded) parent. By checking the boxes that apply, a professional or parent can come up with a percentage of items that are usually found (in clusters) in alienation-related cases. It is important to remember that alienation, if present, may only be one, but significant, factor leading to broken social bonds.[9]

---

8. Elizabeth F. Loftus & John C. Palmer, *Reconstruction of Automobile Destruction*, J. Verbal Learning & Verbal Behavior, 1974, at 585–89.

9. The themes are derived from the research on alienation and the author's experience in about 1,000 alienation-related cases.

Parent-Child Estrangement Inventory[10]

Directions to a Parent: If you have experienced the particular item, place a checkmark (❑) and see the scale on page 87 to determine the percentage of items you checked. Obviously, the more you checked, the greater the likelihood of exposure to an alienation experience. These items can be shared with the Reunification Therapist as guides to your concerns, views, and experiences.

- ❑ 1. My child says things about the past (especially our relationship) that never actually happened.
- ❑ 2. Over time, I've noticed my child is less and less affectionate with me.
- ❑ 3. My child has shifted from calling me Mommy or Daddy to my first name or no name.
- ❑ 4. I have been told by my ex (or child) that my attendance at school or other events is upsetting to my son or daughter.
- ❑ 5. Things that my ex has done in the past are now being attributed to me.
- ❑ 6. My side of the family (grandparents, etc.) is getting less and less time with the kids.
- ❑ 7. My child has reduced or eliminated bringing their friends to my home.
- ❑ 8. When my kids are with me, the other parent calls/e-mails/texts (too) frequently.
- ❑ 9. My parenting is increasingly criticized.
- ❑ 10. My child asked me if I really wanted them to be born.
- ❑ 11. My child told me that I cheated on their other parent and that's what caused the divorce.
- ❑ 12. My child knows more and more about legal issues, but not from me.
- ❑ 13. My views, values, and attitudes are being seen as negative.
- ❑ 14. If my ex does the same thing I do, it is positive for them, and negative for me.
- ❑ 15. My child has said to me or I have heard through others that the child does not want to see me much or at all.
- ❑ 16. My child is using terms like "our family" and "my home" to refer to their life with their other parent.
- ❑ 17. I feel that I am "damned if I do, damned if I don't." If I go to the kid's play I am accused of causing tension. If I don't go to the play then I am told I don't care.
- ❑ 18. I feel like I am losing my parenthood.

10. ©Stanley S. Clawar, Ph.D., C.C.S., 2019.

- ❑ 19. The less time I have with my children, the worse it gets.
- ❑ 20. My kids use phrases and language that can only come from other adults.
- ❑ 21. My authority to set limits/boundaries and make decisions for my kids is decreasing.
- ❑ 22. Some of the professionals I have seen tell me "perception is reality" but I know it is not.
- ❑ 23. Some of the professionals that I have seen do not seem to know what to do to build bridges between me and my children.
- ❑ 24. "Therapy" has made my relationship with my kids worse or it's stayed the same.
- ❑ 25. I feel if it keeps going on like this I will lose my kid(s) completely.
- ❑ 26. I think almost no one "gets it"—kids need two parents who care and guide them.
- ❑ 27. I feel the legal and professional community is set up to keep children enmeshed in conflict.
- ❑ 28. If I have done nothing wrong, how come I am losing my kid(s)?
- ❑ 29. No one seems concerned about the suffering of a parent.
- ❑ 30. The legal system talks about "the best interests of the child." Really? It's in the child's best interest to:
  - ❑ a. Be brainwashed?
  - ❑ b. Lose a loving parent?
  - ❑ c. Grow up with a parent who is "socially dead"?
  - ❑ d. Form an alliance with a parent who damaged their relationship with the other parent?
- ❑ 31. The only ones who seem to "get it" are other parents in similar conditions.
- ❑ 32. Psychological labels have been used to damage my image. Labels like these have been used about me:
  - ❑ a. Anxious
  - ❑ b. Obsessive compulsive
  - ❑ c. Depressed
  - ❑ d. Aggressive
  - ❑ e. Hostile
  - ❑ f. Abusive
  - ❑ g. Other terms:______________________________________
  - ❑ h. I believe that all of number 32 above can be explained by my present parental dilemma.
- ❑ 33. I'm starting to believe this society doesn't really value the parent-child relationship.

- ❑ 34. I am afraid that my children are developing with messed up views of me and social reality.
- ❑ 35. I have been accused of things:
  - ❑ a. Child abuse
  - ❑ b. Sexual abuse
  - ❑ c. Neglect
  - ❑ d. Abandonment
  - ❑ e. Bad morality
  - ❑ f. Stupid decisions
  - ❑ g. Not really caring
  - ❑ h. Using the legal system to hurt my kids and the other parent
  - ❑ i. Being a cheat
  - ❑ j. Lying
  - ❑ k. Upsetting my ex
  - ❑ l. Not paying support
  - ❑ m. Wanting things only my way
  - ❑ n. Narcissism
  - ❑ o. Alienation
  - ❑ p. Not loving my kids
- ❑ 36. I have developed insecurities about my speech and behaviors due to constant criticism.
- ❑ 37. At times my kids feel like strangers.
- ❑ 38. When I try to correct my kid's misperceptions of the past it causes them to become more distant.
- ❑ 39. My kids get defensive of their other parent even if I did not actually attack them.
- ❑ 40. My kids have become spies and report information back to their other parent that makes me look bad.
- ❑ 41. My legal attempts to see my kids have been used against me.
- ❑ 42. My kids don't seem to understand that my time, money, and energy to be with them is because I love them.
- ❑ 43. When my kids talk about events or characterizations of me, I feel like I am talking to a stranger who doesn't know what they are talking about.
- ❑ 44. My children have become hurtful to me when they don't even recognize it or mean to be.
- ❑ 45. I feel like I have become an "out-group" member with my own kids.
- ❑ 46. At times, I see signs that they love me but seem to be afraid to reach out.
- ❑ 47. At times, I hear pleas from the children for peace between their parents but then they "switch back to stranger-like behaviors."

- ❑ 48. When I correct my children's distorted views they seem confused.
- ❑ 49. Sometimes my kids seem to believe my own view of me as a "good guy."
- ❑ 50. At times, my kids will be happy with me after they settle in, yet right before they leave they seem to return to that "distant kid."
- ❑ 51. When I talk to my kids at their other parent's house or a social event they are limited in emotional expression and social contact.
- ❑ 52. The negative views they are developing toward me makes me worry about the future.
- ❑ 53. Sometimes I mentally prepare for what life would be like if I were out of their lives completely.
- ❑ 54. I have had advice from professionals that I should be "patient."
- ❑ 55. Some professionals or judges have suggested that I slowly "phase in" to my child's life. Why? I didn't do anything wrong to get "phased out."
- ❑ 56. When my kids are in "therapy" with me, they mostly repeat nonsense.
- ❑ 57. Professionals have set a tone that they (the professional) are there to respect the child's needs, but if their needs are screwed up then what?
- ❑ 58. I've been given advice to go along like I agree with the kids anxiety but this will make it worse, wont it?
- ❑ 59. Even if I did make mistakes in the past, the kids seem not to be able to balance out the mistakes of their other parent.
- ❑ 60. If I try to correct the distortions the kids have, I'm told "it's not true" or "you're a liar."
- ❑ 61. Guardians ad litem who just represent a child's distortions don't really help me.
- ❑ 62. I think my kids deep down know I love them but sometimes are afraid to connect.
- ❑ 63. The best times we have together are when we are physically (far) away from the other parent (for a good period of time).
- ❑ 64. I sense my kids would like to reach out to me but seem afraid that they will upset their other parent.
- ❑ 65. My ex has put me down in front of the children.
- ❑ 66. My ex has a superior parenting attitude towards me.
- ❑ 67. My kids are coming to see my parenting as inferior.
- ❑ 68. My ex has moved in a new man or woman in the children's lives that is replacing me.
- ❑ 69. Some have advised me to back off and the kids will come back, but I don't believe that this advice is good.

- ❑ 70. The main focus of problems is to put me under the microscope and I can't seem to get out of this position.
- ❑ 71. My defensive position has actually hurt my relationship with my kids.
- ❑ 72. At times my kids seem "schizo," (hot and cold), depending on different settings or things that are happening.
- ❑ 73. My kids don't like going to "therapy" and generally blame me for this.
- ❑ 74. The therapist has not taken a strong enough stance to enhance or validate my parenting.
- ❑ 75. The therapist has not challenged the children's views of me that are inaccurate.
- ❑ 76. The therapist has not told the kids that their negatives can and should change.
- ❑ 77. The therapist seems to side with my ex and the kids more than "building bridges."
- ❑ 78. I have told my kids good contact time will build relationships but they seem stuck.
- ❑ 79. I see my children and myself as victimized by the other parent, the lawyer, the legal system and the "therapists."
- ❑ 80. At times, my children's disrespect is so strong that I know they need correction.
- ❑ 81. I am afraid of being firm or using discipline out of fear of being "reported" to their other parent or some authority.
- ❑ 82. I recognize that the goal of my ex is to damage or sever my relationship with the kids but others don't seem to see it or know what to do.
- ❑ 83. My good deeds, love, and caring in the past are being lost or diminished to my children.
- ❑ 84. If my child asks questions indicating a need to know information and ideas about me or our life I am thrilled to supply it.
- ❑ 85. I have tried clever ways to have conversations that will help the children but it's not easy at times.
- ❑ 86. I feel like I am walking on eggshells and the kids sense this.
- ❑ 87. I can tell that negative information about me is coming from my ex and his/her associates.
- ❑ 88. I always plan(ned) to be in my kid's lives and now I feel that I am being pushed out.
- ❑ 89. I believe that my kids' disrespect and confusion will impact their later relationships. I've told them this and they don't seem to get it.
- ❑ 90. My kids sound like lawyers.
- ❑ 91. My kids have said and implied "they have rights too."

- ❑ 92. I feel my time with them is not natural.
- ❑ 93. When they are with me physically they seem mentally somewhere else.
- ❑ 94. My kids often say "mommy says" or "daddy says." It's like they (the other parent) are here when they are not really here.
- ❑ 95. At night, before bed, with the kids seems to be the best time for closeness.
- ❑ 96. When I see breakthroughs or outreach from the kids, I can tell the ex intensifies their negative message and interferes.
- ❑ 97. Schools and doctors have been told things about me that are damaging to my relationship with the kids.
- ❑ 98. My ex claims they want the kids to have a good relationship with me but (s)he:
  - ❑ a. Limits time with me and the child(ren)
  - ❑ b. Limits communications between me and the child(ren)
  - ❑ c. Tells professionals bad stories about me
  - ❑ d. Spends time and/or money in the legal system to control my relationship and/or access
  - ❑ e. Taints the kids' views of me
- ❑ 99. The kids would likely see me more but seem caught in a loyalty conflict.
- ❑ 100. The kids tell their other parents things that didn't happen here or they modify it to make it negative.
- ❑ 101. If my kids have a good time with me they often don't tell my ex anything.
- ❑ 102. I know my kids get "grilled" when they go back to my ex's house.
- ❑ 103. Joint legal custody has been a joke. My ex makes most decisions without my (meaningful) input.
- ❑ 104. I find out after the fact what's going on at school or other important activities.
- ❑ 105. We can have great times but then they can turn around and sound so cold on the phone.
- ❑ 106. I have hostile e-mails, texts, or other communications from my ex.
- ❑ 107. I've sent cards or presents that have been damaged or disappeared.
- ❑ 108. My children don't have photographs of me at their other parent's residence.
- ❑ 109. My children have joined in on accusations against me.
- ❑ 110. My children don't answer any or very few of my texts or e-mails.

❑ 111. My children have been given too much power to decide family matters.
❑ 112. My ex has damaged my reputation with school, neighbors, doctors, religious, or other therapeutic professionals.
❑ 113. I have been investigated but never found guilty of anything.
❑ 114. I can't figure out how we have good times and all I hear back from my ex or her/his representatives is that they hate seeing me.
❑ 115. My positive history with my children seems to have gotten lost.

Scale

Number of Items	Percentage of Yes	Number of Items	Percentage of Yes
0 – 11	0% – 9%	58 – 69	50% – 59%
12 – 23	10% – 19%	70 – 81	60% – 69%
24 – 34	20% – 29%	82 – 92	70% – 79%
35 – 46	30% – 39%	93 – 104	80% – 89%
47 – 57	40% – 49%	105 – 116	90% – 100%

Alienation Is Present—What Do You Do?

Determine if You Have the Expertise to Assist

If the reunification expert is diagnostically sure that alienation is present, they need to design some specific interventions as part of the overall treatment plan. The reason for this is that if distortions and falsities are present, any future success is highly unlikely or, will, at least, be minimal and compromised. Sometimes, children can still reconnect and then will work through the negative program they have learned.

Prematurely Attacking (Extreme) Distortions or Falsities Can Backfire

If this is done too early in the therapeutic process, it can actually heighten the children's resistance, let alone alarm the alienating parent. Slight misunderstandings can be challenged earlier on (the mother was actually at the play two years ago but the child didn't see her) versus more serious beliefs ("You broke up the marriage by cheating on mom"). *Factual challenges often are not adequate to undermine an alienated child's cognitive and emotional mindsets.* Therapists who understand this will try to build bridges by social-emotional linkages rather than simply factual discussions. Statements from a parent such as, "You know that I have always loved you" will have less impact than sharing an experience where love was clearly present. Alienated children are often "ready," if not prepared (even intuitively) for factual challenges to their problematic beliefs and/or behaviors.

Professional Assistance in Changing Perceptions

The Reunification Therapist can, at times, assist in reorienting a child who has developed beliefs that ultimately have damaged the parent-child bond. A good example of this is an alienated child who used the term "stalking" in regard to his mother's investigation of his school performance. Subsequently, a discussion ensued around the term "stalking." When the child inquired of the Reunification Therapist, "You know what I mean by stalking, right?," the professional answer was "No, please explain it." The child then went on to describe his mother going from teacher to teacher in order to gather what was really (normal) educational performance information. The therapist was then able to explain that following up on school performance was, in fact, a normal parental behavior and that real stalking was more of a criminal term. This brief semantic debate proved useful as there were also many other terms that were used to demean his mother. *The linguistic patterns of alienating children generally could be called "globalized negatives."* This means that extreme terms are used which (virtually always) have a negative implication for the target parent. In this case, the therapist also asked, "Is there ever anything positive about a parent checking up on educational progress?" The neutral language forced a more rational and productive discussion. However, at the end of the discussion, in order to maintain his negativity (which is a common resistance pattern for alienated children), the child said, "Anyhow, I expected you to take my mother's side." It is important to see in this example that working with alienated children in the context of reunification is a process that may take some time. The next session had to deal with the child's (programmed) perceptions of the Reunification Therapist. This happens because alienated children attach negatives to anyone they believe is positively connected to the target parent.

Diversity of Approaches

Alienated children, more so than others, may require a diversity of interventions. Many of these children think they know or can figure out what will happen in a given session. This is a challenge, and providing varied experiences reduces this type of possible (negative) anticipation. Sometimes, they are correct about what is to transpire, and they don't present a cooperative stance. *Remember, just because a child manifests, on the surface, learned hatred or confusion on bonding doesn't meant they don't love that parent and want/need the relationship at some level.* Real attachment is often still present, but buried beneath brainwashing, circumstances, emotional confusion, loyalty conflicts, habitual behaviors, and more.

Coaching the Target Parent

Working with a target parent on new scripts, social positions, ideas, recollections, listening skills, and other communication patterns is crucial so that they are prepared in form and content to deal with the alienated child that is before them. Historically, the target parent has often been worried, scared, and/or anxious about how to communicate with their own child. They frequently say that the child before them is not the one than they used to know. They also say that there was reciprocal caring and love that is gone or damaged. They say that they are damned if they do, and damned if they don't. Helping them through these social and personal dilemmas and hurdles is crucial, as the alienated child will, to some degree, still be reflecting off of them, even if it doesn't look that way in the early phases of contact under professional guidance.

The confusion that alienated children can have is sometimes surprising. An alienated child can tell a parent that they are not allowed or desired to ever come to any of their plays, sporting events, or other activities. The parent then complies, at which point the child issues another message, "I knew you didn't love me because you never show(ed) up for me." *Living in a world of contradictions is indigenous to alienated children and target parents.* The therapist needs the knowledge and capacity to explain and guide the parent through these conundrums. I have often said to targeted parents, "What you see and hear ain't necessarily what you (will) get (or what is underneath)." A generally good principle to follow is that if a child has some positive memories, feelings, and behaviors mixed in with negative memories, feelings, and behaviors, *it is the positive foundational elements that the therapist needs to hear and utilize* (more so than the negative ones).

Working with the Alienating Parent

At times, it is possible to help to reorient an alienating parent, especially if they are doing it unintentionally. Many parents do not want to intentionally harm their own child and if properly approached, they may form a collaboration with the Reunification Therapist because they were unwittingly doing things that were harmful to the relationship of the target parent and child. Some of these parents may have said things like, "I'll do anything for my child." When I have called upon that ethos, they will often then try something new. Also, sometimes the alienating parent starts to experience their own problems with a child that they have due to the empowering of the child against the target parent. In these scenarios, I have been able to *get both parents to join together in a common bond to direct the child's oppositional behaviors.* Many alienated children who start out targeting one parent end up feeling empowered against their siblings, the other parent, teachers, therapists, and others. Arrogance, disobedience, and hostility to rules are not an uncommon behavioral results for alienated children. At times, I've been able to say to alienating parents, "Be careful what you wish for, because you may get it." This "backfire effect" on the alienating parent is common.

Continued Interference

If an alienating parent will not stop performing their problematic role, it may be necessary to enlist the aid of a GAL, the court mediator, or the judge. There have been cases where these parents have simply been issued a cease and desist with sanctions (financial and/or custodial ramifications). This is kind of a "court of last resort" approach, but in the more intense cases (of alienation), it may be a necessity. This should be considered prior to shipping a child off to some of the centers that have arisen and now claim to do radical interventions (in extreme alienation cases).

Enlisting the Help of Others

Sometimes a sibling, aunt, uncle, grandparent, friend of the family, professional, clergy, or other important person in the life of the child can be useful in the re-bonding process. This is especially helpful when the child or alienating parent has a deep respect for that person. A case in point was a coach whom a boy respected probably more than anybody else in his social constellation. This coach strongly desired that the boy reconnect with his father and even went out of his way to make sure that he would say and do everything that he could to make it happen. The result of this was that it did happen due to the collaboration between the therapist and coach. *Thinking out of the box is a necessary skill* for reunification professionals. Using everyone available, situations, scenarios, scripts, and more can be of great service toward reconnecting a parent and child.

If Both Parents Are Sources of Alienation

What I have called *cross programming/brainwashing* or multiple alienation is an additional complication. This is when both parents are performing negative inputs and/or behaviors to a child. Sometimes, one of them is doing *"reactive alienation"*; because it was done to them, they retaliate in kind. The child ends up having no safe haven from negative messages. This experience will "freeze" them developmentally and, possibly, significantly so. Some of these children have asked if "I can live with my grandparents" or "my friend Joey has a sane family, can't I go there? I spend most of my time there anyway." These children sometimes find a surrogate family to stabilize their own lives.

Deprogramming[11]

"The major factors involved in thoroughly understanding the potential for and implementation of a deprogramming process include:

1. *Design of a treatment plan* with a risk assessment;
2. *Knowledge of memory science* and its applications;
3. *Knowledge of the themes* and content of the programme (programming);
4. *Knowledge of the techniques* employed to inculcate the themes (brainwashing);
5. *Knowledge of the duration and intensity* of the programming/brainwashing;
6. *Knowledge of the motives* of the programmer and the child being programmed;
7. *Evaluation of the degree and types of damage* or negative impact of the process of programming and brainwashing upon the child, target parent, and often on the programmer/brainwasher himself/ herself;
8. *Evaluation of the resources available* in the deprogramming process;
9. *Establishment of rapport* between the child who has been programmed/brainwashed and the agent of change;
10. *Knowledge of the potential risks* of implementation of and involvement in a deprogramming process;
11. *Identifying and dealing with the possible "point of no return"*;
12. *Knowledge of the potential for "shutdown"*;
13. *Introduction of objective vs. subjective materials*;
14. *Environmental modification*—changing the amount and type of time the child spends with the programming/brainwashing parent and the target parent;
15. *Change modalities and therapeutic settings*—vacation is helpful in techniques and physical settings.

11. Extracted and expanded from Clawar & Rivlin, *supra* note 1, at 204.

16. *Reeducation, counseling, therapy*—engaging the parents, child, siblings, and/or others relevant to the problem in some forms of informational dissemination, counseling, and/or therapy; and
17. *Measuring the degree/type of changes* that can, will, or have taken place as a result of the deprogramming process."

Summary

Alienation is a process that a parent usually does over a significant period of time. As such, it will not be undone in a day. Unintentional types (20 percent of alienation) are usually more changeable. The Reunification Therapist must be schooled on the theories, methods, impacts, and treatment modalities. Unschooled professionals will often jump to radical interventions with no (or poor) treatment plans or risk assessment. The latter also needs to include risks of interventions to the seeking parent and others, not just the child.

If alienation is a known component of a case, attorneys should so apprise the court because the selection of a Reunification Therapist needs to include this factor as a consideration in the treatment plan and clinical discovery process.

A Message from the Child

I knew my mom's dear heart
Until mine was torn apart;

I knew my dad
When it wasn't a fad;

My parents fought
Certainly not what they taught;

Peace turns to distress and grief
My childhood feelings they did thief;

They wanted me to take a side
Finally, I did abide;

Now I realize all I lost
The absent parent was too great a cost;

Listen up all you kids
Don't take a leap to the highest bid;

You win only then to loose
It can lead you later on to hide behind the booze;

My life was born to the two
This loss leaves me with one too few;

Hatred and anger are the fuel
I only wish they had left me out of their duel;

Mom and dad now seem changed
I wish there was no blame that made seem deranged;

Now my own children I will cherish
So that the blessed love will not perish.

Chapter 5

What Children May Say about Reunification

"It's been so long, what is the difference?"

—15-year-old boy

Sources of Children's Opinions

Folllowing are some of the key sources of children's opinions about reunification and associated therapy (see Figure 5.1).

Concerns and Worries

Frequently, at the beginning of a reunification process, one or more children may issue statements that are negative, or at least problematic, in nature. They usually target some characteristic of the parent who desires reunification; something about past circumstances, commentary as to why their present circumstances are fine without them, and/or some statements of personal feelings that are considered problematic. They may also issue statements about claimed past danger and future worries about safety.

It is the job of the Reunification Therapist to make a careful listing of their concerns and worries. In fact, the initial session may absorb quite a bit of time listening to their worries and concerns about seeing, talking to, and/or being with a parent from whom they have been segregated for various lengths of time. Therapists should not assume the truth or falsity of any particular claim, but hear them as a basis for understanding the child's (perceived) worries and concerns. Of course, the concerns that they raise can be

Are We Done Yet?: A Child's View

Some may say I have many reasons
To oppose Reunification Therapy at this season;

In the first place, I'm not ready
I may still even need my teddy;

Of course, I'm also anxious in my heart
Which makes me feel like opposing the therapist's part;

Anyhow, I have a therapist already
She can keep me quite steady;

Listen up mom and dad, my life is fine
Anyhow, I can't find the time;

You know we have tried to connect before
And it's just proved to be a chore;

My new mom/dad is really great
And that I hope you won't debate;

So let's just tell the judge
That our relationship doesn't need another nudge.

grounded on a factual history and experiential basis or they can be a result of distortions, alienation, misunderstandings, or even historical falsities.

Deciding Session Content

Because Reunification Therapy is based on different types of protocols than other therapies, the concerns raised by the children may or may not be a basis for deciding actual session content with a parent from whom they have been estranged. This can result in a significant difference of methods and procedures from a regular therapist. Many therapists who are not schooled in reunification dynamics operate by what can be called "the readiness theory." Readiness Theory (page 137), in many therapeutic circles, is based on a psychological assumption that children can and will display" various behaviors when they are socially/emotionally ready to do so. The weakness of this theory, of course, is that some children may never be "ready" in reunification cases (and in other areas of social decision making). I have had many cases where children have been in standard therapies for four or five years or more and both they and/or their therapist claim that they are "still not

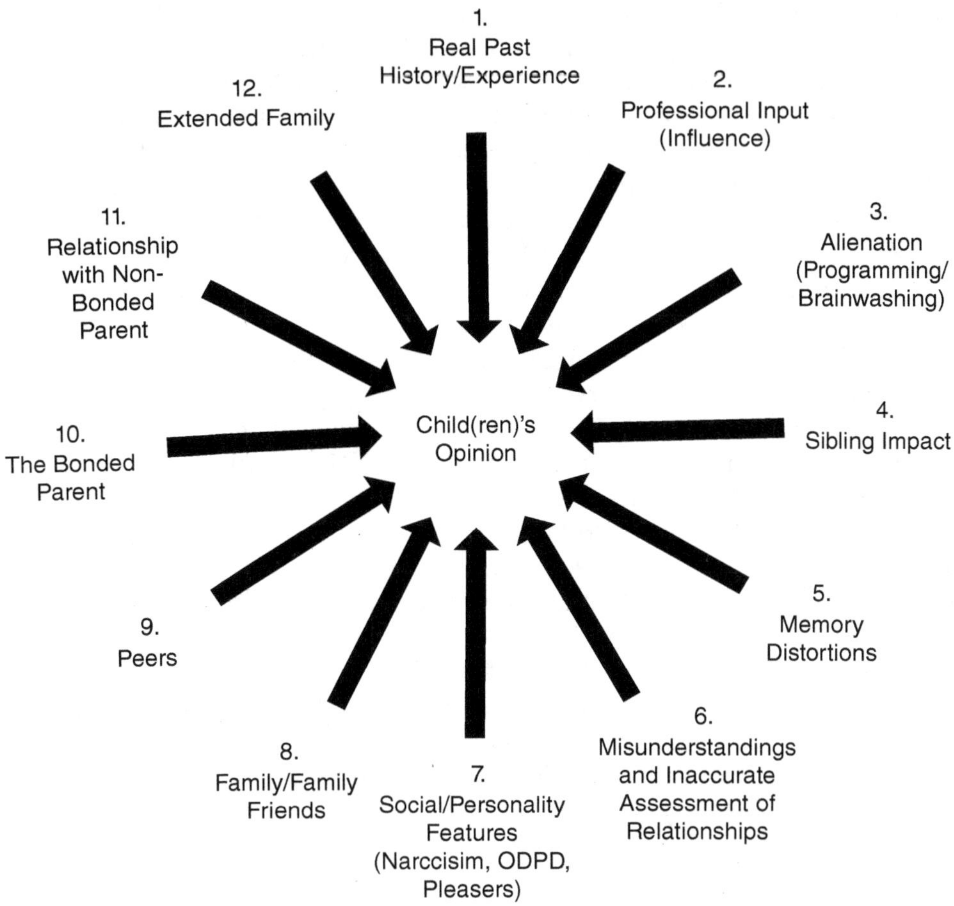

Figure 5.1 Possible Sources of Children's Opinions

ready." In one recent case, which is reproduced by many others, a therapist and child had asserted that the girl who was now 16 years old and hadn't seen her father for years could, when asked, possibly be "ready" when she enters college.

Another problem with Readiness Theory is that it fails to consider that the longer a child is separated from a parent, the more time they have to actually increase their anxiety about contact rather than reduce it. In fact, they also have more time to elaborate problems, issues, and circumstances—some of which may actually have never occurred. Also, children can develop a comfort level with the absence of the relationship, especially when it is substituted by "new family members" such as a stepparent or a parent's paramour.

Additionally, many therapists not schooled in reunification issues may have bought into a distorted history presented by the child and the other parent. So, they are operating on inaccurate or, at least, partial information as to the dynamics of past family life largely because they have had no or limited contact with the parent who is seeking reunification. In other words, they are "not dealing with a full deck."[1] These therapists may present themselves as knowledgeable, caring, and deeply concerned about the well-being of the child. Because they may have also had virtually no experience in re-bonding family members, they are operating out of (technically speaking) ignorance, to some degree. A case in point was a midwestern therapist who informed me that "under no conditions can or should these children (there were three) have contact with their father in the near future due to the 'evil deeds' that he has done." In this case, the therapist had actually filed a report with Children and Youth Services which was subsequently determined to be "unfounded." After a careful review of the case, it was discovered that the therapist had actually helped to triangulate the family relationships by pitting the children and the mother against the father. Additionally, virtually all accusations in her mandatory report were totally explicable without the conclusion of "abuse." The amount of damage repair that needed to be done in this case was substantial. The children had disagreements amongst themselves about their father (because the therapist had shared the "abuse" report, or at least elements of it with the children along with other inappropriate information). The children were bifurcated, to different degrees, with their father. The father and mother had entered into more conflict than they historically had in the marriage. The private school called the father in out of concern for what they heard about his reported "abuse" (even though this was later cleared). The father was split off from his in-laws and there were other significant social damages that needed repair. Of course, this is a case of a technically dysfunctional and probably unethical therapist, but whether intentional or unintentional, it is hopefully an uncommon story. The P.S. in this case is that the therapist did not even have the credentials to undertake an abuse evaluation, prescribe diagnoses, or perform therapy (which also has its own major socio-legal implications), let alone turn the case over to a social agency (and subsequent involvement of the police).

Ironically, in this case, once some reunification methods were introduced, the children (except for one) started to reconnect to their father almost immediately. In fact, one of the children reportedly told the original therapist, "I never want to see you again" when she tried to get her to sign off on the negatives about the father that she entered into her report. However, the bridge-building process needed to continue for quite some time. This example is related to what was mentioned in *Children Held Hostage: Identifying Brainwashed Children, Presenting a Case, and Crafting Solutions*

1. Therapists trained in family (contextual) therapies usually do not make this mistake.

where it refers to "surrogate programmers."[2] Unfortunately, professionals can actually participate, wittingly or unwittingly, in damaging parent-child relationships. I have found judges to be extremely concerned/upset when (solid) information is presented to the court that this has occurred. Judges have said, "Now I have two problems, or maybe three." The first problem they referred to was the historical conflict between divorcing parents and the subsequent parent-child distancing that occurred. The second issue that judges had to deal with was custodial decisions. Now, they have a third issue of damages caused by a professional that will likely need to be corrected by yet another professional. There may even be a fourth issue—finding a qualified Reunification Therapist to do damage repair and heal the parent-child bond.

In Reunification Therapy, children say many things. The following chart shows some examples of what a child might say (and actually have said) that are (initially) problematic and challenging to the re-bonding process

Things Children Say about Reunification[3]

- I'm afraid/scared.
- I don't need him/her in my life.
- I get anxious.
- It's stressful.
- I already have a father/mother (or family).
- I don't have to listen to him/her. He/she is not my parent anymore.
- I have nothing to say. I just won't talk. If I see him/her, I won't say anything.
- It's been so long—what's the difference?
- He'll/she'll kidnap me.
- He/she is mean.
- He/she is just doing this to be in control.
- He/she doesn't even pay the support.
- He/she just wants to see me because of money (child support).
- He/she doesn't really care.
- It's just to hurt me and my mom/dad.
- He/she was never there before. (So what's the difference now?)
- It always has to be his/her way.
- He/she just wants to win.
- I'm old enough to make my own decision.
- You're on my dad's/mom's side (so I can't trust you).
- My life is better off without him/her in it.
- I'm only going to do it so my dad/mom won't be in trouble (go to jail).

2. Stanley S. Clawar & Brynne V. Rivlin, Children Held Hostage: Identifying Brainwashed Children, Presenting a Case, and Crafting Solutions 256 (2d ed. 2013).

3. Parents can also offer up these ideas.

- I want my own lawyer.
- My therapist agrees that it's not the right time/I'm not ready. (Maybe when I'm 18 or later.)
- Therapy has failed before and it (you) will fail again. It will never work.
- What good will it do? I still hate him/her.
- I already have a therapist so I don't need this.
- He/she broke up our family.
- Nobody's listening to me—you can't make somebody like/love somebody.
- I want a different therapist.
- He/she ruined my life so why would I see him/her?
- They don't really care—it's all an act.
- I hate his/her new girlfriend/boyfriend—no way do I want to be there.
- Why would you (the therapist) do that to me?
- His/her girlfriend/boyfriend tries to behave like my real dad/mom. What a phony.
- You don't know what happened before. You weren't there!
- I just want to be left alone and grow up.
- I want to talk to the judge—I have a few things to say.
- I get headaches (or other physical problems) at the thought of seeing him/her.
- I don't care what a judge says
- I'll run away
    - o I'll kill myself
    - o I'll hurt myself
    - o I'll hurt him/her
- I don't know why he/she is doing this.
- When he/she comes in, they will fool you. He/she can put on a good act, but it's not real.
- I want my dad/mom/sister/brother in here with me if I'm going to see him/her.
- Doesn't anyone care what I have to say? I have rights too, you know.
- Even if I do it, once I'm _____ years old I'll never see him/her again.
- When will this stop?
- I don't know why—I just don't like him/her.
- I have a right to my feelings.
- He/she doesn't love me, anyhow.
- This is hurting my Mom/Dad too.
- My Mom/Dad says I have to be brave, but it's hard.
- I'm not getting in the car with him/her.
- My Mom/Dad says things that are nuts—I'll tape it and you'll see.
- He/she made my mom/dad sell the house.
- He/she drank all the time. I used to pick up the bottles.
- The judge didn't hear my side of things.
- He/she can't even hold a job.
- He/she has their own (new) family, so, just leave us alone.
- Even my friends think that he/she is a creep.

- He/she pretend like nothing ever happened.
- It's about what they need, not me.
- I thought you're supposed to help children.
- They don't know how to be a mom/dad so why should I be with them?
- My mom/dad says I shouldn't have to do this, but I still do.
- Even her/his own family (child's grandparents, aunts, uncles) don't see him/her so why should I?
- You know, he or she has been in rehab three times—I don't do drugs. I'm a good kid.

Negatives Have Value

Now that you have reviewed some of the problematic commentary that was gathered by reviewing hundreds of reunification cases, it is important to note that even if the statements seem negative, if used properly, they can be tools for mending relationships. For example, if you look at number 9 in the preceding list, "He'll kidnap me" and then meetings are held where the child was, of course, not kidnapped, that can be used as information for further bonding. Because children often make multiple accusations (whether true or not), they can also be connected to each other. For example, the child who says "He'll kidnap me" and "He's mean" may have to admit that neither of these occurred in the actual (professional) contact setting. So, what we have are behavioral/interactional experiences that belie the opinions that are (initially) presented by the child as reasons for (maintaining) separation. This incongruity is a very important tool to use in individual and collective sessions with children. It does not solve the problem immediately, but, if used carefully, can continue to be helpful in enhancing the comfort factor. So, in a private session with a child who has made both of the preceding assertions, they can be questioned about the social reality that actually occurred—things went fine and there was no kidnapping. However, children who are deeply imbued with negativity will often not stop here. They may then assert, "He's a great actor and can fool anybody, including you." This negative response to a positive experience is pro-forma for Reunification Therapists. The difference is that a Reunification Therapist is not going to make a mistaken conclusion that "perception is (tantamount to) reality."

Perception Is Not Necessarily Reality

In many cases, perception is not reality. For example, a mother who pays the child support she is supposed to is likely not doing it "just to look good." A father who goes to court time after time to see his children is likely not doing it just "to control the family." However, children often make these assertions and expect the therapist to conclude that their perception is reality. Reunification Therapists know that sometimes they have to challenge (if they have the social data to do so) a child's (distorted) perception(s). Children often assert, "He/she doesn't really care." An obvious question arises: How is it that a parent, who has spent years and thousands of dollars to try to see and be with a child, doesn't care? Of course it doesn't make sense, but no one said that positions based on emotions, alienation, misunderstandings, and/or confabulations make sense.

Perception Can Comport with Reality

However, there may be circumstances where a child's assertions have a factual base. For example, children may say, "He was never there when I was younger, so why should I be there for him now?" In many families, parents had a social contract. The contract could have been that one of them is the primary earner and the other attends to childcare and household needs. So, just because a mother or father "was not there" (by agreement), doesn't mean that they didn't care and it also doesn't meant that they can't care (greatly) now. Developing social explanations for past social realities is one of the primary jobs of a Reunification Therapist. In this case, a parent "cared" by keeping to their obligations. They "cared" by earning what the family needed to survive. They "cared" by being with the children in the evenings, on weekends, and on vacations. They "cared" when they expressed and shared their love, ideas, values, experience, and parental decisions. Caring comes in many forms. Children may enter into a temporary state of social shock when confronted with this "novel" set of ideas. As one child said to me, "I never thought about it that way. So, they each did what they were supposed to do?" "You bet," I responded.

Therapy Savvy Children

Children who have been in therapy (sometimes extensively) will frequently spout therapeutic beliefs and jargon. Therapy savvy children will say, "I have a right to my feelings." Of course, they do, but what if the feelings are based on incorrect information? What if the feelings are based on undue influence from someone else? What if the (undue) feelings have arisen out of present (selfish) needs to have a certain lifestyle? This latter point is very common for American teenagers who often target a particular source of authority for acting out. I have seen many cases (mentioned elsewhere in this book) where children wish to be disengaged from a parent because that parent is more of a disciplinarian and provides more oversight on day-to-day behaviors than the parent with whom they are living. So, is it functional (from the child's perspective) if he/she prefers to stay up late at night, be on technology for an infinite amount of time, vape, associate with problematic peers, sleep out without informing where or when, and a host of other behaviors that would certainly not be possible if a surveillance-type parent was in their life and "on duty." This is important because in evaluating what is going on in a reunification case, it may be necessary to look beyond the psychological and historical factors into the (present) social context and parental boundary-setting considerations.

Historical Conflicts

In some cases, children have had a historical conflict with one or the other parent. This conflict may play into present desires to disaffiliate with that parent. We cannot ignore social personality differences that may not have been as visible when the family was together. This may require some special intervention methods to help them identify their differences and how they can possibly blend with a parent today. A good example of this is a recent case where a 17-year-old boy almost completely blocked his father out of his life. The forensic investigation part of the case revealed that they had some substantial differences in the past that could, in large part, account for their present communication and contact issues. Of course, these differences were exacerbated by a divorce situation. When son and father came to learn in the Reunification Therapy that they had these differences, it became easier for them to understand each other. One of their differences was that the father liked elaborate discussions and the son was satisfied with brief, factual conversations. Simply recognizing this communicative aspect brought about a fuller understanding and they learned to talk to each other's specific communication needs and styles. Additionally, the son believed that the father was the cause of the breakup of the family. Through careful discussion, and with no indictment of the mother, he came to learn that, as the saying goes, "it takes two to tango." He also learned to refocus and correct his tried, but untrue, position that "counseling was just another way for his dad to be in control." In fact, it was presented to him that the counseling was occurring because his father loved him very much and was aware that children who grew up without direct loving guidance from a father often have more problems in life—which the father wanted to avoid at all costs. When the father told him this in a loving fashion, the boy broke down and admitted that, "I'm sorry dad. I just didn't see things in the right way. I'm so sorry if I hurt you." These social-emotional breakthroughs are not uncommon in Reunification Therapy and are actually quite positive in nature because they often get to the underbelly of the motivation of the parent who seeks reconnection.[4] From this breakthrough came the opportunity for me to recommend a host of other ways of connecting outside of the office. Once the (negative) social-emotional bubble had been penetrated with love and caring, the boy was able to accept and act on these recommendations for further contact and re-bonding with his dad.

Timeline

Even though children may start out saying negative things, which are grounded or ungrounded, the reunification timeline can often be brief—meaning it is not like other forms of therapy that may be quite protracted. This is often surprising to clinicians who are not schooled in this framework. Many cases may only take a few sessions (like the preceding case) to accomplish the re-bonding goal. Of course, there are others that may require more time, effort, and varied interventions. One of the key factors (mentioned elsewhere in this book) is the degree of support or interference that the non-reunifying parent provides. In fact, some cases may require more actual time with the parents than the child. Customization of interventions is, once again, key. Remember, any changes in the re-bonding of parent-child will have a kickback into the relationship with the already bonded parent.

Collaborative Parents

Not all children have a particular parent who is opposed to reunification. There are cases where both parents, in good faith, are seeking better bonds for their child(ren). However, at times, a child may set out their own course of action with particular goals related to disaffiliation. This is important to note, as a Reunification Therapist should try to identify the social context within which they are providing services. It has been assumed, incorrectly, that all Reunification Therapy is, at base, a one-sided broken bonds case. As noted in Chapter 3, there are a couple dozen other factors that could be

4. However, the bonded parent may hear "the child cried in a session" and challenge the therapist that "they upset the child"—not realizing it was part of a positive breakthrough.

causing a parent-child breach, in addition or exclusion to, alienation. Sorting this out is up to the skills, knowledge, training, and experience of the reunification expert. As noted many times, this is not a job for a regular therapist—in the same way that heart surgery is not the job for a podiatrist—wrong skill sets for the goals of the case. High-level social relationship skills are required amongst others for success.

Thematic Characteristics and Social Identity

In listening to children speak about their lives and the actual or potential relationship with a parent, they can come off sounding as many different types of people in one and will present thematic characteristics of who they are and what they are likely to do. If you listen carefully to the language, they will present as one or more of the following roles: a judge, a therapist, a critic/cynic, an attorney, a prophet (they can predict the future), a moralist (they will tell you what is good and bad), a worrier, a lost person, an aggressor, a confused person, a fearful person, a defiant person, one who threatens self-harm, a sad or lonely person, a potential runaway, a challenger, a physically or mentally troubled person, and/or a person who is in an infantile or childlike state. All of these characteristics and roles can be presented by children of various ages. At times, I have inquired about the theme only to receive a more delineated answer. For example, in saying to some children, "Gee, you kind of sound like a lawyer." Only to have them respond, "I know my rights. In fact, I think I should have my own lawyer." When questioning children who have presented the role of cynic, they have frequently said things like, "It's always been that way and it'll never change." Moralistic children will often assert that, "My mother is just a bad person. She is kind of evil." Some children have referred to their mothers as deceptive, whores, or just terrible people. Fathers may be called losers, liars, and more. The roles a child takes on have significance to a Reunification Therapist. Challenging these roles too early on will usually result in the child solidifying that role and closing off.

It is useful to be able to identify the presence of certain roles and themes in the child's communication. It's a window into patterned thinking that can be quite useful in the reunification process. If a child is by nature, or experience, a worrier, it is a characteristic that needs to be considered in any proposal (plan) that a Reunification Therapist might put forth. Children who are worriers can take a simple fact and escalate it into a catastrophic-type scenario. For example, I proposed to one child-worrier that in our next session we grab something to eat next door with her father as it would be after school and both of them might be hungry. Here is what the child did with this recommendation—"Okay, so we'll go from your office to next door.

We'll order our food and that kind of pretends like everything's fine. We sit down and then talk like we're really friendly. He'll pretend and I'll pretend and then he'll think that everything is fine and he'll say, 'So as long as we had such a good time, why don't we go to dinner without the counselor?' And he'll pick me up at my mom's house. And then he'll file for full custody and everybody will be back in court. And of course my mom will go broke." Children who are worriers often perceive a neutral recommendation as loaded with problematic, if not dangerous (and escalating), consequences.

Summary

In summary, knowing what children say, delineating roles or themes they present, understanding the family context, differentiating Reunification Therapy from other forms of therapy, identifying social realities versus perceived realities, educating children on heightening their social-emotional understandings, listening to the differences between grounded and ungrounded opinions, and a host of other factors can lead to better understandings and a better chance of successful reunification. Of course, as will be discussed elsewhere in the book, "successful" can mean different types of reunification and to varying degrees.

Reunification Therapists must remember in many cases, if not all, negatives have already been aired in court, mediation, therapy, the home, or elsewhere. It doesn't make them any less significant. Reunification Therapists must keep their eyes on the central aspect of the legal order or agreement: reunification. *These negatives presented by a child (or parent) may be hurdles, but not necessarily permanent roadblocks.* The focus is re-bonding, reconnecting, sharing time and love, reaching out, eliminating negatives, and moving on to a better day.

Chapter 6

Impeding and Facilitative Factors

"Knowing what makes it work and what doesn't helps to make it work."

— Stanley S. Clawar

The following list summarizes qualities that impede (restrict, constrain, interfere with, limit, and/or stop) the reunification process. It also itemizes factors that facilitate (help, support, and/or direct) the reunification process in positive ways.

Impeding versus Facilitative Factors of the Reunification Process

Impeding	Facilitative
1. Sociopathic Qualities	1. All Parties Desire Change
2. Surrogate Programming/Brainwashing or Underminers	2. Phase-in Agenda Agreed Upon
3. Litany of Professionals	3. Clear/Strong Court Order—Clear Professional Roles
4. No Sanctions for Violations	4. Protection for the Professionals
5. Violence/Threat of (Self) Harm	5. Measurable Components
6. Lack of Attorney Support	6. Pre-set Appointments/Continuity
7. Traditional Confidentiality	7. Sanctions for Violation(s)
8. Unprotected Professional	8. Varied Methods
9. Judge/Master Indecisive	9. Coaching for All Parties Possible
10. Parents Not Following Guidelines	10. Reframing Social Relations
11. Continued Child Over-Empowerment	11. Strong GAL—if Possible
12. Unrealistic Time Frames	12. Reporting to the Court
13. Child is Parent's "Partner" or "Best Friend"	13. Stamina of the Professional(s)
14. Remuneration Problems	14. Judge/Master Involvement/Decisive
15. False Accusations about a Parent and/or Professionals	15. Broad/Modified Confidentiality
16. Alienation is Present	16. Cease & Desist on CYS/Police Filings
17. Long Gap in Parent-Child Contact	17. Strong Skill Base for the Professional(s)
18. Professional Perceived as Biased	18. Setting Realistic Goals
19. Skills of the Professional(s) are Weak	19. Supportive Other Parent
20. No Reunification Plan	20. Clear Reunification Plan
21. Setting Unrealistic Goals	21. Shorter Time Gap in Breach
22. Personal Parental Issues	22. Identifying the Positive Assets of Parents and Children

Impeding Factors and What to Do about Them

Impeding factors operate to limit, challenge, interfere with, and/or damage the reunification process. They must be considered and dealt with either preemptively or reactively. Note that aside from alienation by the parent(s), there are 21 other factors that can impact negatively on parent-child relationships. Obviously, the opposite of any impeding factors are likely to be positive (sociopathic vs. healthy and stable parents). The impeding factors are described in the following sections.

1. Sociopathic Qualities

These hindering qualities are also referred to as Antisocial Personality Disorder (ASPD) in psychological and psychiatric circles. People with sociopathic qualities tend to lie, be impulsive, break rules/laws, and, in general, could even show a low regard for their own safety and/or the safety of others.

These social-psychological types, especially in the context of a socio-legal conflict, are known to report the belief that many agents are operating against them. This can involve judges, lawyers, guardian ad litems (GALs), therapists, and a whole host of others who "don't get it" or are simply perceived as operating against their interests.

One of their more important features is a very low sense of empathic connection to others. If they do have any empathic connection, they will likely employ it for purposes of manipulation. Their most outstanding feature is a lack of conscience. So, when they behave in a negative, hostile, criminal, or other antisocial manner, they usually don't suffer (any) pangs of remorse, guilt, or regret. They will make statements such as "I did what I had to do."

Sociopaths tend to be controlling, ingratiating, and manipulative. They exhibit a low sense of responsibility for any of their inappropriate behaviors. They have expectations that others will fix problems they have caused. Finally, they can show contempt and, at times, cruelty in their dealings with others.

They also tend to have high levels of narcissism (self-focus and personal aggrandizement), as most of their stories, concerns, and problems revolve around their needs and desires, in exclusion to others.

They can make reunification a very difficult process due to the qualities just described. Reunification often requires a sensitivity to the needs of others (children and adults) and this very quality is often, at best, in limited supply in those with sociopathic tendencies. Any minor mistake by the Reunification Therapist can be blown out of proportion if it is perceived not to meet their needs, perceptions, and definitions of the situation. Sociopaths can be quick to challenge and virtually never take responsibility for any problems in the rebuilding process.

If they break any of the agreements or rules set down, they will likely deny that they did this and/or blame others. *Generally, only people who can accept criticism are capable of change.* This puts sociopaths and the reunification process at a low probability of success. Cases that have parents with no social-psychological pathologies or orientations will be easier to navigate.

2. Surrogate Programming/Brainwashing or Underminers

In high-conflict divorce cases, where there is some form and/or degree of alienation, it is frequently found that there is a primary person (usually a parent) who is operating against the relationship of the other parent. (Please see Chapter 4 on alienation for more on this.) Also, there may be a secondary support system that limits the rebuilding of a parent-child relationship. These secondary support systems, or "surrogates," come in many forms—a stepparent, paramours, an older child, a therapist, grandparents, a neighbor, a relative, and others who often operate in collusion with one of the parents.

At times, these surrogates can be more vociferous than the actual parent. They may assist in strategizing, running interference, stigmatizing, sharing distorted stories, and, in a whole host of other ways, maintaining a vigilance that damages the potential for a child to re-bond with a parent.

Identifying these surrogates may take some time, as they may not appear in the beginning of a case. I have seen all different types of people operate as surrogates, including clergy, teachers, medical doctors, therapists, and more. In other words, almost anyone is capable of performing this function. It is not uncommon for the surrogate's name to slip out in a reunification session (which may or may not be factual). For example, I had a child who informed me that his father's present wife "was the one who destroyed the family." When asked how he knew this, he indicated that "my uncle, whom I trust more than my father, always tells me the truth." Parenthetically, in this case, the father had actually met his present wife after the divorce. This presents a problem for Reunification Therapists as they often have to deal with minor and major distortions (which will be discussed under number 22—Alienation).

The length of time and the type of bonding that a child has with a surrogate has to be assessed in order to build a careful treatment plan. Reunification Therapists often think they're making progress only to find that there is major slippage. If this transpires, and it often does, they really need to investigate the potential that there are other "players" above and beyond the parents and the children.

If these surrogates, or underminers, of a parent-child relationship are known prior to the beginning of the reunification process, it is often useful to have them identified in a court order in terms of "putting them on notice" for cooperation. I have cases where a judge has been willing to identify a stepparent or others who are already known to be problematic. A warning and real action for contempt with "teeth" can often help. But it also can cause the surrogates to go "underground" and develop new ways to issue their negative messages. This is especially complicated when the surrogate feels that they have become the "real father" or "real mother" and believes that the child's other parent really deserves to have a damaged or even no relationship.

At times, it is possible to incorporate surrogates and draw them into a positive alliance. This "alliance" can often serve to make the difference between success and failure. I have had stepparents say to me, "Thanks for offering to see me as we've been to four counselors already and I was basically ignored."[1] Asking these stepparents for help and support can often prove to be a simple and effective solution. However, professionals need to be aware that if the surrogate changes their position or belief, it may meet with a challenge from the child themselves. When I've told some children, "It's nice that your stepfather would like to help." I've been met with quizzical looks and questions like, "What do you mean? He knows my father is a bad guy. Why would he say that?" These kinds of scenarios will require teaching the adults new scripts and explanations for what appears to the child as a radical shift in the labeling of one of their parents. There will be social adjustment on many fronts.

The absence or reduction of the impact of surrogates will clear the path to focus on the key parties. However, be sure to check if there were surrogates who are no longer in the picture. A case in point was a father and son who needed re-bonding but there was a stepfather who was now divorced from his mother for some time. He was a significant negative/disruptive parent that impacted on the boy's view of his father. In fact, he still saw him on occasion.

3. Litany of Professionals

Commonly, the longer cases go on, the more numerous the list of professionals that get involved. Psychiatrists, psychologists, clinical sociologists, social workers, pastoral counselors, parenting coordinators, social agencies, GALs, forensic evaluators, child advocates, sequences of lawyers, judges, school counselors, teachers, principals, and more continue to be a larger and larger group surrounding the family problems at hand. The impact of all

1. In defense of the counselors, they may have been limited by the court order or agreement to only see certain parties.

these proliferating professionals is generally problematic, especially for children. Here's why.

The children have to tell their stories, the same stories, to varied professionals over different periods of time. For many children, this creates a typecasting, not always positive, about the professional roles, caring or lack thereof, and, most importantly, the ability to really help and change things for the better. A kind of *child cynicism* can set in that makes each subsequent professional have a more difficult time in their therapies and/or evaluations. Adults can develop the same type of cynicism.

A scenario comes to mind that may be instructive. A boy of about 13 years of age was asked to come to my office because his mother and others thought he was "in some kind of depression."

Therapist: "What's going on?"

Child: "I don't want to be here."

Therapist: "Then I won't keep you long, just a couple of questions. Okay?"

Child: "So what's the question?"

Therapist: "Could you share with me why you don't want to be here?"

Child: "Sure, you're all the same."

Therapist: "Who's all the same?"

Child: "I've seen lots of therapists like you and they all say the same thing, ask the same thing, and nothing really changes."

Therapist: "Could you give me an example?"

Child: "Sure. The last guy heard what's going on with me visiting my dad on weekends and the idiot came up with a brilliant idea. You know what this guy said? He said, 'you know it could actually be a good thing.' The good thing to this idiot was that I saw my father for what he called 'quality time' and tried to tell me that it was actually more time than I saw him when he and my mom were together. Can you believe how dumb somebody can be?"

Therapist: "Is that the end of the story?"

Child: "Of course not, I turned on him and I said look, when my dad lived here I got up in the morning (tears in his eyes) and I would follow him to the bathroom and I'd watch him shave. He had this way of doing the same things in the same way each day. And then he'd go into the kitchen, see, and take some orange juice and some coffee, you know what I'm saying? And then after a little while he'd put his sport coat on and I'd walk him to the front door (now profusely crying) and he'd lean down, kiss my head, and he'd say, 'I love you son.' And I'd say, 'I love you too dad.' And then he'd say, 'I'll see you tonight.' And I'd say, 'You bet.' So, some idiot therapist is gonna tell me that a thing called 'quality time' was better than seeing my father every single day of my life. What a f***ing idiot!"

Child: *now crying profusely*

Therapist: "I'm so sorry and I will try to never be disrespectful to how you feel about your father, your family, or the time that you spent with them."

Child: "No, it's not your fault. You didn't do it. But thanks for trying to understand—nobody else sure did. Nobody got it so far. Can you believe it?"

This story reflects not only a series of professional involvements, but one professional who confused meaningful daily connections with "quantity of time." Time sequence and regularity build bonds. The child got it, the doctors (at least one), with all good intent, did not. Usually, the fewer professionals involved now and in the past, the less complications for the Reunification Therapist—a luxury often missing.[2]

4. No Sanctions for Violations

Unfortunately, many reunification cases come to professionals after a long series of court actions, mandatory conciliations, arbitrations, negotiations, evaluations, and therapeutic interventions. The results of this litany of activities is that one or both parents may feel that success is unlikely because there (also) has been "no teeth" put into any of the court orders and/or other formats for solution. Therefore, the idea that there are no consequences for noncompliance, manipulation, or overt aggression can come to hinder the very bond-building process that is now at hand.

Negative sanctions are not always a tool that guarantees success, but I have seen heightened levels of cooperation, at times, when there were financial, custodial, and/or other sanctions in place. There is a saying that you can't legislate morality, but, of course, morality is legislated all the time. The Civil Rights Act was a morally based law. "Thou shall not kill," derived from the Ten Commandments and turned into criminal laws, is a moral imperative. When the court decides which parent is behaviorally and attitudinally

2. Many professionals give it their best, but legal, family, and other circumstances limit their path to fuller success.

more functional, they are making a moral judgment. Therefore, a legally based sanction has the appearance of a moral mandate. Cooperating on behalf of the children, because it is in their best interest, is clearly a moral imperative. In other words, is it good or bad to rebuild the bond between a parent and child? With some exception, I haven't seen too many argue against the morality that it is "good" to (re)connect a parent and child.

At times, the Reunification Therapist may be asked for conditions that they think would facilitate progress. They may (should) want to review the history of the case and, if appropriate, recommend that relevant sanctions be put into place. If this is done, then specific behaviors need to be identified that are *compliance behaviors* versus those that undermine a mending process. These behaviors can include:

- Attendance
- Punctuality
- Respectful behavior toward all parties (including the Reunification Therapist)
- Doing the arranged therapeutic homework
- Applying new recommended behaviors/scripts
- Challenging/deleting dysfunctional behaviors
- Sharing relevant information with the therapist and the parent(s)
- Being part of the solution
- Moving past the past

5. Violence/Threat of (Self) Harm

Increasingly, the courts and reunification counselors are being confronted with cases that have real, imagined, and/or accused threats of violence. Of course, these must be taken very seriously. Just because a child threatened suicide before and did not act on it does not mean that it is to be discounted. Problems can arise because of the mandatory reporter laws in many states. The simple threat of harm (or perceived harm) can be a basis for reporting the situation. This can be further complicated by the fact that Reunification Therapists may receive a case that already has an active Protection from Abuse order (PFA) and a child or parent reveals a corollary incident to the Reunification Therapist. This is where a legal consult for the Reunification Therapist may be necessary, as there may be more questions than answers.

- Does an active PFA protect a child, if it has a no contact clause, even if the same or new (related) incidents are reported to the counselor?
- How does the counselor differentiate reports that are motivated by manipulation (including children who are capable of this)? "I know you have to report this," said one adolescent.

- Once an investigation is completed and determined to be false or unfounded, how do you reactivate a therapeutic environment when a parent or child still holds on to the unfounded accusation?
- What are the risk factors to the therapist for proceeding in the face of accusations that may then result in negative experiences to the child?

Reunification Therapists need a clear set of ethical guidelines that help them to explain when, how, and why they proceed in such cases, and when they don't proceed.

Because many Reunification Therapists appear to operate from a professional bias that the history is to be minimized and that they are to simply follow a court order to reconnect the parent and child, they may err on the side of operating with limited information. There are many Reunification Therapists who do not even read previous evaluations and reports. This can present its own problems. In fact, there are cases where Reunification Therapists have refused to speak to the present or past therapist(s) and other parties that may have meaningful information (in terms of risk assessment).

All Reunification Therapists should have resources available for immediate consultation. For example, a threat of suicide by a child should necessitate an immediate psychiatric consult or referral to a local hospital with psychiatric facilities. Reunification Therapists need to be cautious about making a judgment that such threats are just a matter of grandstanding. Their motto should be "if in doubt, check it out."

Another recent case example was one where a mother reported to me that her daughter (who didn't want to live with her, but was ordered by the court to do so because of alleged abuse by the father) was having violent thoughts. She told her mother that the scissors on the counter made her want to pick it up and stab her in the neck. The court and the mother wanted Reunification Therapy. The son, who was still with the father, had also threatened in the past to attack his mother. The daughter in this case had, some time ago, observed the mother trying to kill herself. Reunification Therapy? I had recommended psychiatric and possible law enforcement interventions. The mother reported that the daughter was "placed under psychiatric care and was now out, and was reported to not be under any psychiatric emergency." Is this a case that a Reunification Therapist now wants to engage in? Possible threats and actions to the Reunification Therapist and the parties can include:

- Suicidal actions
- Assaulting a party
- Runaway actions
- Exiting a car when it is moving (on the way to Reunification Therapy)

- Obtaining a weapon or having access to one
- Verbal assaults
- (Perpetual) dangers to the therapist

6. Lack of Attorney Support

Attorneys can clearly make or break the reunification process. If a court order is in place and they support the directives and conditions, clients will have higher degrees of compliance. Often, the attorney is the only person whom they may trust, and that makes the influence of the attorney very significant. Most attorneys that I have worked with will abide by the court's directive as officers of the court. However, as in any occupation, there are some who, even if unintentionally, undermine or limit the reunification process. Clients who do not wish to engage in the process or even provide support from the sideline are the ones who need clear/strong direction from their attorneys. Interpreting the spirit and context of an order or agreement can be most instructive to some clients. This may need repeating. The more specific the attorney is in terms of behaviors that are compliant (and noncomplaint) the better.

I have found that explaining to the attorneys the goals, methods, and levels of respect that will be shown to the parties can help them greatly with their clients. In fact, some Reunification Therapists will not take cases without a release that says they may speak to the attorneys as per their discretion. Caution needs to be exercised, as some attorneys may wish to continue their (legitimate) adversarial role via phone or e-mail. Clear boundaries need to be set here for the Reunification Therapist. Most attorneys will then collaborate.

A pre-reunification conference with both attorneys can help to set the groundwork for the parent-child meetings. It should be made clear to the attorneys that this meeting is not to rehash litigation issues and positions; it is to let them know what and how things will be done and how they can assist in the process. Obviously, if they have key information that will impact the bond building, it should be heard.

The downside of enlisting attorneys is that they may come to feel that they have open access to raise any and all issues with the therapist. Therefore, the degree and type of contact needs to be defined early on in the process. Generally, the best guideline is that, short of an emergency, contacts will be initiated by the Reunification Therapist for progress update information, client compliance, and related issues.

Reunification Therapists need to be extremely careful about ex parte communications. In fact, they should virtually never do this. If there is an extenuating circumstance where a contact is made with one attorney (ex parte), then an immediate follow up by phone or e-mail should be made to balance out the information with the other attorney. It is an important principle—all such communications go to both attorneys equally.

7. Traditional Confidentiality

Following are 21 reasons that traditional confidentiality can be problematic for reunification cases. This is especially true where there have been periods of high conflict (and distance) between the parents and/or between a parent and child.

- Confidentiality may have already been tried and failed.
- High-conflict types are usually focused on power and if the professional has no influence, the parent(s) may fill the power vacuum. Open communications to the relevant parties can be empowering for the Reunification Therapist.
- The high-conflict person(s) feels there is no oversight for negative, noncompliant, or disruptive behaviors. Professionals cannot report which parent is most compliant with the court order under traditional confidentiality. There is no potential for sanctions, as no information can "leave the room." Professionals cannot report success or failure of court-ordered goals and objectives.
- The high-conflict parent is more likely to feel that the professional forum is for ventilation, nonresolution, or disruptive behaviors.
- The high-conflict parent has likely frustrated previous professionals.
- The professional is more limited in bringing about change or closure. The therapist has nowhere to turn for back-up support or for reinforcement for relational changes (if traditional confidentiality is in place).
- Continued conflict and/or negative alienation of one parent against another can be a form of child abuse, but professionals are less likely to report this (compared to other forms of abuse).
- It allows the court order to be more easily manipulated or even countermanded. "It's just a counseling session," says a parent.
- It actually makes no practical sense because by the time "counseling" takes place virtually all issues are already known to the courts, GALs, other family members, schools, sometimes police, CPS agencies, and so on. So what is the confidentiality about?
- Custodial modifications, if required, are hindered due to the lack of valuable information that the counselor is permitted to share.
- The parent who executes the most conflict-based behavior can control the outcome.
- The professional is more protected if they feel the need to externalize information and opinions (on behalf of the child[ren]).
- The presence of the court is felt to be more present in each session as a guiding force.
- Parties know the professional has tripartite obligations:
    - o To the court/GAL

  - o To the parents
  - o To the child
- Reunification professionals can share information with other professionals, teachers, and so on that befits the best interest of the child.
- It is a clear message to a high-conflict parent that the professional will not be party to damaging the health and welfare of a child.
- It reinforces the fact that, under serious conflicted conditions, the ultimate custodian of the children is the court.
- It makes clear that parents are not there to "just talk things out," but to prove they can change for the betterment of their children.
- Most cases at the high-conflict level are not counseling or therapy in the traditional sense. They are advisory, guidance, mediation, conflict resolution, or some other social intervention. Therefore, traditional confidentiality is often not relevant to the issues and/or goals of Reunification Therapy.
- A conflict-based parent is more likely to summarily discuss or make up stories about the counseling process that cannot be controlled because the professional is silenced.

In summary, making sure a nonconfidentiality clause is present in a court order or attorney agreement is helpful. Some Reunification Therapists will no longer accept cases that are bound by the traditional confidentiality restrictions.

8. Unprotected Professional

Many knowledgeable and skilled forensic therapists have left the field due to the threat of and/or actual legal actions against them by clients. Therefore, to provide an opportunity for the professionals to operate somewhat smoothly, it is important for them to be protected during the process of providing reunification services. In some cases, courts have granted absolute or common-law immunity as established by the particular case law in that state.

Furthermore, it is functional to have placed in the court order that the professionals shall receive no threats, intimidations, accusations, and/or other interferences with their professional duties.

Many professionals have their own releases and the courts should direct the parties to also sign them as further role clarification and protection. Additionally, it may be helpful to specify support for the way the professionals wish to have contact. Is the contact to be in person, by e-mail, text, phone, Skype, Facetime, or other means? This is important because some clients, especially today, like to make their points by (long) texts and/or e-mails. This can consume large amounts of professional time and lead to misinterpretations. Reunification Therapists need the right to set limits on e-mail proliferation.

Any further delineation that sets boundaries around the professional-client relationship can be helpful. For example, directing the clients to use respectful language during the intervention process is a guideline the therapist can refer back to. The parties can also be directed to abide by all of the interventions/suggestions provided by the professional.

Reunification experts should be permitted to articulate the various and sundry types of contacts with other professionals and lay people that they feel will expedite the process.

As noted earlier, explicitly stating that traditional confidentiality is not extant in this type of forensic therapy is important. Many clients believe that this is always operational.

In summary, any and all factors that can be made explicit that surround the professional-client relationships are important. The more exacting and detailed, the better. Little should be left to individual interpretation, as this is where conflicts, manipulations, and misunderstandings can arise. Vague delineation of professional actions and protection impedes the process.

9. Judge/Master Indecisive

One of the single largest complaints that I have heard over the years from hundreds and hundreds of clients is that they felt adequate information often existed for a clear decision to be made by a judge or master, yet, no such decision was made (according to them). The frustration that results from this perception can and does spill over into the reunification process.

Quite frequently, clients will view the Reunification Therapist as a quasi-judicial agent. This, of course, must be clarified, but that may not stop the covert or overt desire for more delineation that the client possesses in this regard. At times, a court order might actually provide the authority for a Reunification Therapist to make a decision that has to do with frequency and type of contact that will be operational between a parent and child. Some Reunification Therapists do not want this level of authority.

Many judges are extremely protective of this decision-making power and never relinquish it to a non-judicial professional. On the other hand, there may be others involved in the case, like GALs, who do have various levels and types of authority. The Reunification Therapist must be very clear on the extensions and limitations of their decision-making rights (and obligations).

There are times when a Reunification Therapist will need the support and decision making of a GAL, child advocate, master, and/or the judge. Therefore, the mechanisms for access to these professionals is extremely important. Must they go through the attorneys? Do they have permission to directly call the GAL? Are there conditions where they can have direct access to the judge? All of these access issues can and will influence decisions that need to be suggested, issued, and/or executed. The more decisive the legal and professional involved, the clearer the guidelines are to conduct required in the reunification process.

10. Parents Not Following Guidelines

This factor, possibly more than many others, will impede and potentially damage a re-bonding process. This issue is actually relevant to both parents, as the parent who may not be directly involved (in most of the sessions) will need to support whatever process and content the therapist recommends. If they don't—or worse, they work against the content and process—the chance of success is greatly reduced. There can also be compliance issues on the part of the parent who is trying to reconnect. Sometimes they don't like the suggested scripts, speed of the therapy, or the approaches of the Reunification Therapist. All of these issues have to be methodically worked through for continued progress to take place. This is where the "therapeutic alliance" skills are key.

These compliance issues should be addressed up front with all relevant parties so that they understand their responsibilities and impact on the ultimate outcome. These "parties" include any individuals who have been party to the ongoing breach. Therefore, parties may include stepparents, grandparents, other counselors, educators, and maybe others.

Of course, the clearer the guidelines are, the easier it is to measure compliance. In other words, therapists should be able to say what each of the parties are to do and not to do that will lead to higher rates of success. These compliance metrics are especially key if the counselor is obligated to report to the court exactly who has supported or undermined the reunification process—the who, how, when, and what of the process. Following are some examples of guidelines for parents:

- Don't speak about the other parent unless it's positive.
- Don't talk about legalities, court, and/or trials.
- Don't interrogate or question kids about the other parent's home and/or conversations.
- Don't favor kids who spend more time with you over those who don't or who seem to favor one parent right now.
- Accept the children's re-bonding and support it with each parent.
- Know that the children have different views on parental contact.
- The above item is not to be, anymore, a basis for divisiveness.
- The children deeply want a sibling comradery.
- The children are tired of divided camps, court, litigation, and feeling like middlemen.
- The children were most appreciative of the recent group session because "it was theirs."

- Parents should not push for details of the children's sessions, just what they children choose to share.
- A joint session with the father and children will likely follow.
- A joint session with the children and mother will likely follow (already discussed with both).
- Effective communication between parents (even if limited to details of children's lives) should be done. More examples will be offered when we meet.
- When Dr. Clawar has made progress on the sibling reunification, please support it.
- Give Dr. Clawar feedback, in session, on these initial guidelines.
- Help each of the children to regain the lost elements of their childhood (even though they are young adults). They are aware of this loss.
- The children prefer to live in the present and move forward, even though there were historical crises that needed resolution.
- Both parents need to take more ownership of what transpired at her home for the children that was hurtful.
- Reunification Therapy has some different procedures; please ask questions and then support them.
- Do understand the court order (if any) or legal agreement and follow the guidelines.

11. (Continued) Child Over-Empowerment

There are a number of factors that may have facilitated child empowerment and that can impact on this dimension of impeding the reunification progress. They include, but are not limited to:

- The child's personality and social style—some are controlling and influencing types.
- Others choose to work against the reunification.
- Bad experiences with past professionals.
- A misunderstanding as to how much of a say they (the children) have in the process.
- Lack of clarity on the goals, methods, and content supplied by the Reunification Therapist.
- The degree of case compliance supplied by the respective parents and other possible support systems.
- Parental conflict—no unified front on key issues.

Children sometimes confuse their input with the right to set directionality to a case. It is up to the therapist to clarify the degree of influence that all parties have. Obviously, it is best to get the buy-in from the child, but if they come with a previous history of feeling that they "call the shots," this can severely compromise the (initial) potential for progress.

In some cases, children have felt they need to be empowered because they hold a litany of negative stereotypes and opinions about the parent with whom they have a breach. These are cases where these stereotypes/distortions/misguided facts have been corrected quickly and resulted in a prompt turnaround on the outreach by the child. For example, there have been many cases where children believe that if they reconnected with a parent, this would result in them having to live with that parent more full-time. Some children have believed that custody will be given to a parent with whom they re-bonded. There are other cases where children believe that the broken bond situation was legitimate because "they (the parent) broke up the family and are responsible for the divorce." When these are clarified in diplomatic terms, changes in attitude and behavior may result.

Therefore, it is very important for a therapist and a lawyer to understand what they may be observing in terms of anger, silence, myths, and a whole host of other presentations that, on the surface, look like child empowerment or a desire to obtain it is really something else.

Children sometimes seek power when there has been a power vacuum between their parents. They may also assert power positions when the legal system has presented itself as too vague or indecisive. As many children have said, "Somebody has to make a decision, so I did."

Previous failures in reunification can also result in children looking very decisive because they are tired of the serial, but failed, attempts to reunite. Some of these cases involve a deeper level of analysis and require high levels of sensitivity skills on the part of the therapists and lawyers.

Some ways to reduce child over-empowerment can include:

- Having the parent who is seeking reunification apologize for some misdeeds. (This can be a double-edged sword.)
- Getting the two parents to agree that reconnection is important.
- Teaching the child how to participate in a session so that they can present issues that are important to them.
- Doing reverse role play with the child so that the child takes the position of the parent and the clinician (or the parent) becomes the child.
- Educating the child on the positive and negative consequences of a disengaged versus a reconnected relationship.
- Sharing with the child that the end result of linking is not, in of itself, actually negotiable, but the various methods and timing may be negotiable.
- Finding ways from their respective parent/child histories that they can talk effectively and partake in specific activities together.

12. Unrealistic Time Frames

Some reunification orders set a time frame of one to three months. This may or may not be realistic, depending on the severity, complexity, and duration of the parent-child separation. It often takes a number of weeks just to get a sense of these factors in order to estimate potential time frames for different interventions and set a (tentative) treatment plan.

Many of the children who are vested in keeping the parent-child separation ongoing sometimes employ a predetermined time frame to their advantage. In other words, they will run the three months out and hope that "this too will fail" as many children said to their therapist. So, the children (and/or a parent) go through the motions with the full intent of helping the process to fail because they know there is a given end point in time. This can be called "surface action." Time estimates need to be carefully assessed with flex time built in, if it befits the case.

13. Child Is the Parent's "Partner" or "Best Friend"

It is commonly the case that the child who is segregated from one parent is over-integrated with the other parent. These children will often refer to their favored parent as "their best friend." There are positive and negative aspects to this "friendship." In many of these cases, the friendship is used as a rationale that, "I really don't need another parent because my mom is not only my mom, but my best friend." Similarly, another child said, "My dad does everything for me and with me, so I really don't need my mom."

It's helpful to socially educate a child that the definitions, meanings, love, caring, and sharing of every parent is different in style, content, frequency, and importance.

14. Remuneration Problems

Before any professional process begins, all financial details should be presented and clarified. This includes:

- Total costs.
- Hourly costs versus retainer structure. Is there a retainer or are the fees paid for at time of service?
- Is there a charge for phone and technology communications?
- Are reports an extra cost?
- What are the fees for interfacing with other professionals?
- Is there a cost for going to court?
- Which parent or parents are obligated to pay what percentage of the various fees?
- Who is presented with the updated billing and who has access to it?

- What happens if fees are not paid within the time specified?
- What happens if money is left over?

The clearer the fee structure is from the beginning and the more it is adhered to, the less conflicts and misunderstandings arise. At times, a parent who is opposed to reunification will create conflicts over fees in the hope that the professional will disengage or make an ethical mistake in terms of their own social-emotional responses.

Fee releases that clarify all aspects are a safeguard against problems in this area. The respective attorneys have a right and need to know how the fee structure works on behalf of their clients. Court orders that delineate this obligation precisely are extremely helpful.

15. Threats and (False) Accusations about a Parent and/or Professionals

In highly conflicted divorces, there is a relatively high rate of (false) accusations of various kinds. These accusations can be about a parent's moral character, sexual behaviors, selection of paramours, financial obligations, work histories, behaviors during the marriage, (alleged) physical abuse, neglect and/or abandonment, love and/or interest in the child, and a host of other accusations.

There are cases where false or unfounded accusations play a main force in the parent-child bonds that are damaged. *Children have often been party to these accusations, directly or indirectly, and may carry them as part of their "armor" against re-affiliation.* Working through these is one of the more difficult parts of a reunification process. Some children hold on to these "for dear life" and have developed associated feelings and behavioral reactions. These beliefs, even though (possibly) factually incorrect, help to shape the perceptual base, attitudes, and behaviors of the child. It is not uncommon to hear some of the following:

- "You cheated on mom."
- "Dad said he gave you plenty of money for us, but you stole it and spent it on you and your boyfriend."
- "You caused the breakup of the family and I will hate you forever for that."
- "Mom said you made us lose our house. How could a father ever do that to his kids?"

Accusations can be equally as powerful against professionals. Examples of these include the following:

- "I understand that you generally favor mothers (or fathers)."
- "If you don't do this correctly, I need to put you on notice that I'm watching to see if my son/daughter is under more stress from the counseling."

- "I'll tell you up front that no doctor (or court) can tell me what to do with my child."
- "You know, my kids are going to tell me everything that goes on in here."

16. Long Time Gap in Parent-Child Contact

The longer a separation has occurred, usually the more problematic the reconnection. Children develop routines, lifestyles, habits, and various beliefs over time. The perceived necessity of a particular parent in their life may diminish and they become solidified in their present mode of living. Sometimes, they will seek a contact out of "need." For example, I had a case where the child was disconnected for about 12 years and then needed money for college and reached out to her father (and paternal grandmother). I referred to this as a reconnection based on situational needs. After much discussion back and forth, including commentary about the child's lack of accepting any contact before, the child came up with a question. The question was, "How do I know who to believe about what really happened and whether they (Dad and his family) really are good people?" (She learned from her mother "they were all bad.") The answer that I shared with the rejected side of the family was to tell her this, "See us, talk with us, have some holidays with us, and in other ways share some time and you will then be able to come up with your own decision about what kind of people we are."

Time gaps are not always as predictable as they may seem. For example, there was a child who hadn't seen his grandmother in 13 years and likely had a longing all along to know who she was (as he was cut off by his father at the age of five). She was very well-known in the community and even though the father spent years in an alienation process, the child maintained a curiosity, interest, and need to know his paternal grandmother. Finally, when he reached 18, he worked with his mother to do an outreach and finally see her and talk with his grandmother. These affiliation needs are pent up for many children to connect or re-connect with all types of relatives. It is part of their biological, ethnic, racial, religious, and family histories and (possible) identities. I refer as it to the *N.T.K. (Need to Know) factor.* I have seen this as a driving force in many children. At times, it has resulted in a backfire effect on a parent who may have hindered their connections over a period of years.

As a result of big gaps in time, children develop a curiosity about the looks, behaviors, activities, careers, and other aspects of a parent that has long been out of their purview. Sometimes physical resemblances have been shockingly similar. In other cases, they can see a blend of their joint parental biological contributions. Some had even selected careers that were, unbeknownst to them, similar to the missing (estranged) parent. These factors were used therapeutically as "bridge builders" between parent and child.

Generally, time is an enemy in these kinds of cases. Unfortunately, many parents hold on to the belief that "they will eventually come around, even if it's years later." That is not my clinical nor research experience. I have found the opposite to be true—*the longer the breach, the less likely there will be mended ways. This is why prompt intervention is generally indicated and preferred.*

17. Professionals Perceived as Biased

The parent who is opposed to a reconnection can come up with (imagined) bias claims. They can assert gender bias, experiential bias, case bias, and a whole host of other ways in which the professional will not be seen as neutral. Of course, professionals who dedicate a lot of their life to rebuilding family relationships are not neutral, but it does not mean they are for or against a particular parent. *The professionals are value based precisely because they value family bonds.* Muddying the waters is a common technique of parents who are trying to disrupt and contaminate the professional activity.

Professionals can frequently be sure that once one aspect of bias is raised and set aside that others are (or may be) lurking in the wings. Reunification Therapists need to document these claims and encounters as they will surely come up later (in court or some other forum).

18. Skills of the Professional(s) Are Weak

Reunification counseling has now expanded into a larger category of forensic specialty. Because of this, and as some other areas of counseling diminish, there has been a draw that is attracting many who do not have the training and/or experience in the necessary forensic areas. Just because someone is a psychologist, social worker, family counselor, clinical sociologist, and the like does not mean that they are qualified to engage in reunification efforts. They should have significant experience in family dissolution, alienation, mediation, therapeutic assessment, treatment/risk plans, and many other forensic skill sets. Most of all, an ability to relate to children of all different ages and backgrounds in terms of their interests, as well as their present social-emotional and legal status is crucial.[3]

19. No Reunification Plan

All professional interventions should operate by designing a plan that identifies the directives (legal context), issues, methods, metrics, timelines, and

---

3. For more on this, see Selecting a Professional in S. S. Clawar & B. V. Rivlin, Children Held Hostage: Identifying Brainwashed Children, Presenting a Case, and Crafting Solutions (2d ed. 2013). Association. Also see Chapter 8 in this volume, "Skill Sets and Qualities to Look For in Selecting Reunification Experts."

goals. Also, alternative diagnosis (e.g., child's social styles/personality problems versus alienation) should be considered, as this would change the proposed interventions. Plans can be designed in phases, such as the one that follows.

A Sample Plan: Reunification Phases

I. Assessment/Evaluation Phase
   a. Explain the Reunification Therapy process to parents and their particular roles
   b. Court/legal context
   c. Releases (court ordered and professional required)
   d. Identifying problem behaviors
   e. Alternative explanations for the Broken Bonds
   f. Past professional efforts at reconciliation, if any
   g. Failures—success (degrees and types)
   h. Reunification versus unification
   i. Relevant histories (social, family, legal, professional, educational, and medical)
   j. Parental perspectives
   k. Child perspectives
   l. Parent/child contact—historically and present
   m. Reporting requirements (GAL, court, mediator, therapist, attorneys, etc.)

II. Planning Phase
   a. Articulate goals (short term versus long term)
   b. Micro–macro perspectives (individual, relational, familial, and socio-legal)
   c. Explain the Reunification Therapy process to parents and their particular roles again
   d. Buy in—compliance factors
   e. Reunification versus unification relevance
   f. Risk assessment
   g. Metrics of progress (for child and parent)

III. Implementation Phase
   a. Who is involved?
   b. Singular versus joint sessions
   c. Methodological/Interventions—samples of some relevant interventions
      i. Parent coaching
      ii. Desensitization
      iii. Scripting
      iv. Role collaboration—parents

v. Safety/comfort elements
vi. Involvement (social) school, etc. (direct/indirect)
vii. Chronicity and social setting considerations (meeting times/place)
viii. Other methods[4]

IV. Progress Assessment Phase
a. Compared to original orders, goals, directives, and/or agreements
b. With parents/child
c. Summary memo (to gatekeeper, GAL, court, attorneys, clinicians, etc.)
d. Future considerations, recommendations, and other termination considerations

The preceding is only one sample of a four-phase plan (assessment, planning, implementation, and progress assessment). Sometimes the topics are performed in different sequences.

If there is no plan, the so-called therapy ends up as "seat of the pants" chitchat with guesstimates on interventions and their impact. No medical and or therapeutic work should be done without a plan, but my clinical experience in hundreds of these (researched) cases is that the majority of previous intervention attempts involved no actual systematic plan whatsoever. If I asked the clients what plan they were following, they usually indicated that they were not made aware of any plan. If I followed up with the professionals, I often found out that there frequently was no plan or a vague one, at best. *This is one of the more serious impeding factors, and probably accounts, to some degree, for the high failure rate that is reported among clinicians for Reunification Therapy (especially in high-conflict cases). No plan means no metrics.* Without metrics, progress cannot be accurately measured or explained.

20. Setting Unrealistic Goals

Because many professionals start out with no plan, they do not have graduated goals. Graduated goals include a sense of positive progression. Positive progression is initially exemplified by the following items:

- The child's understanding as to why they are there.
- Talking to the child about themselves (sometimes with no reference to parenting issues).
- Talking about their present state of contact or lack thereof with a parent.

---

4. Benjamin. D. Garber, *Cognitive-Behavioral Methods in High-Conflict Divorce: Systematic Desensitization Adapted to Parent-Child Reunification Interventions*, 53(1) Fam. Ct. Rev, 96–112 (Jan. 2015).

- Sharing with them some information, concerns, or interests of the disengaged parent.
- Reviewing photographs with them of past history and contact.
- Having a joint session where they can each talk about themselves, but not necessarily the relationship.
- Scripting each of them to say things that the other can accept (after learning their respective linguistic style and "hot points").
- Correcting and connecting on historical misunderstandings.
- Connecting and possibly having a meal together (in the office or outside of the office) with the therapist present.
- Getting them to agree to some form of brief written communication (e-mail, text, etc.).
- Possible agreement on having a brief meal outside of the office by themselves.
- More progressive contacts/communication, up to and including full normalization.

Many therapists attempt to go to immediate contact and talking about the relationship problems and suggesting ways for reconnection. Some children (very few) who have been disengaged from a parent will react favorably to this form of (radical) immersion conversation. It can create anxiety and further disengagement on the part of the child. Adults who have lost time and contact are often ready for quicker/more serious topics and direct involvement than the children. This phase-in approach may be quite different from the approach of radical immersion in circumstances of high conflict custody cases. Many children will agree to lower level contact (goals) whereas they will not agree to an all-day visit or an overnight early on in the reconnection process. Caution needs to be exercised here so as not to symbolically signal that the parent is a danger (as some are accused of) to the child. Facilitating social and emotional adjustment is not synonymous with messaging a "bad" or "unsafe" parent implication.

21. Personal and Parental Issues

There are many idiosyncratic factors that can impede a reunification process. Parents will vary in the specific issues and their intensity to which they are held. Knowing what some of these are can be helpful as they commonly appear in many divorce/reunification cases.

Perceived or realistic extra-relational affairs. Where this is a belief of a past or present transgression, there is a high emotional charge to the parents' interactions and acceptance of each other. In many cases, there was not, nor is there presently, an actual affair. *However, the perceived affair can be just as real in its consequences.* A case that exemplifies this latter issue is a wife who accused her husband of three past affairs and one that was allegedly ongoing. The historical analysis of the marriage suggests that the only likelihood of a real affair was a one-night stand over a decade ago, to which the father readily admitted. The animus of the wife continued to contaminate the reunification process; this accusatory element was not present until far into the Reunification Therapy. Whenever progress was made in the therapy within the office, it would often be undermined outside of the professional setting.

Feeling devalued as a parent. Some parents felt that they were underappreciated, under-recognized, or disrespected during the marriage. Their possible rigidity of positions during Reunification Therapy may stem from an attempt to gain status and recognition as a full-fledged parent at this juncture of the dissolution.

Scared and fearful. Many parents have fears of financial insecurity, impeding loss of a residence, and other fears that can impact on their ability to be helpful participants in reunification counseling.

Fear of the Future. This is related to the preceding item, but may have its own independent existence. A concern for parents is, what will it be like to be uncoupled in the future? They may never have envisioned themselves as a single parent and this unknown factor can facilitate anxiety that spills over into the Reunification Therapy.

Fear of losing the children. This specific fear is very common for parents. Therefore, anything that would come up in Reunification Therapy that deals with the amount and type of time they will share (or lose) with the children can create anxieties and positional rigidities. The loss here may not just be in physical time but also in the depth of connectivity to the child and in decision making related to the various aspects of the child's day-to-day life.

Revenge and hostility. Sometimes the various aspects of a divorce or uncoupling is loaded with feelings of retaliation for perceived grievances. This is especially the case for the parent who did not initiate the separation/dissolution of the family. These elements of social-emotional reactivity are not always fully conscious. Parents who harbor these feelings will often rationalize them in terms of some need that the child allegedly has. Clearly, this can also relate to old marital grievances that are transferred into present negative social-emotional reactions.

Mental health dimensions. Some parents have had long-standing conditions of depression, anxiety, bipolarity, addiction(s), or other diagnostic labels. Divorce and separation can exacerbate already existing conditions, or even create them anew.

Presently involved in a new relationship. This aspect of a parent's personal life regularly impacts, positively or negatively, on Reunification Therapy. In some cases, the paramour can contribute positively to a smooth re-bonding process, or they can be (extremely) problematic. The latter condition may manifest itself by imposing themselves as "the new parent" or in other ways introducing tensions that interfere with a re-bonding process. It is therefore, at times, important for the Reunification Therapist to know about their positions and even meet them to judge the degree of cooperation that can be obtained. I've had cases where judges needed to warn the new adult in the life of the child to cease and desist from any negative input that they have issued. Sometimes, just their adult existence is a lightning rod to a (threatened) parent.

Desire for residential relocation. Due to job opportunities, reconnecting with extended family, and/or a desire to start a new life, a parent may wish to move a significant distance from the other parent. This of course creates physical custody dilemmas. Even if Reunification Therapy is successful, the issue of frequency and type of contact between parent and child introduces an element to be considered. The greater the physical distance, the more likely the custodial divide becomes one of school and weekly contact with one parent while the other parent is relegated to vacations, holidays, and summers. However, the nature of the re-bonding process is still the key element, no matter how much time is allocated to each parent. Parents who might receive less physical time with the child often end up with two problems. One is the amount and type of time and the other is the nature of the social bond itself. Interestingly, parents who have the majority of time under these conditions often complain that they do not have enough "quality time" and want to argue over vacations, summers, weekends, and the like. Their argument often revolves around the fact that they are doing the "task and discipline time" versus the other parent having the "fun time."

The preceding personal issues are only a few in order to exemplify important dimensions that impact on, if not contaminate, the Reunification Therapy venture. Being knowledgeable and sensitive to these issues is often fundamental to the potential success of reconnecting a parent and child. Sometimes, the Reunification Therapy experts can deal with these directly (in private sessions); other times they may need to refer them out in order to decontaminate them from the particular task at hand of mending the parent-child relationship.

22. Alienation Is Present

Alienation is one result of a programming/brainwashing (or over-influencing) process that results in the estrangement of a child from the target parent as well as negative behaviors and attitudes. This process can be intentional or unintentional. It can be mild or intense, frequent or infrequent. There are a litany of techniques that parents can use to create a damaged relationship between their child and the other (target) parent. The end result is that the child has absorbed the negativity and desired (physical, social, and/or emotional) distance from the target parent that matches the brainwashing parent's perspective and belief structure. For a more complete understanding of the process, motivations, techniques, detection, impact, and deprogramming strategies see *Children Held Hostage: Identifying Brainwashed Children, Presenting a Case, and Crafting Solutions.*[5]

Alienation has become the diagnosis du jour. This means that many legal and therapeutic professionals have come to believe that behind the need for (all or most) reunification is alienation. This is not true. Please see Chapter 3, "Casual Considerations: Broken Bonds—How Did It Happen?" on page 25. However, even though there are about 26 other causes for parent-child separation other than alienation, it is still very important that the therapist be extremely well versed in evaluating, diagnosing, and treating alienation. In recent years, I have seen a large number of reunification cases where the professional may have assumed alienation but never objectified it beyond just issuing an opinion. This kind of professional behavior can actually create secondary problems. Parents who are not and did not alienate become estranged from the professional process and feel that they are unjustly labeled. This damages the potential for a "therapeutic alliance," which is important in rebuilding parent-child bonds.

Where alienation does exist, it is a strong impediment to re-bonding and must be dealt with systematically. Who is the alienator? What is the specific content contained in the belief system of the child? How long has it gone on? Has it been previously identified? Has there been any previous intervention(s)? How has the accused parent responded? What techniques of inculcating distortions has the alienating parent employed? What specific damage(s) can be identified in the child as a result of being involved in this process? These and many other questions need to be researched and answered in order to be able to design an alienation intervention plan (which may then become part of a larger Reunification Plan).

The presence of alienation lowers the probability of successful connectivity, but does not mean that it is impossible.

Because many cases of reunification involve alienation, to some degree, it is important that the Reunification Therapist be schooled in this social problem and its solutions. They should not jump to radical interventions without (first or not at all) trying other alternative methods.

5. S. S. Clawar & B. V. Rivlin, Children Held Hostage: Identifying Brainwashed Children, Presenting a Case, and Crafting Solutions (2d ed. 2013).

Facilitative Factors

Where possible in the previous listing of impeding factors, we also mentioned ways to turn them into positive tools. The additional factors cited and explained next can make a positive contribution to the reunification process and outcomes.

1. Identifying the Positive Assets of Parents and Children

It is helpful to identify attitudinal and behavioral assets of both the children and parents for whom the reunification process applies. On the positive side, parents can be collaborative, communicative, supportive, insightful, flexible, child-centered, and a whole host of other characteristics that help the process. Children also have assets, which could include being bright, creative, sensitive, enthusiastic, communicative, curious, emotionally expressive, and more (see Appendix C starting on page 253 for a listing of children's assets). Too often therapies of all kinds focus on problems, issues, and negatives alone. A comprehensive listing of the positives can also provide important guidelines for the Reunification Therapist.

2. All Parties Desire Change

In some cases, although they are not necessarily the majority, both parents would like to see a better relationship. Although they agree on this general idea, there may be minor or major disagreements over the process, interventions, time frames, and social arrangements.

By using their common support for the ultimate outcome—a parent and child re-bonding—any differences that arise can often be negotiated in a positive way by explaining that they are the details rather than the substance. For example, the parent who is trying to re-bond may insist on overnight stays early on in the Reunification Therapy. The other parent may agree that there should be a reconnection, but might not support overnights at all or not at that particular time.

By the Reunification Therapist always keeping the key agreements of the parents in mind, as well as the ultimate goals, they can keep the process moving. Parents who have this type of desire often can be helpful in planning various combinations of meetings. This means that some meetings will include both parent and child versus the child with either parent versus the child only with the parent seeking re-bonding.

3. Phase-In Agenda Is Agreed On

However the parents arrived at participation in the Reunification Therapy process, it is helpful when they can actually agree on the progressive phases of normalizing the relationship between parent and child.

4. Clear Strong Court Orders/Professional Goals

The more articulated the order is in terms of parties, goals, timelines, compliance expectations, possible sanctions, and a whole host of other delineations (see the same court order starting on page 227), the better it is for moving the case forward.

The more professionals involved in a case, the more that each one should be identified in terms of their specific obligations and limitations. This includes GALs, regular therapists, Reunification Therapists, psychiatric checkups, and the like. Clarifying professional roles in a court order gives the Reunification Therapist a framework to rely on when interacting with clients.

5. Measurable Components—Metrics

As mentioned throughout this book, this is one of the key elements that should be present in virtually all reunification cases. For details of why, what, how, and when, see Chapter 9, "Measuring Success: Min/Max Metrics" on page 167.

Progress may come in small increments in the beginning and then arithmetically or geometrically expand as the social bonds are rebuilt. See the section Measuring Progress in Chapter 9, "Measuring Success: Min/Max Metrics" for the details of this measurement phenomenon. Global statements by professionals that "progress has been made" are fairly useless to the court, the lawyers, or others without specific reference to exact attitudes and behaviors. Just as the presence of metrics is seen as a positive support for Reunification Therapy, its absence or poor articulation is a clear negative. *Detailed metrics allow for precise discussions and also for assessing what should be done in the next steps of the healing process.*

6. Preset Appointments/Continuity

It is most helpful to reunification if appointments are set up significantly in advance with exact time frames attached to them. The more regular the appointments and the longer the lead time in knowing them, the greater the chance of different types and degrees of success.

7. Varied Methods

The more varied the methods, techniques, and approaches, the greater the flexibility to customize cases as per the case characteristics and personalities/social styles of the parties involved. Singular methods, which are often the stock and trade of non-Reunification Therapists, can limit the degree and amount of success. See the list starting on page 6 in Chapter 1 of this book for examples of some reunification activities. Even established Reunification Therapists sometimes develop habitual approaches like just employing talk therapy. In addition to the fact that it may not work, it can lead to boredom for the clients fairly quickly. This is especially true for children today who are used to constant and varied entertainment-type stimuli. I have often found that when I change the methods (sometimes from week to week), the mental engagement and interest factor rises radically. Actually, when a child says, "This is not like my other therapy," that may in itself be a compliment. This is not meant as a "put down" to other therapies, but to reinforce the notion of some meaningful differences.

8. Coaching for All Parties Possible

A good part of the reunification process is to coach (help with scripts and ideas to use) in order to interact with each other. There is a "lexicon of reconnection." Phrases such as "being with you," "doing things together," "remembering fun times," "missing our goodnight talks," and many more that continue to reinforce social bonding are key to the healing process. *Coaching parents and children to use relational lexicon* as well as when to be silent helps them to develop new skill sets that will help them not only with the parent-child re-bonding but also with other relationships. *Teaching them the difference between thoughts, feelings, beliefs, attitudes, and behaviors can be most instructive.* The child who says, "I hate my mother" often benefits by getting them to label the particular emotion that they employ(ed)—"hate." It is a feeling, not just a thought, not necessarily an attitude yet, nor is it an actual behavior. Once the parties learn a better labeling process, they often start to reconfigure what they say, how they think, and ultimately how they behave. For example, if a child didn't get a baseball glove that he desired and issues the statement, "I hate my father for not getting me the baseball glove," he can come to learn how thinking and feeling this has led to his desire to not see his father. In other words, thoughts and feelings can have consequences in action. In this scenario, the child was not aware (called "consequential thinking") that by disengaging from the father, he developed an unconscious plan to actually never get the glove. He needed to be educated on reframing the problem so that a dialogue could take place that might lead to his attainment of the desired glove. "Dad, I'm really feeling sad and sometimes angry that you wouldn't buy me the glove. I don't understand why. Can you tell me?" After possessing this newfound verbal ability, he discovered that a more solution-oriented discussion took place, including actual interaction with his dad.

9. Reframing Social Relations

In helping children to reframe their relationship with a less bonded parent, they come to be able to accept a redefinition of statuses (positions) and roles (expectations). A clear example of this is the child who constantly complained (and stayed distant from his mother) that his mother was always wanting to supervise his homework and time schedule for extracurricular activities. He defined her as "a pain in the neck," "a policewoman," and "a member of the Gestapo." Because of his terse definitions, he also thought it was appropriate that she do none of these school related behaviors. "And then maybe I'll see her." A discussion ensued both with the Reunification Therapist and the mother that revolved around duties and obligations of being a parent. She came to learn that being a parent does not mean agreeing with the child all the time nor does it mean that the child gives direction to a parent on key issues of the child's life. In fact, it's the other way around—parents give direction (even if there is opposition) to the child. This, according to sociologists, is called "role clarification." Reframing the child's understanding of what a parent does proved helpful, as it assisted in reaffirming legitimate boundaries that often become confused in separation, divorce, and custodial conflicts. A common criticism by parents seeking to re-bond is that, "I've lost my authority and ability to have a say in what happens in my child's life." Reframing parental skills, obligations, and authority under this condition can be extremely fruitful, but not easy.

10. Strong GAL—If Possible

The presence of a knowledgeable, directional, and experienced GAL can make all the difference in a case. For a detailed analysis of their many functions, see Chapter 12 "How GALs Can Help in the Reunification Process" on page 235.

11. Reporting to the Court

The right to report the success, or lack thereof (in terms of any preset metrics), is important. Parents who know that the court is in a state of surveillance tend to behave more appropriately. This is not always true, as some adults have a consummate disrespect for the law and its representatives. Fortunately, these are a relatively small minority. It should be clear to all parties what, how, and when things will be reported and why.

12. Stamina of the Professionals

This is a personal human quality that can have significance to the outcomes. Being physically and mentally facile, persistent, and durable are the personal intangibles involved in reunification work. Professionals should always look "on top of their game" and ready for the professional activity at hand. However, many of the Reunification Therapy sessions are held in late afternoon to early evening due to student schedules, sports obligations, and homework demands. This means that these professionals need to make sure that their personal life is in relative balance. Their diet, exercise, social relationships, and obligations need to be in a condition of (at least relative) homeostasis (balance). Clients can tell when a professional is distracted, tired, misremembering case facts, and a host of other personal "reads."

13. Cease and Desist on CYS/Police Filings

If accusations of abuse, neglect, and other negative behaviors have been set aside (or already ruled on) by social agencies, police, and the courts, it is important that the clients stop using this information against the other parent.

14. Supportive of Other Parent

It is extremely helpful if the parent without the Broken Bonds is or comes to be supportive of the process and goals of reunification. A lot of the work of reunification experts is to help the child make the reconnection. Homework, discussions, and activities can be suggested by the Reunification Therapist so that the office is not the only setting in which the re-bonding is to take place. In fact, if it is the only setting, it is likely to have lower success rates and take longer.

Summary

It is rare to have all of the facilitative factors or even all of the impeding factors present in any one case. However, using them as a reference can be a useful guide. They can also be used in the legal arena to craft a customized court order. Reunification Therapy can be helped by determining the presence of both the strong, supportive facilitating factors and the weak, problematic impeding factors of the case.

Chapter 7

Nineteen Popular and Professional "Theories" That Can Be Problematic to the Reunification Process

"I can tell you one hundred reasons why this won't work."

— 14-year-old girl

"A theory is only as good as its ability to explain all or most aspects of the phenomenon it is addressing. All theories are open to challenge with new or contrasting evidence."

— Stanley S. Clawar

The theories or assertions that follow are commonly issued by children, parents, and/or various professionals. They need to be dealt with because they can be impediments to an even, well-articulated reunification plan. Linear (head-on) debates or counter assertions to them may not be the best initial approach in dealing with them. The Reunification Therapist needs a litany of responses, depending on the case, as they may have worked before in stymying past reunification efforts and professionals. Some assertions within these popular theories may have a history that is important to understand (whether factual or not).

1. Readiness Theory

This is a theory that has been floating around in mental health circles for a very long time. The basic idea is that people cannot/will not/do not perform behaviors until they are "ready." It is based on a few other theories that will be noted later. Unfortunately, it is one of the most common professional and now popular theories that are employed to challenge, redirect, or impede Reunification Therapy.

The obvious question that arises for reunification is "when is the child ready?" This can be exemplified in a recent case where a child had not seen her father for about two years and when I checked with the child's therapist, he informed me that she is still not "ready." I inquired as to when her therapist thought that she might be ready and he proffered, "probably when she's done high school and about to begin college." Of course, there is no guarantee that she would even be ready at that time. What he likely didn't know was *the longer there is a breach, the lower the probability that re-bonding will occur.*

All Reunification Therapists need to be "ready" to deal with "readiness theory." Reunification court orders do not usually contain the explicit or implicit idea that tolerating a long readiness period is in "order." Some non-forensic clinicians have dealt with this by using another theory called phase-in theory, which will be discussed later (theory number 17).

Reunification professionals should have at hand their own scripts ready for adults and children to explain that if readiness has failed before, it may, in fact, fail again. James Thurber, a famous humorist, has said, "This has unworked in the past, and it will unwork now."[1] An important question to ask is, why is the child not ready? There are many answers to this important question. They could not be ready because they have had a gap in their contact with a parent that has become habitual. They may not be ready because they have adults and siblings who are supportive of them not being ready. They may not be ready because they have a long history of social and/or personality conflicts with a particular parent. They may not be ready because they have distorted or misinformation about one of their parents. They may not be ready because the parent they haven't seen exercises more discipline (and they don't like it). They may not be ready because another adult has supplanted that parent (in meaning and function). They may not be ready because they're an oppositionally defiant child. They may not be ready because they are blaming one parent for the divorce. They may not be ready because a professional told them they are probably not ready. This is just to cite a few reasons as to why a child may "not be ready."

This is a key hurdle for Reunification Therapists, attorneys, and judges. So, be ready!

1. James Thurber, *The Last Clock: A Fable for the Time, Such as It Is, of Man,* 35(1). The New Yorker 28 (Feb. 21, 1959).

2. Anxiety Theory

It is regularly presented by professionals and parents that re-bonding has failed and/or cannot take place at the present time because a child has various levels and types of anxiety. As with all other theories, there may be kernels of truth contained within the assertion. But the more important issue is not just whether there is anxiety but where and how it developed. Were there periods in the child's relationship with the now distant parent that were anxiety free? Were there times when they were closely bonded? Therefore, the question arises as to when and how did this change? Reunification Therapists need this information so they understand that the relationship (quality) may have been different during different time frames. Also, it's important to know that one of the ways to reduce anxiety is to help someone face the source of that anxiety. We cannot help people being afraid of crossing a bridge without, sooner or later, approaching the bridge. Holding sessions with a now distant parent where the parent is properly behaved and did nothing to induce (further) anxiety may be a very important (safe) social experiment. It is not uncommon to have these encounters where a child is surprised to find that "it was okay." On the other hand, if (serious) alienation is a factor in the case, a child may report not only continued anxiety, but may present distortions about what actually happened in the session. Children may report that the parent or even the professional used profanity—and, yet, it never happened! I'm aware of professionals who report that some children have hyperventilated in the presence of a parent they have not seen for a while. Teaching them to breathe properly and reregulate their respiration can be helpful in these situations.

Some children have symptoms of Generalized Anxiety Disorder (GAD), which can be triggered by novel situations. If this is mixed in with a dose of alienation, you have a potent combination of factors. If the child is or has been treated for GAD, it would be proper to contact the diagnosing professional for information and interventions found useful.

The (unacceptable) alternative to many of the theories, if they are taken as absolutes, is for the child to never encounter the parent because some problems may arise in the initial reconnection. We teach children to face anxieties every day of their lives and can do so with respect, appropriate cautions, and forward movement. It's called maturity.

3. Scared Theory

It is commonly reported that if a child knows they are going to see a parent from whom they have been disengaged, that they will be scared before, during, and after the encounter. Obviously, we are addressing the majority of cases where abuse has not been found, as it is understandable that in these cases, legitimate fear could be induced at just the thought, mention, or sight of that parent. Unfortunately, in many family law cases, filings made of emotional, physical, and sexual abuse that are unfounded or false are not infrequent. It is the job of the Reunification Therapist to create an environment that is safe and comfortable. However, even if this is accomplished, children can still assert this social-emotional concern. Again, finding periods of time when they were not afraid of that parent is important information. It is also not uncommon that the children will report all kinds of social-emotional reactions that may have an underlying factor of guilt. Many children feel guilty for not talking to, seeing, or, worse, testifying against a parent. *Guilt alone can create the need or desire to not encounter that parent.* I've had children say to me, "I feel really sorry that I told the custody evaluator about my dad's hollering. He didn't really do it that much, but I heard that what I said was made to sound like he did it all the time—and he didn't." At that point, the child cried and said, "So you see why I can't see my dad, don't you?"

4. Feelings Are Important Theory

This theory connects to all of those theories just described, but is usually articulated as a general emotional statement with assertions like "I just don't feel like seeing her," "I'm not feeling this is a good time," "I don't feel like doing homework with my dad is going to be comfortable." It's interesting because one of the aspects of social maturity is understanding that feelings may not be the best guide to conduct. So, if a child says, "I'm not feeling like going to school this week," we often tell them that the feeling is not a guide to conduct and that it is going to occur (going to school) in real time. If siblings are fighting, and we ask them why they are fighting and one of the children says, "I felt like hitting my brother in the face," we do not usually concur that the action should follow from the feelings. In other words, *feelings can be a guide to constructive or destructive behaviors.* Therefore, the feeling that you don't want to see a parent who cares about you, loves you, and wants to help guide your life should not necessarily be honored. If it is, it may result in one of the major losses in the child's life. Feeling theory is pervasive both professionally and popularly. Teaching children the difference between listening to feelings that help us versus listening to feelings that hurt us (and others) can be most instructive. Popular culture strongly supports feeling theory. A large percentage of popular music caters to the idea that feelings are one of the most important parts of life. This is not necessarily false, but not much of a distinction is made between feelings that lead us in the right direction versus those that take us down the wrong path.

5. Separate Therapy Theory

This theory asserts that Reunification Therapy is not necessary because the child, was, is, or will be in some separate type of therapy. Of course, there are literally hundreds of different types of therapies in the United States. One quick survey that I did identified (in excess of) 200 separate types of therapies—none of which necessarily have the same goals, format, skill sets, or content as Reunification Therapy. Anyone who has done reunification for any period of time has had cases with children who have been in therapy for one, five, ten, or even more years—sometimes with no meaningful impact on a parent-child relationship. In many cases, a child is involved in a separate therapeutic experience (and possibly a custody evaluation simultaneously) while asked to undergo reunification efforts. *It is important to identify where and how these separate professional experiences may be collaborative, or even potentially in conflict with one another.* A therapist who has no, or limited, knowledge of forensic social-science therapies is often the least helpful in collaboration with the reunification expert. Even explaining to the regular therapist that there is a court directive on the nature of the parent-child contact that must occur within a specific timeframe can be confusing or unsettling to them. They are not used to these kinds of parameters (or constraints) surrounding a therapeutic relationship. *The idea that the goals may drive the method is different or even alien to some therapists.* A case in point is a teenage girl who entered private therapy while undergoing Reunification Therapy and a custody evaluation. After one session (and inadequate history taking), the private therapist suggested that the child may want to block her father from texting. Nothing was inappropriate about his texts. So, we have one therapist recommending a child cut the father off in contradistinction to the very goals of the Reunification Therapy court order and goals. On the other (positive) hand, it is possible to work with fellow professionals who understand that *forensic-type therapies have special modalities and goals*; these therapists will try to share information that is helpful to the re-bonding process. An example of this is a case where the forensic therapist was in regular touch with the child's psychiatrist (who not only monitored medication but also was providing specialized therapies for ADHD). Their professional interface facilitated a positive parental reconnection.

6. Don't Need Him or Her in My Life Theory/ My Life's Fine Theory

This position is not infrequently articulated by children of various ages, but is especially by adolescents who have been separated from a parent seeking re-affiliation. They will pose a number of reasons as to why they don't need that parent. This theory can also be called the "My Life's Fine Theory." The subset statements of these theories are "I'm doing well in school," "I have good friends and I'm not in trouble," "I have a stepdad who is like a real dad," "My life's in place and I don't have to run from house to house," or "If my life is fine the way it is, why change it?" This, on the surface, is not so easy to navigate because there may be surface truth to it. Of course, it's missing the additive dimension of having another loving, caring parent in their life. Kids who proffer this usually imply the additional effort of seeing their parent will involve a "hassle" due to time and logistical issues. The latter issues are procedural and can usually be addressed methodically.

7. Can't Change Theory

Parents and children can assert that the parent who is desiring a reconnection couldn't change in the past, so they likely can't and won't change now and in the future. Statements like, "They say things in an office that sound good, but then no change happens on the outside" and "We've been through a number of doctors and there has been no change. So why bother?" are examples of this stagnating dialogue. Interestingly enough, clients who assert this rarely mention what role they have had, if any, in the noted limited change process. When asked how they have changed or could change, their responses range from silence to "I don't know" to "Why should I have to change? I'm the child." The already connected parent needs to understand that their degree and type of support for change could be the "secret sauce" to the case. Helping the distanced parent with scripts and behaviors to deal with this can prove quite constructive.

8. Failed Before Theory

This is often connected to the theory above (can't change theory) where citations are presented of the various attempts to rebuild the relationship having met with failure, or worse, more problems. Some resistant parties to the process will cite chapter and verse about where, when, and how things have failed. References to the amount of time, money, and aggravation are also presented during these kinds of discussions. Although some of the negativity that surrounds this theory (and others) may appear unimportant on the surface, it is not. It may be true that failed attempts can or have caused more problems. It may be true that excessive amounts of time and money have been spent. Reunification Therapists need to be cautious about simply discounting negative commentaries. Certainly, this theory is one that, if true, can make the present reunification attempts more complicated and more difficult, but there is important and relevant information that can be gleaned from these historical experiences of (perceived) failure. Reunification Therapy needs to be respectful of these possible reactions and have plans to deal with them.

9. We Never Got Along Theory

Citing past difficulties in a relationship is also commonly heard. The assertion may be valid or invalid, and sorting this out can be quite helpful. I've had many cases where extensive videos and photographs exist showing years of happy and collaborative moments between parent and child.[2] If alienation is involved, a child may actually rewrite the objective reality that is (and was) before them. For example, in one such representative case, when a child was confronted with massive written information (holiday cards, videos, and photographs) he indicated, "That's something my father does well." When asked what that means, he further explained, "He's a great actor and all of those pictures are just phony smiles. They're not real, so don't be fooled." However, it is possible that because of social styles and personality differences and other family dynamics (including children being turned against a parent during a marriage) that there may be some validity contained within this assertion. Reunification Therapists need to be open to all possibilities, but must come back to refocus their charge—reunification. Also, if it is true to any degree, *the future doesn't have to recreate the past.* This is a hard, but important sell to make.

10. Maybe Later (Put Off) Theory

Reunification Therapists hear what may also be called the put-off theory—reunification can't and shouldn't be done now, but may be possible sometime in the future. The future is usually an undefined space of time. When asked why later and not now, a litany of reasons and excuses are put forward. Some of these include, "I'm in the middle of midterms," "I have an important social event (prom, vacations, etc.) coming up and I don't want to be upset," "It just doesn't feel right at this time," and "I think when I'm a little older, I'll handle it better." A famous religious proverb, "If not now, when? If I am not for myself, who shall be for me? If I am for myself alone, what am I?" may apply here. This is also related to "readiness theory" noted earlier.

11. You Don't Really Know Them Theory

This is related to the idea that the particular client (a parent and/or child) has knowledge and information about past events, problematic morality, reputational issues, and other factors that suggest that the parent desiring a reconciliation is, in fact, a bad candidate. If pushed further, some children can actually provide more specifics, such as, "He broke up the marriage," "Everybody hates him—even in our church and in his busines," "He's a porno freak," and "She's an alcoholic." As with other theories, there may be different degrees of validity or information that is valid and useful. Even if

2. Make sure your permission to view or hear videos, texts, phone calls, and other forms of communication conforms to state and/or federal law.

the ideas are false or were previously true, they also reveal the perceptions and beliefs of the child and/or the other parent. This is all useful information that can be utilized in an articulated treatment plan. True, false, distorted, or otherwise, it is data that can be applied for bridge building. However, it should not be determinative of the (initial) judgments of the Reunification Therapy.

12. Nobody Gets It Theory

This assertion is that judges, attorneys, guardians, therapists, and any others connected to the case are really "stupid," "ridiculous," "crazy," "paid off," "they're on my mom's (or dad's) side," or "they don't care about kids." Many of these children, but not all, have learned comments like these from various adults. Certainly, some can generate these feelings and thoughts by themselves, but when the statements have been properly researched, children will often admit the source is other than their own brain. These types of comments make it harder for Reunification Therapists, as they are often considered guilty by association. Therapists can also hear, "You're probably just like the rest of them and you won't get it either." One child recently said, "The only reason I'm coming is because if I don't, my mother will be in trouble with the judge. So, I'll come, but I won't look at him (the father), talk to him, or anything else. You probably won't get it either." This type of positioning is difficult, as it represents an initial defensive or hostile attitude. Reunification professionals need to be objective and find out exactly what the other professional "didn't get." Incidentally, getting it and agreeing with it are not the same thing in Reunification Therapy.

13. You Didn't Live My Life Theory

Many children will tell their Reunification Therapist that their past experiences were so problematic that they are simply better off not knowing or being with the parent who wants to see them. They will recount real or imagined stories that they deem problematic enough to rationalize their temporary or permanent disengagement. Again, this kind of assertion may require additional social research in the event that some of the accusations have possible validity. Even if they are valid, the Reunification Therapist may still have the task before them of rebuilding the relationship (while considering or incorporating these problems into consideration). These children (or other parents) often want an empathic response from the Reunification Therapist. If extended, empathy is often confused by clients as agreement. Caution is warranted here for Reunification Therapists, as children or parents will quote them with statements such as, "They said they understood, so I know they agree with me."

14. I Have Rights and Want My Own Lawyer Theory

Generally, children will assert this from approximately age 10 on up. Some have been privy to courtroom hearings, evaluators, attorney contacts, GALs, overhearing discussions about legal issues, interviews by Children and Youth Services (CYS or CPS—Children Protective Services), and a whole host of other related involvements. Either by coaching or of their own accord, they can generate this opinion or demand. These children may be some of the more oppositional as they are looking for another intermediary between them and the reunification process (or both parents). It's important to explain to some of these children, when a GAL is in the case, that they serve the function of overseeing and protecting the interests of the child (and the therapist, if so stated). In some cases, attorneys have actually been appointed to represent the child's interests. Reunification Therapists need to understand that they have to respect those court-connected agents and consider their questions and concerns on behalf of the child. Knowing when to accept and/or suggest that a child (and parent) can or should speak with their GAL or attorney is an important procedural and ethical obligation.

15. They're "Abusive" Theory

As mentioned elsewhere, a number of cases involve founded, unfounded, or false findings of abuse. Reunification Therapists must understand the difference between sexual, physical, emotional, and social abuse. They also need to know the difference between covert and overt abuse. For example, overt sexual abuse might involve touching, fondling, or penetrating a child. It can involve exposure to pornography and/or using the child as a photographic model. Covert sexual abuse may not involve any necessary physical contact, but could involve lots of discussions and suggestions about sexually charged themes. The latter (overt abuse) can be extremely difficult to determine, because many parents take on the role of "sex educator" (when and if the other parent opts out of this important function). I've had cases where one parent will discuss menstruation, growing breasts, sexual acts and scenes (sometimes seen by the child in the media), contraception, disease transmission, and other sexually loaded topics. In one case, a father was turned over to the police and Children and Youth Services for a more complete investigation. It was quickly set aside as unfounded. However, the damage to the relationships between the children and the father had to be incorporated into the Reunification Plan. In this case, it was found that the therapist had actually coached the children to say negative and incriminating things and to perceive their father as a source of danger. So, the problematic therapist's accusation of the father as a "groomer"[3] could, in a way, possibly be applied

3. Grooming is a process purporting to actual abuse.

to himself, the therapist. Ironically, he was actually one of the most involved, caring, and appropriate parents one could find—by many measures of effective parenting.

16. One Good Parent Is Enough Theory

There has been little doubt over the centuries, if not forever, about the centrality and importance of the mother's influence and impact on children. More recently, there has been a concurrent development to document the importance of the father's role and involvement with children. One of the better sources that draws on a wide range of scientific studies is Paul Raeburn's book *Do Fathers Matter?: What Science Is Telling Us About the Parent We've Overlooked.* The conclusions are very clear that a father's involvement facilitates better language development, lowers the risk of problematic behavior, and has other positive influences on the mental and physical health of the child. This and other research should put to rest any issue that may arise as to the father's equal, but significant, impact on child development. The fact that Raeburn draws on many disciplines lends additional support to his observations and conclusions. In other words, we are in an era where the importance of both parental figures is well established.

However, Reunification Therapy experts may still encounter covert or overt beliefs about the importance of one parent or the other. Sometimes providing a parent who holds reservations about the other can be handled by assigning them clear, focused, and well-grounded readings. This doesn't always solve the belief, depending on how entrenched a particular belief may be.

17. Phase-In Theory

Many bonded parents assert that the Reunification Therapist needs to proceed slowly—usually to build trust with the child. Although this may have some validity in selected cases, it also can be employed to retard the therapeutic process. Professional discretion is key in this area. Different cases lend themselves to different contact speeds; some necessitate a slower (phase-in) than others that can tolerate more immediate immersion.

18. The Chemistry Isn't There Theory

Bonded parents present this as a dilemma on behalf of the child. They often make statements such as "They never really were close," "They just don't connect," or some other assertions suggesting a non or mal fit between parent and child. Even if this is true, not all parents have a perfect blending with a particular child. However, by good bridge building activities, the "chemistry" can improve. As in all areas of parent and child input, the Reunification Therapist listens, respects, and employs professional discretion toward the ultimate goal—better parent-child bonds. Children can also make these assertions with and without alienation as a component.

19. (S)he Doesn't Even Listen to Me Theory

It can be asserted that Reunification Therapy shouldn't take place or will fail because the less bonded parent brought it on themselves due to their poor listening skills and ability. The "not listening" complaints can come from a parent, a child, or both. *Some confuse not listening with the idea that the parent didn't comply.* Clearly, compliance and listening are two separate things. "When my daughter told me to get out of her room while I'm talking about homework—I listened, but I didn't do it," said one father. However, listening skills can always be improved on. Some degree of mutuality is necessary to develop here in the Reunification Therapy process.

Summary

In summary, the preceding theories can be both problematic but also a source of useful information, even if some of them are not well grounded in reality. They are also instructive to know because attorneys, judges, therapists, GALs, and others will confront them and need to have appropriate scripts ready when they are recited and presented as part of (possible challenges to) Reunification Therapy. A good professional doesn't start out with a bias that these are all manipulations or untruths. They may or may not be. But, either way, they must be dealt with as part of the social context of the particular case that is before them. It is also important to recognize that in some cases, only a few or even one of these will be asserted. However, in other cases, many or all of them may be presented to the legal and therapeutic professionals. They commonly appear in court, so attorneys and judges need to be on the ready. They require, at times, forensic investigatory skills with a high sense of neutrality, objectivity, and an unbiased perspective. Knowing them will help lawyers and forensic experts to be prepared. Judges will also often hear these arguments as a basis for not issuing a reunification order or even to cease Reunification Therapy.

Chapter 8

Skill Sets and Qualities to Look for in Selecting Reunification Experts

"Who am I? What am I doing?"

— Stanley S. Clawar

The above two questions are used to train clinicians, mediators, and other professionals. They must be asked obsessively to keep one on track or accomplishing the mission. The answer to the first question, in regard to reunification is, "I am a Reunification Therapist ordered by the court or agreed upon by various parties." The second question is the task focus—reunifying family members. Keeping these two questions in mind prevents getting sidetracked. One is not doing "therapy," but Reunification Therapy. One is not rehearing a legal case (it's likely been done or about to be done). If the Reunification Therapist is clear and consistent, the clients can be more focused on the task at hand.

Those searching for a Reunification Therapist would benefit by considering the requisite skill sets needed to accomplish this demanding but important function—bringing family members (back) to a closer, better, more loving and mutual relationship.

As noted throughout this text, the first thing to recognize is that no particular clinical discipline need be a mandatory requirement for working in this field. So, forensic psychiatrists, psychologists, social workers, marriage and family counselors, clinical sociologists, pastoral counselors, and other disciplinary backgrounds may all have knowledge and skill sets that can serve as a basis for working on reunification issues. Clearly, they have different perspectives on human behavior, but that does not necessarily exclude them from the goal of healing damaged relationships between a parent and child. Following are some of the key areas of consideration that are important in identifying, selecting, and working with reunification professionals.

Mediation, Conflict Resolution Skills, Credentials

Having training and experience in mediation and conflict resolution is extremely helpful (if not mandatory), as many of the cases revolve around real or imagined conflict between a parent and child (let alone between the parents). Knowing the skills and jargon of mediation provides a base for staying calm in the face of expected and unexpected information and conflicts. It allows the professional to maintain a sense of calm amidst possible high tension situations. People with this skill set can also prioritize issues so that the more solvable issues are worked through first. They also can identify what are called "set asides" whereby the therapist sidebars certain issues because they cannot or should not be dealt with at that particular time. Progress, however, moves ahead on other issues and topics. Mediation experts can also draft clear and focused documents concerning what has been agreed to and what is yet to be improved upon. This skill set includes dozens of techniques for resolution of differences and conflicts.

Forensic Knowledge

No matter what the discipline, a Reunification Therapist should have training and extensive experience relating to the forensic component of their chosen field. A regular psychologist is not necessarily qualified to do forensic work, nor is a regular psychiatrist, social worker, or any other field of behavioral science. The forensic component means someone who has the knowledge of the law, the legal system, the various players and roles in the legal system, family law issues, how to work with a GAL, ability to read and understand court orders and reports, and a whole host of other socio-legal knowledge and related skill sets. Many people from various disciplines have moved into "forensics" because it is exciting, challenging, and potentially income producing. However, a reunification case in the wrong hands will create more problems than it solves. True reunification experts have received many cases where they have the original problem of building bonds as well as the new overlay problems created by a non-forensic behavioral scientist who did not know the proper procedures, methods, and approaches.

Substantial Case Experience in Successfully Re-bonding Parents and Children

This is not just a matter of numbers, but emphasizes the word "successfully." Not all cases end up meeting the maximum goals set by the courts or a parent. However, success can be measured in outcomes that resulted in better relationships defined by different types of progress and to varying degrees. It is important to note that just because someone has been doing something for 20 years, does not mean they have done it correctly. The analogy would be a golfer who has been golfing for decades and is approached by Tiger Woods, one of the world's greatest golfers, who says, "By the way, do you know that your backswing is wrong? Here's how you follow through." Again, just doing something over time doesn't mean that it has been done correctly. In selecting a reunification expert, requests should be made of their relevant "track record." Judges, attorneys, and GALs often have information that is helpful in this regard. Please note that a one-off criticism on the Internet should not necessarily disqualify them. Some clients will use the Internet as part of their assaultive behaviors against a professional.

Reputation for Non-Adversarial Practice

Truly objective reunification experts have the majority of their cases court appointed, attorney agreed upon, GAL recommended, or mediator referred. A very small amount, if any, of their practice should be of an adversarial nature. This means that they are respected by people in the socio-legal occupations as well grounded, knowledgeable, ethical, and objective. They are not a father's rights person, a mother's rights person, nor do they abide by any particular category of favoritism. Speaking occasionally to a mother's rights or father's rights group does not necessarily exclude or disqualify them, although most professionals in the field avoid this appearance of bias, where possible. They do, however, enjoy bringing families together, where possible, and can create comfort across age spans.

Respected by the Courts, GALs, Attorneys, and Fellow Professionals

As noted earlier, respectability has usually been earned over years of handling basic and more difficult cases. They have been seen as knowledgeable, honest, ethical, and with a high degree of integrity. They have also garnered respect by admitting their limitations and identifying cases that are not amenable to the reunification processes and methods, as well as ones that are. It's not an intervention process that fits all cases. Obviously, the expert may need a diagnostic session or two in order to assess a case's viability. This respect theme can be called the "reputational factor."

Ethically Based Practice

One of the worst things that can be said about a social behavioral expert, if true, is that they are "unethical." Good professionals abide by ethics on a number of levels. In the first place, most professionals belong to at least one professional society that has its own set of articulated ethical guidelines. Whether they are (forensic) psychologists, clinical sociologists, psychiatrists, social workers, or from many other disciplinary backgrounds, they should know and practice the ethics related to their professional associations.

In the second place, there are legal ethics in which they should be grounded. This does not mean they are attorneys, but that they understand the ethical parameters of judges, lawyers, GALs, and others in the legal-related professions. For example, if it is unethical for an attorney to have an ex parte communication with the Reunification Therapist, they should know this and will remind anyone who tries to cross that boundary. In the third place, there are also communal ethics that exist, often by regional or cultural differentiations. Knowing these ethical differences can be very important. This could even relate to the ways in which attorneys and experts are seen by the courts in a particular community. In some locales, the experts come in with a high level of respect and credibility. In other places, they are seen as adjunctive, at best.

In the fourth place, individuals may have their own religious basis as a source of ethics. These religious guidelines can set some structure for mundane things such as what days they will and will not testify; this can happen when a special holiday falls on a court date. In other matters, some experts may not be able or willing to testify in regard to cases on same-sex couples or where abortion is a topic. Eliminating any potential area of bias is a professional mandate.

In the fifth place, individual experts may have their own ethical guidelines in terms of what kinds of cases they can do or choose not to do. They may prefer to exclude themselves from cases that have a history of physical violence, domestic abuse, drug addiction, or any other area that is problematic for them (in terms of training, experience, or personal proclivity).

The ability to have a coherent practice while integrating five different levels of ethical standards can prove a challenge in itself. Many attorneys and other legal functionaries come to know which experts prefer and function better in different types of cases. However, attorneys would do well to check this out prior to the beginning of a case.

A professional I had to deal with in a custody case a few years ago labeled himself as a "forensic psychologist." He was a member of the APA (American Psychological Association) and should obviously subscribe to their ethical standards, including their forensic standards (which has a separate code). In looking at his work on the case, he violated many, if not most, of the key ethical standards in both the regular and forensic APA standards. One of the most important guidelines as far as custody is to not issue definitive statements, conclusions, or recommendations without access to both parents. In this case, the professional was hired by and only talked to the father before writing a substantial report in excess of 100 pages; the report commented extensively on the mother's behavior without ever speaking to her. This is an ethical violation pro forma.

Part of another ethical principal of the APA, Principal A: Beneficence and Nonmaleficence, is to "take care to do no harm." In this case, he also made many assertions about the mother that were harmful to her image, and his recommendations about custody would place the child into situations that could prove potentially harmful to both her safety, health, and general welfare.

One of the most egregious violations though was the lack of scientific basis for his (professional) judgments. In this case, the professional concluded that the mother was an alienator. He did virtually nothing to prove that the mother was an alienator besides write a report. The bases for his conclusions were strictly from document review and speaking to the father. He spoke to no other professionals involved in the case—neither the mother, the child, nor any of the dozens of doctors that treated the child for medical and mental health issues. Standard 9.01 of the Forensic APA Guidelines states, "Psychologists base the opinions contained in their recommendations, reports, and diagnostic or evaluative statements, including forensic testimony, on information and techniques sufficient to substantiate their findings." This overlaps with Standard 2.04, "Bases for Scientific and Professional Judgements" which is also part of the Ethical Guidelines of the APA. In this case, the professional's opinions had inadequate scientific proof in order to make his rather extreme claims.

These are only a few of the ethical violations that this professional made in this case. Unfortunately, this is not an uncommon scenario. These "experts" are open to serious cross examination given their ethical missteps. Attorneys are increasingly examining the ethical dimensions of experts' opinions, methods, and conclusions. Experts are now starting to be challenged (in the courts) as much on their ethical mistakes as on their content, procedures, and conclusions.

Capacity to Diagnose the Difficulty/Complexity Levels of Cases

Not all experts desire or are capable of handling cases with certain types of diagnoses. Some children may have social-psychological diagnoses (including children with special needs) that are quite serious and this may be beyond the ken of the particular practitioner. Of course, this diagnostic issue can also apply to one or both of the parents or siblings. Some experts don't work well with dual diagnosis and some do. Some do not have the interest or capacity to deal with different types of addictions when they are presented as part of a reunification case. Furthermore, the complexity of the case can be from minor to major. As the level of complexity increases, the challenge to the Reunification Therapist also increases. Cases that have been in litigation for years, with multiple diagnoses, with a litany of previous experts, with a litany of attorneys including representation for the children, including the presence of a GAL, and many other factors are certainly not appropriate for a novice.

Experts should clearly state their interest and capacity in regard to social-psychological diagnoses, case histories, and other aspects of case complexity.

Even the level of acrimony and, at times, overt hostility when a parent is ordered to participate can be a non-starter for some counselors/therapists.

Verbally Articulate and Performs Well-Crafted Reports, Memos, and E-mails

In an era where writing skills have diminished nationally, it is becoming harder and harder to find people of all professions who write clearly and succinctly. The ability to draft a coherent and focused forensic report (which usually has to be done in these reunification cases) is extremely important. In many cases, memos have to go back and forth between the therapist and the attorneys, GAL, parents, courts, co-parenting appointees, and others. Poorly written memos and reports can actually introduce new problems due to a lack of clarity, direction, precision, and specificity. Knowing that all communications issued and received by a Reunification Therapist have legal implications is certainly basic, but may not necessarily be appreciated by all mental/social health professionals. Clear, focused professional language helps all case functionaries. In cases of public record, attorneys can see samples of their professional levels of spoken speech and written abilities.

Formatting a Report and Related Materials

- Court Order, Agreed Upon Order, Mediation Guidelines
- Listing of Parties
- Documents Reviewed

- Intake Interviews—All Relevant Parties
- Treatment Plan with Metrics (Tentative)
- Measuring Progress (Stabilization), or Regression
- Reporting to Parents, Child(ren), Lawyers, Court, and Orders as Appropriate to the Case
    - o Compliance
    - o Status
    - o Metrics
    - o Conclusions/Recommendations
- Termination, Referral, and/or New Treatment Plan

Published/Acknowledged in the Field

It is not mandatory, but useful to have an expert who has written objective materials (research and/or clinically based) to be shared beyond their own practice. It shows an acceptance by other professionals and knowledge that has likely been critiqued. Popular and professional articles and books can also provide a window into the thinking and perspectives of the expert. Professional presentations on topics relevant to reunification cases are also a positive. Accreditations may continue to develop for reunification practices. Hopefully, different disciplines will be involved as only one professional society having a monopoly on certification will narrow the range of theoretical, research, and application modalities. Now, we have some individuals issuing certificates that are not grounded in a large enough professional matrix of colleagues. Some are creating their own self-serving certifications. Court time, presentations, and other (professional) activities may or may not be a clue to skills, ethics, and effective interventions. Some audiences may not be a good basis for evaluating their professional recognition, but represent certain biased constituencies—mother's rights and father's rights groups are two such examples. The Internet has facilitated the proliferation of many groups with varied agendas. For example, the Internet is loaded with parent alienation groups of varied quality and professional grounding.

Can Write a Treatment Plan

A treatment plan is a (highly articulated) document that identifies the presenting problems, issues, procedures, and court directives. It considers relevant historical material. Every case has family, educational, legal/forensic, medical, social, psychological, drug, and other possible histories. The historical information is not as complete nor as detailed as in, for example, a custody evaluation, alienation evaluation, or abuse assessment. However, the Reunification Therapist must know how to ask and abstract key historical factors that will impact on the plan's goals, methods, procedures, and possible outcomes.

A good treatment plan considers all relevant players in the present time frame. This can include GALs, other therapists, teachers, parents, grandparents, siblings, mediators, and a whole host of other possible functionaries. What roles did they play historically and are they presently active in regard to the present clients?

A good treatment plan also considers the details of the present situation very carefully. Is the child presently seeing the parent in question or have they had a significant gap in time since they have had meaningful contact? This relates to understanding why and how long the breach has occurred. Was it due to social circumstances, such as parental job demands? Was it due to (alleged) alienation by a particular party or parties? Was it due to accusations (founded or unfounded) of abuse? Was it due to a conflict resulting from social-personality differences? Was it due to the pressure to take sides in an acrimonious divorce? Reunification Therapists understand that the stated reason for the breach may have a base in reality or not. Also, even if the breach is based on well-grounded problems, it still may be reparable.

1. Metrics

All treatment plans need to articulate (if not already done so by a judge or someone else) specific behaviors, attitudes, and interactions that would be considered as "progress." It could be anything from a child that was willing to talk about the parent, to reviewing family photographs, to accepting a text message, to having lunch with the parent with or without the therapist present, to accepting a parent coming to a sports event in which the child is a participant, to going to the movies together, to planning a birthday party, to accepting a Christmas gift, to spending a weekend together, to dealing with a possible distortion that a child may hold (such as the fact that the parent reportedly does not pay support). In other words, *any behavior or attitude can be articulated as an aspect of progress, which means that the breach is diminishing.* Some therapists may try to go from no contact to high levels of immersion. Some cases may require phase-in, while others may work perfectly well with immediate contact sessions dealing with face-to-face interaction. Also, it must be remembered that some treatment plans are easier to execute, such as a scenario where a parent and child are both desirous of reconnecting but don't know how to do it. In these cases (and they do exist), I have put parent and child together from the beginning and recommended outside activities. Frequently, in these cases, improving the verbal communications, understandings, and/or misjudgments can quickly result in a re-bonding that approaches the normal interaction between the parent and child. See Chapter 9 of this book, "Measuring Success: Min/Max Metrics," on page 167.

2. Actual Interventions

The actual methods that are used to deal with the metrics should also be identified. Office visits, home visits, restaurant meetings, viewing videos, reviewing letters, storytelling, role playing, challenge sessions, and many more techniques should be articulated as possible approaches. Clearly, changes are often made in process as it is discovered that some techniques work better than others for the particular parties involved.

Once the preceding history, skill sets, and qualities are in place, the treatment plan can begin. There is often a mixing and matching of the methods in order to find the right combination for a particular case. For example, I've had children who work well by having them share their own view of the family history and how they got to this point in not seeing a particular parent. Other children cannot deal with this direct approach very well and may need different techniques that allow them to discuss other aspects of their life first. Some children present a hostile, negative, and rejecting attitude, whereas others come in with a sense of confusion, anxiety, and concern, but not hostility. Letting children and parents know how the Forensic Therapist will work is extremely important, because many children and families have been in multiple types of therapies before. Explaining that forensic therapies are based on particular goals, often directed by the court, guardian, or other outside force, is extremely important, as it helps them to understand it is a directional process with specific measures of success. It is not "regular talk therapy" where some chitchat may be interpreted as an end in itself. It is also important for the clients to understand that forensic therapists will often make clear recommendations, provide advice, measure the success of that advice on a regular basis, and report this where so ordered.

3. Changing Methods or Approaches

It is important for clients to understand that particular methods or techniques will be changed from time to time and explaining when, how, and why this happens is helpful. So, in a recent case, I had to change the method from an in-office discussion approach to having the parent and child spend time together outside of the office. The rationale and intended result was clearly explained. The teenage boy's response was, during lunch, "I see what you're doing. You're trying to make things folksy and, like, I have a regular relationship with my dad. It won't work. I don't want lunch, I don't want to eat with him, I won't order any food, and I won't talk." At this juncture

I quietly signaled the cook, who came over, and addressed the boy directly with his Italian accent and said he would like "to make something special." In the meantime, he brought over some pasta which the boy commenced to ravenously consume. As he ate, we talked and things did "normalize." Forensic Therapists do not always do what they are told to do by children and they clearly know when and how to disobey the directives of a child. In another case, a 10-year-old boy told me he would not sit in the same room with his father. Rather than using the ancient, but often failed "readiness theory," I invited the father into the room. He behaved most appropriately. The child cried, ended his tears, and told his father that he was very sorry if he had hurt his feelings. But, "I just didn't know what to do with you and mom fighting all the time and I knew mom couldn't handle it if I saw you a lot." The father had been pre-scripted (a very important technique in Reunification Therapy) to say and do exactly the right thing. They ended up hugging each other on the sofa, at which point I exited the room for a while only to return a little later. The session was ended at that juncture as the goal of verbal and physical re-bonding had begun to take place. Reunification Therapists need to know when to disappear or do or say nothing further. *The technique of silence needs to be taught more pervasively* in our (clinical) training institutions, workshops, and meetings.

4. Progress Assessment

Assessing progress takes place on a regular basis. In fact, it should be done after each session. Knowing when to share this progress with the clients is also an important skill. An example of this was when I said to a 14-year-old boy,

> Let's take stock—so far, we have talked about why you can't talk about your father. We have talked about what you saw in the conflict between your mother and father. We have talked about your past therapies and why they didn't work. We have talked about the social characteristics that you and your father have in common. We have talked about the differences between you and your dad. We have talked about whether your dad loves you or not. We have talked about the fact that the longer you don't talk to your father, the longer you will likely not talk to your father. We have talked about your anxiety in actually meeting with your father and not knowing what to say. I have shared particular scripts with you so that you will feel less anxious in initially talking to your father. So, John, my strong opinion at this point is that we are ready to talk to your father. And I say "we," because I will be here if you need me to help with that conversation, but I don't think you will.

The result of this review of progress helped this adolescent remember and reframe everything that was done prior to the actual physical meeting with his father. It also helped him to see "progress" in a new light. The father had been scripted ahead of time, as is often necessary, so he would say and do the right things. The conversation was a little stilted in the beginning (they were told this might happen) and eventually normalized to the point where one could not tell they had a two-year breach in their relationship. So you get "ready" by understanding, guiding, and ultimately doing—not waiting ad nauseam in these cases.

5. Summary and Termination

Summarizing the progress for the clients, the court, and (especially) for the parent and child with whom there was a breach is the final stage of intervention. It is often a good idea for Reunification Therapists to put something in writing, even if only in bullet points, reviewing the progress, making suggestions for the future, and identifying the level and type of cooperation that led to what is hopefully a successful conclusion. However, in some cases, one parent may be so intent on damaging a reunification that they would do almost anything to interfere with the process. This will have to be identified in any summary report to the attorneys, GAL, and/or the court. Some cases require multiple starts as they have to go back to court for a parent to be held in (possible) contempt and a judge to reaffirm what they expect at the next treatment phase. Many failures in reunification work occur because of an interfering parent who will, directly or indirectly, miss appointments, come late, start conflicts with the therapist, make false accusations about the therapist or their procedures, set up outside appointments to conflict with the reunification appointments, have conversations with the child that undermine potential progress, have other parties call the therapist with information that contaminates the process, make and/or file false accusations against the other parent, and in a million other ways, intentionally or unintentionally, damage the process, therapist, and/or content of the reunification. So, what this means is that while Reunification Therapists will confront parents who are extremely positive in supporting the process and will comply with almost any and all requests to make it work, the polar opposite is parents who have been, both in the past and present, in opposition to any type or level of reunification and will exercise any and all maneuvers available to them in order to disrupt the process. The latter parent category is often deeply enmeshed with the child, so that even if the child wants to re-affiliate, they may reflect off of the anxiety ("reflective anxiety") and/or hostility of that disruptive parent. You can tell this is the case when the child uses the same words, profanities, arguments, distortions, and historical inaccuracies of the negative parent. They often "speak as one." This is bonding over negativity and presents a real challenge.

Elsewhere in this book I have spoken about mechanisms to regulate the interfering parent. For more discussion on regulation, see Chapter 12 "How GALs Can Help in the Reunification Process." Also see the sample court order in Chapter 11, "Guidelines for Judges (and Masters)."

Knows the Importance of Filing Progress Reports

Although mentioned earlier within the important features of a treatment plan, this filing of reports needs to be sectioned out for specified emphasis for Reunification Therapists. Progress reports can take many forms. There can be brief memos to attorneys. This can be extremely helpful, as attorneys are (unfortunately) often kept in the dark until a later point in the reunification work. I found that keeping them regularly informed allows them to be helpful in maintaining some directionality for their clients. Progress reports can be in written form, by telephone conference, or Skype/FaceTime. In-person meetings are (even more) effective with both attorneys present. Keeping attorneys out of the process is an old and likely failed method. Progress reports are also helpful for the clients and child as it gives them a framework for what has been accomplished and what more there is to do. Progress reports should be objective and not accusatory. However, if there are issues of compliance or interference, they need to be identified. Progress reports should also contain suggestions for future behaviors that would be helpful to either maintain the positive progress or to change possible non-progress. Progress should be stated with reference to the original goals in terms of how close or far away the clients are from accomplishing them.

Willingness to Say When a Case Is Not a Candidate for Reunification Therapy or Counseling

At times, cases may not, from the onset, be good matches for this re-bonding approach. There are many factors that are "red flags." For detailed discussion on this and related matters, see Chapter 4 "Alienation," Chapter 6 "Impeding and Facilitating Factors," as well as the Chapter 9 "Measuring Success: Min/Max Metrics" section entitled "Point of No Return." Parents who have sociopathic qualities (which may not be discovered until the case has already begun) are problematic, to say the least. Parents who have sued one or more previous therapists are poor candidates. Parents who have already been found guilty of parental alienation may continue this process during the treatment and therefore will (attempt to) damage it. These and other factors need to be considered. However, cases that have multiple attempts with little or no success are not necessarily to be ruled out. A new methodology, new scripting, a new approach, and sheer stamina on the part of some professionals might lead to types of and degrees of success not previously obtained. This is why an initial meeting or so is really an assessment time of potential problems and a tentative judgment of the relevancy of Reunification Therapy or Counseling for this particular family.

High Frustration Tolerance

If a reunification professional needs any one personal characteristic (and they need many), it is the capacity to have a high frustration tolerance. These cases involve forward movement, backward movement, stagnation, big spikes in success, plateaus, and many other variations in goal attainment. These professionals need to be able to have the capacity to hang in for the long run as case histories, child behaviors, parent interference, scheduling problems, and many other dimensions of the case can all be frustrating from a human point of view. "Quick fix" personalities will generally prove fairly ineffective.

Cannot Be Intimidated

It is common for reunification professionals to be directly or indirectly threatened, challenged, sued, reported to professional organizations, harassed, and in many other ways, confronted. The ability to stay centered and focused is important. It is also important for them to have the full backing of the court, attorneys, or guardians. Backing by others is an important message to parents who would (try to) intimidate the professional and reinforce that they are not alone; also, that there may be consequences to performing such interfering behaviors. Because of this problematic dimension in execution of the profession, many reunification professionals, as noted, have simply left the field. All parties need to sense and know that the Reunification Therapist is "on the job" and comfortable in seeing it through. Interfering parties will try to judge the "fear factor" in the Reunification Therapist. Court and professional indemnifications are also key.

Can Read, Comprehend, and Execute on Legal Documents, Including Court Orders

Many non-forensic professionals have extremely limited knowledge of legal process and language. The ability to execute a court order means that one clearly understands the directives and conditions. Many therapists have made mistakes in assuming they have realms of power that do not exist. The judge, in some cases, did not say that a professional could not change a custodial arrangement as per their discretion. The judge did not say that a professional could be the child's therapist. The judge said to perform Reunification Therapy for a child and a parent. The judge said that the GAL will make the final recommendation emanating from the reunification process. This, of course, limits the recommendation power of the reunification professional. Some therapists may not understand the difference between an arbitration agreement versus a mediation agreement. For a sample court order, please see pages 227 to 229 of this book.

Can Keep the Parties on Track

Because reunification work is usually guided by specific goals and objectives, it is important to keep the parties focused. It is very easy for this professional activity to slip off into some other form of therapy, socio-legal discussion, or historical regression. Regularly reminding the parties about the goals, methods, and metrics for progress is important. By the time parents and children come into reunification settings, they have often been through conciliators, mediators, arbitrators, legal meetings and conferences, court appearances, and even possibly previous therapies. Because of these multiple experiences, they can and do easily slip into different roles and content that are not relevant to the reunification process. I frequently have to say to clients, "Remember, you are not litigating in here. We are having a discussion about going to the movies." or "You're not negotiating whether you will see your father, as a judge has already said you will. We are working out the how and when, not the if." Performing this function is not easy for the professional, as they have to be constantly vigilant that professional meetings could be slipping into some other format or agenda.

Can Testify Clearly

It is not uncommon for a reunification professional to end up in court, on a judicial/master's phone conference, or in some other setting where they have to present testimonial skills. The ability to be concise, objective, and helpful is mandatory. The court is most interested in solutions and, therefore, in any kind of testimony, it is important to share the metrics of the case. Identifying who complied with the process, clear suggestions on what can be done moving forward, or explaining why the case was not or is not a candidate for reunification work are all of interest in the socio-legal settings. Judges do not need, nor necessarily seek, diatribes on the social-personality characteristics of a particular parent. Judges want to know where they are in regard to their directives. They want to know if different approaches are helpful other than what has already been undertaken. They want to know who can build bridges with the least amount of trauma to all parties. They want to know what will bring the case to conclusion. Judges are mostly interested in being educated with information that they previously did not have which could help the family in distress that is before them. They take this obligation seriously, and so must all others in the case.

Judges do not like pontificating, bias, poor ethics, unexplained procedures, or any loss of professionalism. They want answers with strong clear rationale to meet their obligation of doing "what's in the best interest of the child."

Innovation

The ability to create novel conversations, interventions, assessments, and suggestions are fundamental to Reunification Therapy. It aids the customization dimension while still maintaining common ethics and professional practice guidelines. One boy was asked, because of many teens' obsession with music, to pick a song that best represents his relationship with his dad and he cited "A Boy Named Sue" by Johnny Cash. We played it and discussed its implications for his relationship with his dad. This became the basis of a great conversation that led to new insights.

History of Educative Functions for Legal and Mental Health Professionals

Presenting seminars, panels, workshops, CLEs, and classes to professional audiences is a plus. It means they are recognized and accepted as respected professionals who are up-to-date in their fields. Often their professional papers and commentary can be related to the case at hand. It also means they have a professional network from which to draw ideas, opinions, and challenges.

Clues You May Have the Wrong Professional for Reunification

Following are clues that you may have the wrong professional for reunification. Use it as a checklist. The more checks, the more problematic the choice.

- ❑ 1. Disobeys or Does Not Follow Court Order(s)
- ❑ 2. Often Operates with No Exact Treatment Plan
- ❑ 3. Jumps to Radical Interventions without More Moderate Approaches First
- ❑ 4. Limited Knowledge of Alternative Methods
- ❑ 5. Demonstrates Biased Behaviors
- ❑ 6. Retries the Case or Allows It to Be Done
- ❑ 7. No or Inadequate Relevant History Taking
- ❑ 8. Poor Rapport with Children or Adults
- ❑ 9. Blames Others for Progress Limitations
- ❑ 10. Rejects Ideas from Others That May Be Helpful
- ❑ 11. Always Employs Exactly the Same Protocols in All or Most Cases with No Customization for the Case Specifics
- ❑ 12. Their Practice Has Been Largely Adversarial
- ❑ 13. Limited Number of Court Appointments[1]
- ❑ 14. Not Well Respected by the Legal or Mental Health Communities
- ❑ 15. Has Not or Cannot Develop a Risk Assessment
- ❑ 16. Believes That All Cases Are Candidates for Reunification
- ❑ 17. Does Not Understand the Functions of a GAL or Has Limited Coordination with Them
- ❑ 18. Will Not Testify or Has Limited Experience in This Area
- ❑ 19. Works with Only a Few (and Often the Same) Attorneys
- ❑ 20. Too Connected with Father's Rights or Mother's Rights Groups Either Historically or at Present
- ❑ 21. Not Up-to-Date on the Latest Forensic Research Related to Their Tasks
- ❑ 22. Does Not Abide by the Professional Ethics of Their Field
- ❑ 23. Doesn't Know That Traditional Confidentiality Does Not Apply or Believes Traditional Confidentiality Applies to Reunification Cases
- ❑ 24. Promises (Amazing) Results before Even Knowing the Case

---

1. Less experienced professionals may be capable of handling less complex cases.

The Professional

They call me a professional
But I have a confessional;

So here it is in a nutshell
I sometimes have clients who ring my bell;

Composure I must keep
Never to appear that I need sleep;

The obligations are many and I must keep them straight
The court, the lawyer, the pastor, the children, and even the new client's mate;

All are telling a story
They believe are full of glory;

Kind, steady, and respectful I am
No one must even feel like they have been shamed;

A balancing act at its extreme
Calmer in the face of mean;

The upside of it all
Is to see a child leave with his parents walking tall.

Chapter 9

Measuring Success: Min/Max Metrics

"If you can't measure it, you don't know and can't explain what's happened"

— Stanley S. Clawar

Definition of Metrics

A metric is any objective or subjective factor(s) that can be used as a measurement of relational success, failure, or progress. An objective measure, for example, would be that a child proactively seeks to be with a parent. A subjective measurement might be that a parent reports their child said, "I really miss the time that we weren't together and I do love you."

Ultimately, reunification is about either realigning a present relationship that at one time may have had positive qualities, or improving a relationship that previously had problematic qualities. In either case, it is important for the professional to understand the positive elements contained in any social relationship. Following is a list of some of the qualities of a functionally happy and healthy social relationship.

- Caring/Concern
- Respectful/Responsible
- Offers Help
- Facilitates Growth in Others
- Focus on the Other, Not Just Oneself
- Sees Self-Limitations (Can be Self-critical)
- Not an Other Blamer/Takes Responsibility
- Shares Common Activities
- Sharing (Ideas, Resources, etc.)
- Can Set Aside and Forget Minor Issues/Conflicts

- Conflict Reduction Skills
- Provides Protection (Social-Psychological, Physical, Reputational, etc.)
- Issues Appropriate Compliments
- Respects Individuality (Joint and Separate Time Can Be Experienced)
- Possesses and Utilizes Empathic Qualities
- Accommodates to Change
- Can Live in Different Timeframes (Past, Present, and Future)
- Can Make the Other Person a Priority
- Prioritizes a Happy, Peaceful, and Balanced Life
- Admits Mistakes
- Effective Communication (Including Hearing, Listening, and Feedback Skills)

It is obvious that probably no relationship has all of these qualities at the same time. However, to have the list as a guideline can be helpful as an aspect of developing and applying parent-child metrics. I have frequently used these social characteristics as a way of asking questions, guiding behaviors, and ultimately helping people come to an understanding of a healthy social relationship and its goals. The terms themselves can be used by Reunification Therapists as part of the language of rebuilding parent-child connections. Eventually, the child comes to understand there actually is a discrete language used to describe good relationships. I've had many children say to me (after some repetition on my part of the terms in the list), "I know what you're going to say. That behavior by my mom was caring. That's what you were going to say? Right?" My answer was, "Yes, you're right and I'm glad you could anticipate me." Proper language is often a precursor to proper behavior. Many children and parents do not have what sociologists call *a language of relationships*. This is one of the educative functions of a Reunification Therapist.

Why Are Metrics Important?

Metrics are important because they provide a base to measure success, failure, and other stages of progress. Generally, Reunification Therapists need to report their progress, or lack thereof, to judges, guardians, attorneys, mediators, other therapists, parents, and even to the children. *Unfortunately, the articulation of exact metrics is one of the weakest areas of practice for Reunification Professionals.* Also, if they end up on the witness stand or having to answer detailed questions from GALs or others, they are more capable of delivering the exact information that is being sought. *Also, if they have no objective measures, it is also not possible to create a treatment plan.* Treatment plans include (among other components) the problems or issues, methods or techniques, timeframes, alternative procedures, risk assessments, and goals. Often, the presenting problems and goals are key issues in reunification. Generally, either a lack of contact and/or negative emotions related to the level and type of contact on the part of the child are present. Subsequently, the goal is to improve the frequency and quality of contacts. The metrics can be any of the ones mentioned in this chapter, but in any event, should be clearly identified. For example, if a child will not allow a parent's name to be uttered and they eventually come to permit this—this is progress. If they not only permit it, but later on initiate the parent's name—that's progress. If they deny having any memory that is positive and at a later time are able to recall events, ceremonies, or family gatherings that have positive elements to them—this, too, is progress. If they will not be in the same room with a parent, but then are able to—this is progress. If they have blamed a parent for the entire divorce process and its consequences and are then able to understand that the family situation may have been more complicated than that—this is progress. If they have refused to answer texts from a parent and then start to respond—this is progress. Not all progress is slow and of a phase-in nature. Sometimes once one hurdle is overcome, a larger breakthrough may occur quickly after that. An example of the latter situation is a father who had virtually no contact with his teenage son for more than a year and did a sermonette about his love for the child. This changed their relationship rather quickly. The prepared sermonette went something like this:

> I've tried to reach out to you, but as you know, you virtually never answered, and that's why we're here. So let's set the record straight and even if you don't speak back to me, I would like you to go off knowing this. In the first place, I dearly wanted you to be born. In fact, your mother and I planned everything together including my full participation in childbirth classes and me being present at your birth. Jack, it was the greatest day of my life. I'm sorry if I get choked up while I'm speaking, but I'll push on anyhow. You were the joy of my life and I did everything with you from changing diapers to being excited when you took your first step to playing with you before you could even speak to going to daycare before you were even eligible for kindergarten. We did everything together including all of your sports. I helped you with homework projects wherever I could. Anyhow, to have this break in our relationship is so shocking that I can't put it into words. I don't want it, I don't understand it, and I want us to be back in each other's lives where we belong. Life moves on quickly and I believe we should be doing things together like we always did, primarily because I love you and you are my son. Did you hear me? You are my son and nothing, Jack, will ever change

that. There, I've said my piece, so if you want to leave, you can, but know that everything I said is true and in your heart you know it's true.

At this juncture, the boy had tears in his eyes and sobbed uncontrollably. He reached out for his father who reciprocated the contact. I left the room and told them I'd return in a while.

Of course, not all cases go like this, but Reunification Therapists have to be open for this possibility and know how to set the stage. It's a good example of *coaching a parent to penetrate the negative veil* that surrounds many children who have had broken bonds. Frequently getting to the underlying truth and past reaffirming social-emotional connectivity brings about a positive return.

The metrics in this case were easy as they had been set up as measuring all of the different types of communication that parent and child could have. Subsequent to the sermonette session, they communicated electronically, reactivated being together during events and holidays, and, in general, reconciled as though nothing had ever happened. It's also a good case in point of *not over-reading or accepting an aura of negativity surrounding a child.* There are many prophecies that have been given, sometimes by professionals, sometimes by family members, that "this child will never reconnect with that parent or if they do, it will be a long time in hell before that happens." Nevertheless, it is clear that those cases necessitate specific metrics just like all others. Reunification Therapists should listen to, but not buy into all the prophecies of doom—as some cases turn quickly or slowly, but still turn toward the positive. The case just cited was over in a few weeks with a full re-bonding.

Figure 9.1 reveals the element that can facilitate a positive outcome in reunification cases. Figure 9.2 is a gross procedural map in reunification cases.

Range and Intensity of Issues

Unlike the preceding scenario, many cases have months or years of relational damage prior to coming in for professional guidance. Some cases have had long periods of alienation, abuse accusations, litigation, serial professional involvements, and a whole host of other (negative) experiences. Filtering through these to rekindle a positive emotional and social relationship is not easy. The more serious the history and the longer the history, the more important it is to have a delineated court order (see the sample court order in Chapter 10 on Guidelines for Judges (and Masters)), the relevant professional skill level of the Reunification Therapist, a greater amount of patience

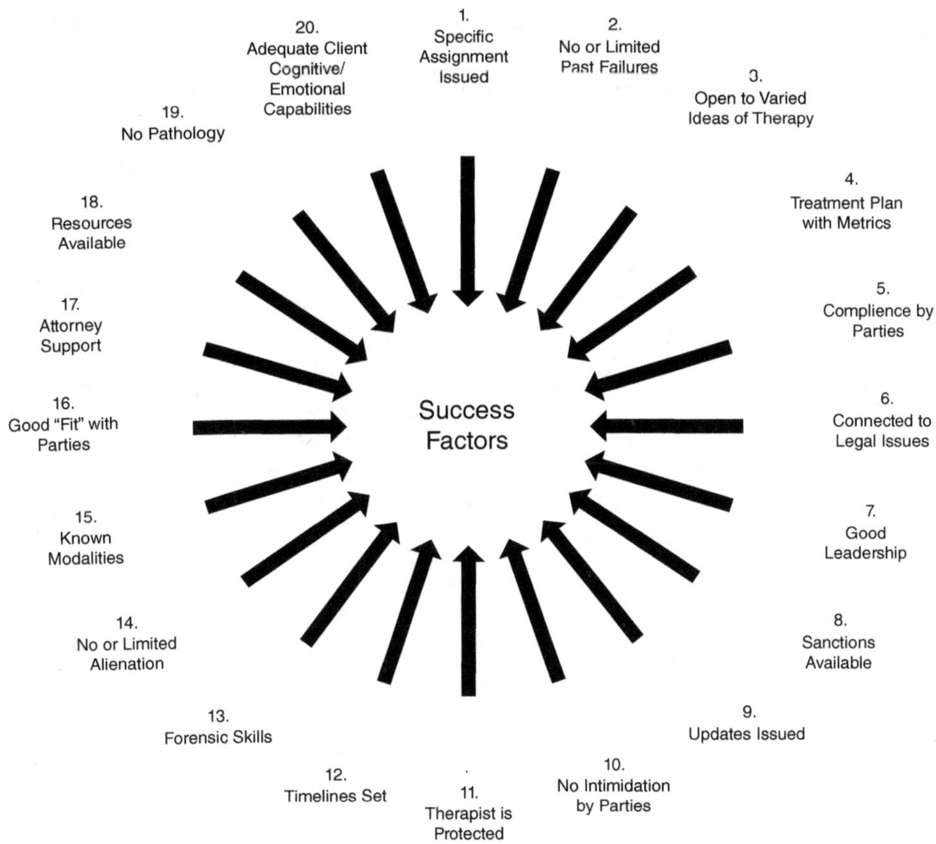

Figure 9.1 Twenty Selected Factors That Impact on When and Why Therapies Succeed

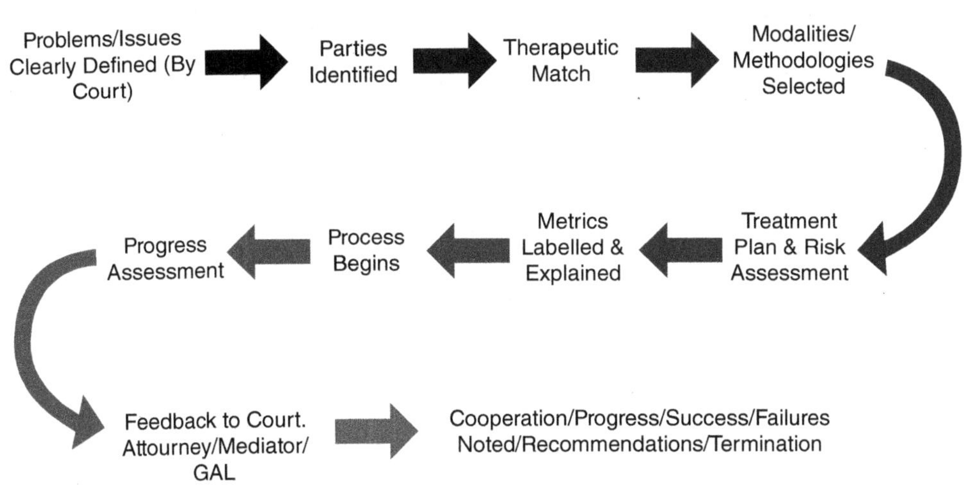

Figure 9.2 Evidence and Goal-Based Therapy: A Sequential Model

required, and a more precise set of metrics for progress. It could be that a child just speaking negatively in a professional setting is a measure of progress in these kinds of cases. They wouldn't talk to, but they may then talk about, the parent. Therapists dealing with what they have called "basket cases" need to practice what Theodor Reik called "listening with the third ear."[1] *Children may reveal information in their dialogue that can be used for future bond building.* As one child said in a fit of anger, "My dad broke the marriage and ended my family by cheating on my mother." This commentary was very interesting because the divorce occurred when the child was only one year old. So a question that presents itself is how did he know (let alone if it was true) this historical and social fact? Actually, some forensic research led to the finding that it was his mother who actually had serial affairs but had implanted the idea into the child over many years (a process of inversion or other-blaming) that the father was a philanderer. Obviously, this kind of case is more difficult because the child has distorted and incorrect information stored over many years. Correcting the "information" in the beginning of building a relationship would likely prove counterproductive. It is very common in reunification cases for children to have "facts" that they believe are a solid grounding for their hostility and social distance from a particular parent. See Chapter 5, "What Children May Say about Reunification" on page 95 for more examples of what children commonly say in reunification work.

It's important to know that some historical statements by children may be valid. This might necessitate some (coached) confessional presentation by a parent to a child, demonstrating that some change or correction can be made. Some children remember correctly that their father was always at work and "not around that much." "So, why should I be around for him now?" In these types of cases it can be helpful to educate the child that there is something called a *social contract.* This means that mother and father agreed that either the mother (or father) would stay at home to raise the family and that the other parent would work to earn money to support the family. When I've discussed this with some children, they have found it revelatory.

It's important to know that some children may find it hard to accept recommendations for various forms of communication and contact because they harbor different degrees and types of guilt. *They could even have guilt for not seeing a parent for a period of time* and, consequently, simply not knowing what to say or do. Coaching these children becomes part of the process of reunification. The coaching is matched on the other side by helping the parent to have appropriate answers and comments to the child's concern(s). Many children have made statements like the following:

- "I don't know what I'd say if I saw my mom again."

1. Theodor Reik, Listening with the Third Ear: The Inner Experience of a Psychoanalyst (1949).

- "I'll bet my dad really hates me for not talking to him."
- "It's going to be really uncomfortable seeing my mom after all this time."
- "What do I say about all the bad things I said about my dad? I know he didn't forget them."

These and many other statements reveal the *normal anxiety about reconnecting*. Interestingly, they are one of the easier issues to deal with in mending the relationship. Providing the child with reassurance and actual commentary by the parent often eliminates the initial anxiety. Letting them know there are no wrong answers in a discussion can also be helpful. In one case in point I said to a child, "Your dad holds no grudges. Did you know that?" The boy asked, "How do you know that?" I responded, "Because he told me and he really just wants to see you and be your father. He also said that the only feelings he has are feelings of sadness for missing out on times with you and most of all he has the feeling of continued love, which he has never lost. You shouldn't feel guilty at all."

In the more extreme cases, a child will come in and be extremely allied with a parent to the point where they express verbal hatred and hostility that seems unremitting. The parent with whom they reside reinforces all of the negative stories possible and does everything they can do to interfere with the reunification efforts. These cases especially require (extreme) judicial oversight and may even necessitate sanctions (which will be discussed in Chapters 10 and 11). These cases are not for novices, as the therapists themselves may be attacked by calling the police, reporting the therapist as abusive, attacking credentials, illegally recording the therapist, using the Internet for defamatory purposes, and a whole host of other negative attacks. Once again, there are times when the professional has to temporarily terminate the re-bonding process and receive assistance from a guardian or refer it back to the court in ways that have hopefully already been predefined by the judge. Some parents are so committed to the total damage and destruction of the relationship with the other parent that they will stop at nothing to accomplish their mission. These parents have been called poisonous, toxic, extreme alienators, and a whole host of other terms. But, they all have something in common—they have usually spent years, a great deal of energy, and other resources to keep a child separated from the other parent. These children may present what looks like legitimate anxiety reactions to even mentioning the name of the despised parent. These are often cases where extreme measures and interventions are recommended (not necessarily by this author). There are usually a litany of other interventions prior to shipping a child off to a setting in a strange place with strange people under strange conditions. This should never be done without an articulated risk assessment. Even then it may be a questionable procedure.

Measure Is the Measure

I'll try to explain my success
With a general sense of the mess;

"So where are we now?" says the judge
"And I'd appreciate no fudge";

"Better than before your order
Maybe we're on the recommendation border";

"That's not clear." says the lawyer
"So is the parent a destroyer?"

"Wait one minute." says the guardian of the child
"This dialogue is hard to tell. It's from nowhere to heavily piled";

"If we had some precise measures
We might be able to see the growth in possible parent-child treasures";

"Do they talk, question, eat or do things together
Compared to the past with now... is it better?"

"Do they smile, go somewhere as a team?
Or are things still so mean?"

"Let's get precise and then we will know
If the therapy is good or a no go."

Risk Assessment

All mental health and social interventions (just like in the field of medicine) have attendant benefits and risks. "There are risks incumbent in any process; however, *a decision has to be made as to what is the greater risk*."[2] In undertaking a reunification process, the professionals overseeing this process should

2. S. S. Clawar & B. V. Rivlin, Children Held Hostage: Identifying Brainwashed Children, Presenting a Case, and Crafting Solutions (2d ed. 2013) at 218.

articulate a risk assessment as best as possible. This includes the projected positive and negative outcomes for the procedures that will be utilized. In this specificity of outcomes, there should also be an itemization of alternative methods should one not work or bring about negative consequences. The negative consequences should have a backup plan of help and protection with associated ideas and resources.

A case example is where a judge ordered a risk assessment, but the therapist did not perform one. In this case, there was a long history of data relevant to possible spousal and child abuse by the father. The mother, in fact, spent a few years during the marriage visiting a domestic violence center. The Reunification Therapist decided (though it was never adjudicated) that the mother was an alienator, and, as such, needed to be "put in her place." So, the clinician set up a sequence of activities leading to the child being taken away from the mother and grandparents (who were also historically the child's primary caretakers). The mother continued to caution the therapist that the child has emotional breakdowns at the slightest mention of the father or any potential contact with him due to the (alleged) abusive history. The primary issue here is not just that the therapist was proposing the most radical intervention possible, which included isolation from the mother and grandparents, taking the child out of town, placing the child in unknown surroundings, and having her (the child) spend time with professionals whom she never met nor trusted, but the serious procedural issue was that she never designed an effective risk assessment. If she did, and knew how to do it, the assessment would have included potential downsides, rescue efforts, emergency care, and a whole host of safety and support services should the mother's predictions actually occur. By disrespecting that downside possibility and not drafting a proper risk assessment, she created a plan that did not really attend to the potential needs of the child and instead just told the mother, "She will be fine," which, of course, could not be guaranteed. This would be a case of sloppy intervention, at best. All professionals involved with children have an obligation to second guess their own procedures and potential outcomes.

Ironically, in the preceding case, the judge's order still stands in terms of wanting a risk assessment. Therefore, this professional actually stands in violation of the outstanding order. This now takes on possible legal dimensions that could have been avoided had the therapist simply executed the judge's initial directive.

A risk assessment is the least articulated item of reunification plans—and yet, should be one of the most visible. They should be able to address and answer the following concerns and questions. Each area of risk generally has the same concerns and questions to answer and consider. *A risk assessment should include both preventative and reactive measures for each possible risk.*

1. Social Risk Assessment

- How is the child's social life?
  - o Are there any current problems (with peers, siblings, etc.)?
  - o Family relationships—functional versus dysfunctional
- Has reunification been attempted previously?
  - o What impact did it have on the child's social life, if any?
  - o How will the new procedures impact on the child's social life, if at all?
  - o Should (insert specific intervention) be implemented, what specific risks are there to the child's social life?
  - o What are the preventative measures to be put in place to avoid these risks?
  - o Should these risks come to fruition, what recommendations are made as reactive/corrective measures for safety and welfare?

2. Educational Risk Assessment

- How is the child currently performing in school?
  - o Are there any current problems?
    - Examples: study skills, learning differences, retention, executive functioning, organization, project completion, authority, or peer issues.
- Has reunification been attempted previously?
  - o What impact did it have on the child's school performance, if any?
  - o How will the new procedures impact on the child's school performance, if at all?
- Should (insert specific intervention) be implemented, what risks are there to the child's school performance?
  - o What are the preventative measures to be put in place to avoid these risks?
  - o Should these risks come to fruition, what recommendations are made as reactive/corrective measures for safety and welfare?

3. Psychological Risk Assessment

- How is the child functioning psychologically?
  - o Are there present or past issues of:
    - Anxiety
    - Depression
    - Suicidal ideation (and actual attempts)
    - Hostility

    - Mood volatility
    - Panic attacks
    - Eating disorders
    - Other psychological considerations
- Has reunification been attempted previously?
  - o What impact did it have on the child's psychological well-being, if any?
  - o How will the new procedures impact on the child's psychological well-being, if at all?
- Should (insert specific intervention) be implemented, what risks are there to the child's psychological well-being?
  - o What are the preventative measures to be put in place to avoid these risks?
  - o Should these risks come to fruition, what recommendations are made as reactive/corrective measures for safety and welfare?

4. Medical Risk Assessment

- Does the child have any relevant medical problems?
  - o Allergies
  - o Dietary restrictions
  - o Asthma
  - o Gastric problems
  - o Sleep problems
  - o Migraines
  - o Medication needs
  - o Other medical concerns
- Has reunification been attempted previously?
  - o What impact did it have on the child's physical health, if any?
  - o How will the new procedures impact on the child's physical health, if at all?
- Should (insert specific intervention) be implemented, what risks are there to the child's physical health?
  - o What are the preventative measures to be put in place to avoid these risks?
  - o Should these risks come to fruition, what recommendations are made as reactive/corrective measures for safety and welfare?
  - o Are their doctors known and available should need be?
    - Who?
    - Contact information?

The preceding lists should help to outline the risks of the intervention in question. However, a successful risk assessment should also include the possible positive outcomes should the intervention be successful. This will help to create a fuller picture in order to the weigh the pros versus the cons and allow for a more informed decision to be made as to whether the intervention should be undertaken and/or carried out.

Some examples of positive outcomes are:

- Improvement in communication skills
- Heightened feelings of closeness
- Rise in trust levels
- Desire to be proactive
- Reconnection to family lineage
- Gain additional adult guidance
- Burdens of conflict or guilt may lessen or go away completely
- Improvements in personal identity
- Correction of past distortions
- Knowing and accepting that they are loved
- Accepting the redefinition of the family under conditions of separation/divorce
- Child is able to continue their social-emotional development/growth

For an Inventory of Risk Assessment Factors, refer to the Appendix L starting on page 281.

What If It Fails?

- Permanent loss or social damage can occur for both the parent and child.
- Custodial shifts/changes can be considered.
- Other professional interventions or assistance can be considered.
- Importance of the Reunification Therapist's report takes on special significance.
- Emergency plans may need to be articulated.
- Why did it fail? Explanations should be performed.
- Need for levels and types of cooperation that occurred.
- Recommendation of a break with other activities for the parties then reconvene at a later time.
- Options should be provided to the court/GAL.
- Include risk assessment with positives and negatives.
- Is it worth another try?

Measuring Progress

Measuring the success of Reunification Therapy necessitates an understanding of the different dimensions by which a parent and child can become separated. Once we understand these areas, we can then objectively look at (and measure) their reconnection. Separation can be on the verbal, physical, emotional, social, or spiritual levels. In addition to understanding these categories of connectivity, it is also true that cases of reunification can vary in their intensity. Some cases can actually start out on a goal of preventing disintegration of the relationship. Other cases may have only experienced a slight degree of slippage. Yet, in other scenarios, the degree of separation can be almost total. This means that some children have no verbal dialogue with a parent at all. In fact, they may refuse to speak to, or even about, them. These more extreme cases are also represented by no affectionate physical contact. On the emotional side, they may represent extreme degrees of negative emotions. This includes the absence of all (visible) positive emotions such as love, caring, and acceptance. On the social side, they may have very limited or no actual interaction with a parent—some for long periods of time. Some parents believe there is a spiritual bond that forms between parent and child that is a very special form of connectivity, unlike any other aspect of their bonding. This special dimension is also damaged in the more extreme cases.

Following is a sample profile in checklist form that Reunification Therapists, the courts, lawyers, and GALs can use to identify areas of forward movement in the re-bonding process, or lack thereof. It is set up with various types of interaction and degrees of receptivity that can take place between a parent and child.[3]

Checklist of Forward Movement between Parent(s) and Child(ren)

Activity	Suggested	Observed	Successful
Willing to Talk about the Parent	❑	❑	❑
Willing to Talk to the Parent	❑	❑	❑
Texting	❑	❑	❑
FaceTime/Skype	❑	❑	❑
Length of Conversation	❑	❑	❑
Physical Contact Handshake Sit Close Hug Kiss Hello/Goodbye	❑	❑	❑

3. They are not necessarily in order of depth of contact.

Activity	Suggested	Observed	Successful
Listen to Stories by Parent	❑	❑	❑
Share Their Own Stories	❑	❑	❑
Communicate over Family Photos/Videos	❑	❑	❑
Share Information about School	❑	❑	❑
Share Information about Peers	❑	❑	❑
Share Information about Life with Their Other Parent	❑	❑	❑
Accept Help on a School Project	❑	❑	❑
Accept Help with Sports or Extracurricular Activity	❑	❑	❑
Ask Parent about Their Life	❑	❑	❑
Talk about Future Goals School Travel Vacations Hobbies Others	❑	❑	❑
Share Food In Office Out of Office	❑	❑	❑
Drive to Session Alone with Parent	❑	❑	❑
Drive Back to Present Residence with Parent	❑	❑	❑
Plan Daytime Contact	❑	❑	❑
Plan an Overnight	❑	❑	❑
Plan a Weekend	❑	❑	❑
Plan Midweek Dinner(s)	❑	❑	❑
Go to a Concert/Show/Movie	❑	❑	❑
Take an Extended Trip	❑	❑	❑
Visit with Grandparents or Other Extended Family	❑	❑	❑
Call When Away with Residential Parent	❑	❑	❑
Accept a Present	❑	❑	❑
Offer a Present	❑	❑	❑
Demonstrate Humor	❑	❑	❑
Normalize Eye Contact	❑	❑	❑
Initiate More Time	❑	❑	❑
Tell Residential Parent They Want to See the Other Parent More	❑	❑	❑
Tell Residential Parent to Stop Saying Negative Things	❑	❑	❑

Activity	Suggested	Observed	Successful
Share Their Birthday with the Parent or Vice Versa	❑	❑	❑
Attend a Religious Service with The Parent	❑	❑	❑
Utilized Music/Lyrics as a Tool	❑	❑	❑
Personal Notes/Letters	❑	❑	❑
Full Normal Regular Reconnection in All Aspects of Parent-Child Relationship	❑	❑	❑

Progress is usually not measured in just a straightforward and upward fashion. There can be forward movement, stabilization, backward movement, followed by forward movement again. The therapist needs to be looking at the overall positive features of reconnecting versus any particular slippages that might occur. *One of the most significant factors that will determine the progress is the degree of support or opposition that the child has from outside forces.* These outside forces include the other parent, siblings, extended family members, the court (when involved), and other professionals. Even with some back and forth movement in the re-bonding process, the overall direction should be upward and positive. If this does not occur, see the section in this book on "Types of Reunification Activities and Techniques" in Chapter 1 on page 6 for examples of the various interventions that should facilitate progress. Therapists need to set a reasonable timeframe in which to measure the verbalizations and actual behaviors that are identified as important in the re-bonding process. Reunification Therapy is not meant to go on and on, and the professional may need to make a judgment as to when the therapy should be terminated due to its success or lack thereof. If a parent's goal is to have many overnights in a row and they are starting from a base of no contact, and the therapist succeeds in having the parent and child re-bond except for that final overnight goal, the therapy is not necessarily a failure. Setting realistic (but modifiable) expectations as the therapeutic process proceeds is part of the job of the professional.

Timeframe

It is helpful to set some limits and boundaries in terms of time elements. How many times per week will the child be seen and with whom? How long is it projected that the reunification process will last? Of course, sometimes it is hard to tell the latter until an assessment of the case is made, but even with this condition, some fair estimates should be offered. At times, judges will control this by indicating that they want reports on a monthly or quarterly basis. It is even better if the judges also help to specify what they consider to be "progress." I have seen cases where the child has been "in therapy" for four or five years with no progress. This is probably more common than one would guess. Often the reason for this protracted experience is "the child is not ready" (see Readiness Theory on page 137). Sometimes it is helpful to have more sessions clustered in the beginning stages so that a child is seen more regularly with and without the parent(s) in question. The usual once a week sessions, in the more serious cases, sometimes do not work because the defense mechanisms get reactivated in between the long gaps of time. It is not inappropriate to apply some commonsense understandings to setting time boundaries. If therapy is going on for six months and proper metrics are applied with no progress whatsoever, it is fair to raise questions as to why even smaller progress measures could not be accomplished. The lack of progress could be due to "chemistry," procedures, cooperation, interference, or other factors. Whatever the reason may be, *a reappraisal of progress, or lack thereof, should be done every three months, at minimum, if not sooner.* It is also possible that within the same timeframe, progress could be made with one child but not with another. In other words, progress is not necessarily even for all siblings within the same family. Progress reports should individuate on this sibling factor. The same methods do not necessarily work on different children within the same family.

Picking the time of the sessions can also be important. Children are usually in school during most of the day and then have extracurricular or co-curricular activities and homework obligations afterward. Setting *appointments when children are busy, tired, or distressed from other life obligations does not make for a very good base for building a professional relationship,* let alone reconnecting them to one of their parents.

Cases with high degrees of obstructionism are not uncommon. These parents, and sometimes even the child(ren) will "go through the motions" if there is a preset limited number of sessions and intentionally try to accomplish nothing. In a recent case, a child was ordered to participate in Reunification Therapy with her father "for a minimum of five sessions." The mother made it very clear that this was not going to be just the minimum, but the maximum. This ended up in her being back in court on this issue and many others, including her hostile and negative interference with the actual sessions. She was found in contempt, fined for legal fees and her share of the sessions, and in other ways chastised to return in a more serious and supportive fashion to the reunification endeavors. This resulted in her doubling down on her hostile and accusatory behaviors. This then resulted in a second contempt hearing and so on. Many of these parents who are highly obstructionist to the process are just as happy to end up in court as they are still being successful in restricting access and further damaging the parent-child relationship.

Some Ways to Measure Effective Parenting

Parenting is actually an interactional metric. Following are 24 factors that can be measured, more or less precisely.

1. Parental Attentiveness

This factor has to do with the degree of attention given to children's needs, interests, and questions. Attentiveness can be either proactive or reactive. In its proactive form, a parent is reaching out and initiates the interaction around the child's needs, interests, or questions. Attentiveness is also related to supervision, because when a parent is attentive, they will be able to identify problematic areas in order to supervise the child. In its reactive form, the child is initiating requests or demonstrating needs that would, in turn, require the reaction of the parent. Attentiveness can range from neglect (the absence of attending to children's needs, interests, concerns, and questions) to "the helicopter parent" who is, in effect, over-monitoring everything that goes on in the child's life. These types of parents have also been referred to as "snowplow parents," "lawnmower parents," and "tiger moms." It's important to note that all families have their own culture of parenting, involvement, discipline, pressures, and sanctions. A middle point seems to be the healthiest in terms of identifying important needs and interest of the child while also allowing them to explore their environment without excessive oversight or adult participation. Some parents simply "over-parent."

2. Patience

This has to do with a sense of persistence and the ability to have a high frustration tolerance. Patient parents are generally easy going and even tempered. They are the opposite of precipitous. Demonstrating patience with homework, peer relationships, and many other facets of a child's life are very important for the healthy growth of the child. This can be measured by observing play, interaction at meals, discussions, and other activities. If permitted, children have a high capacity for asking questions and revealing infinite curiosities. A parent becoming easily exasperated or intolerant are signs of impatience, whereas a parent remaining composed is a sign of patience when dealing with a child.

3. Convivial/Friendly

The ability to maintain a sense of warmth and approachability is an important part of parenting. Being friendly means being able to provide companionship and build closeness without confusing it as an actual friend on the child's age level.

4. Physical Contact

This varies greatly by a number of social factors, including regionality, ethnicity, and nationality, as well as individual family cultures. What is considered appropriate and common in one group may be defined negatively in another. There are numerous studies identifying the cultural differences that are considered normative within particular groups. One such study compared Hispanic and Anglo samples surrounding the importance of physical contact and affectionate touching for infants. The findings revealed that Hispanic and Anglo mothers both touched their children on a daily basis. Even though Anglo and Hispanic mothers both touch their children, the rate of frequency varied. Anglos reported "very often" while Hispanic mothers reported "all the time." However, Hispanic mothers were found to touch more frequently and reported "being more affectionate with their infants and having more skin-to-skin contact." "Emotional involvement is more typical for Hispanics compared to Anglos." "Other studies have shown that differences between Anglos and Hispanics exist even when demographic variables including income, acculturation, family size, area of residence, and education are a controlled statistic."[4] Using this one cultural difference, we can guess how incorrect interpretations could be made for Hispanic parents as being "over enmeshed with their children" when no such definition exists within their culture. In fact, this type and frequency of contact is expected and rewarded. This suggests extreme caution when using only psychological variables to explain behavior in forensic-related matters. So, extensive physical contact in terms of body against body, tight hugs, baby's head resting against the mother, touching the mouth and face, and issuing kisses are all cultural imperatives.

It has been known for quite some time that good contact with a baby during its first year of life leads to a stronger immune system and feelings of safety and security. We are creatures of touch and this can be initiated by parent or child. Children of all ages, especially in times of distress, will seek healthy contact. In a recent case, I could tell that a father and son were reuniting because as I went into the waiting room, I saw them playfully punching and holding each other on and off the sofa. This physical contact (of a playful nature) was revelatory; I assumed that the session was going to start off with a report that things were going fine. Indeed they both offered the observation that, "We're back on track." I joked with them if we should end the session then and there, which brought about a humorous response from both as they looked at each other. "No" said the son, "we can talk some more cause this is helping me and my dad and I'm really glad." With

4. Fabiana Franco, Alan Fogel, Daniel S. Messinger, & Christopher A. Frazier, *Cultural Differences in Physical Contact between Hispanic and Anglo Mother–Infant Dyads Living in the United States*, 5(3) Infant & Child Development 119–27 (1996).

this commentary by his son, it was clear that the father had tears in his eyes but was trying not to break out into a full-blown crying jag. So, even the physical distance that parent and child keep in the office can be symbolic. Clinicians have long noticed that as people feel closer together, they often sit closer together. It is common in the beginning of Reunification Therapy for a parent and child to find the greatest distance possible without being outside of the room. Sensitive clinicians will often find excuses for them to be closer together as physical proximity can reignite old positive feelings (if used appropriately). Eye contact also usually increases with feelings of closeness. This also has cultural variations as it may be disrespectful in some Asian cultures to stare too long in an adult's eyes.

5. Statements of Endearment

Issuing statements of affection are part of a healthy interchange between parent and child. Terms such as love, you're special, you're the best, I really like you and what you stand for, and a whole host of other types of commentaries from parent to child are relatively easy to measure. Additionally, when children become alienated and/or non-unified with a parent, this is one of the first things that gets deleted from their vocabulary. In fact, in many cases, children stop referring to their parent as their father or mother. Calling them by their first name, if they haven't done that before, is kind of an anti-endearment signal as well as a rejection of their parental status. (The exception is in subcultures where parents are called by their first name.)

6. Listening Skills

Good listening skills are indigenous to all functioning relationships. A parent who possesses these skills can make it clear to their child that they understand what the child is saying prior to them responding. Good listening skills involve using a feedback process whereby the parent lets the child know that they may need further clarification on any particular message. This allows the child to feel understood and have a safe and comfortable forum for communication. Reunification Therapists sometimes have to teach these skills to both parents and child(ren).

7. Discipline

The ability to delineate boundaries and limits is one of the hallmarks of effective parenting. Discipline is sometimes confused with punishment, but it doesn't really mean that. A parent who can set limits or boundaries is actually preparing the child for realistic relationships outside of the family. Setting clear expectations on behaviors is part of discipline. The ability to follow through on homework assignments, making appointments, being on time, and other measures of accepting responsibility is key to the child's growth process. Part of discipline is correction; correction of language, peer-related behaviors, keeping promises, overuse of technology, forms of address, proper attire, and dozens of other behaviors require a teaching process with possible consequences and rewards. Parents often lose this parental right and duty as a function of their isolated situation in reunification cases; they feel damned if they do and damned if they don't exercise discipline.

8. Rule Setting

This aspect of parenting relates to discipline, but is more specific in terms of the rules for life in various social situations, for example, when to enter a conversation and not to interrupt another, rules for proper eating behaviors, rules for gaining the attention of adults, rules for wearing proper attire in accordance with the outside weather or social setting, rules for not running at poolside, and dozens of other examples—as rules exist in every sphere of life. When these rules are forgotten, ignored, violated, or unknown, it should be asked, "Was the parent effective in issuing proper reminders and bringing the child back into line with the appropriate expectations?" This is often easily observed even in the office setting, although the observations can be expanded upon by the parent-child conduct outside of the office and through third party input (schools, relatives, therapists, clergy, and others). Rules make school possible, they make the family life possible, they make good peer relationships possible, and in turn, make society possible. It is not hard to measure this aspect of parenting as each parent can simply be asked what rules they have set for the child in different spheres of the child's life and how do they enforce them. This too can be a lost function for a non-reunified parent. Many such parents are afraid to set or remind the child of rules due to their tenuous parental status.

9. Proper Manners

The old term for this would be etiquette. Society functions by the implementation of manners in many ways. Courtesies, politeness, and terms of respect for position are all part of social etiquette. Parents are the guardians of etiquette and implement this by teaching the child their greetings, farewells, thank yous, sorrys, and many other social graces that are the lubricants of social relationships. They are very notable today in regard to their absence. By parents teaching these niceties, they are also (subliminally) teaching the child elements of respect for members of the family, teachers, the law and its representatives, people from different backgrounds, peers, and all other social functionaries. It is not uncommon in reunification cases for children to demonstrate low levels of proper manners and respect (even if they were present before). This may be a sign of their negativity toward the setting and/or their parent. It's also one of the first things that Reunification Therapists need to address as to what they define as appropriate decorum. Some children will substitute proper manners with rudeness, profanity, or hostile remarks. Addressing this helps to define the respectability of the setting as well as of the parties present.

10. Safety

Historically, and even through to today, safety is a primary parenting responsibility. There are many forms of safety, from physical to medical to social to psychological to economic and to reputational. Rule-setting, noted earlier, is a specific way that safety can be measured. Are there safety rules for the pool (public or private); play patterns; not throwing objects in the house; curfews; having friends alone in the house; use of kitchen utensils; seatbelt use; Internet cautions such as social media, chatrooms, games; selection of food and drink; sex education; and more? This is often one of the common complaints by the parent who is not the one being reunified. Real and imagined safety issues can be proliferated and may necessitate some research on the part of the Reunification Therapist. It is important for the Reunification Therapist to differentiate between allegations that have already been litigated and adjudicated versus new concerns that have not been previously addressed. Reunification Therapists are not there to re-litigate anything nor override previous findings. If the court has accepted the reports on abuse allegations as "unfounded" or "false" (or "founded"), then that is the context in which the therapist must operate. Many make a mistake and allow these issues to be reopened outside of the confines of the courtroom. Parents who are insistent that abuse (another term for a safety concern) has occurred may continue to pressure all professionals with whom they come into contact with in order to share and accept their views and worries.

11. Encouragement

Parents who encourage children tend to reinforce positive behaviors and either ignore or limit negative ones. A metric for this aspect of parenting can include the degrees and types of support, assurance, help, pep talks, uplifting language, cheerleading, and/or inspirations for the child. These can be measured through the use of language and actual parental behaviors. Encouragement exists through all possible domains of the child's life, from play to intellectual pursuits to peer relations and to their family relationships.

12. Educational Dimensions

Educational opportunities involve all areas of a child's life from which they can learn new things and use them to navigate their physical and social environments. Education does not exclusively refer to institutional learning. Some parents can turn regular play into a learning situation with ease. They use toys for learning (puzzles, computers, books, and more). Parents vary from allowing children to have realms of self-exploration versus guided learning. Each of these can be measured and commented upon by a Reunification Therapist. Some parents have a much more restrictive view of learning and believe that that is really the job of the formal educators. The most powerful and longitudinal of all types of learning is what sociologists call role modeling. Many parents are aware that what they do, what they say, how they resolve issues, whether they are physically active or inactive, the respect they show for the other parent, their religious practices, and their philosophies of life are absorbed by their children through "social osmosis." It is not hard in professional settings to identify the linkages that come from role modeling between parent and child. Frequently, parents will say (and it may be correct), "They are or used to be my clone." One of the great losses in parent-child segregation is the loss of this social osmosis. Of course, this invisible absorption process includes, at its core, the values and beliefs of the parent that gets transferred to the child on a moment-by-moment basis. Keeping parent and child separate disallows this growth in knowledge, ethics, values, beliefs, and behaviors.

13. Responsibilities/Performing Basic Parenting Tasks

Measuring parent responsibilities can be quite easy if we identify core areas—medical, social, educational, economic, spiritual, familial, ethics, crisis assistance, and nutritional are only a few of the core areas. These are areas for which a parent can and should be held accountable. Have they been conscientious and dependable in exercising these responsibilities? These are often very helpful to identify, as they can become a source of discussion with a child who may be resistant to reunification. Many parents can articulate their exact behaviors over the life course of the child in each of these core areas. The loss on the part of the parent due to their separation from their child is that they can no longer (freely) execute in these domains that would be helpful to the child. Being excluded from educational, religious, sports, and meetings of all types is not infrequently experienced as painful by the nonbonded parent. There could be significant loss because many of these parents have great commitment, ideas, and energy to share in these core areas. In fact, they may have been the key parent and effectively executed in one or more of these important zones of their child's life. Attending to falls and minor injuries, caring for an ill child, shopping for and with the children, getting children up in the morning, ready for their schooling or day's activities, and getting ready for and celebrating holidays are all important basic parenting tasks.

14. Humor

Good and regular humor is important for healthy social relationships. In fact, when Sigmund Freud was reportedly asked if he could study only one thing in a culture or a society that would tell him the most about that culture or society, what would that be? His answer (and he wrote a book about that) reportedly was the humor of a society.[5] When asked why, he answered somewhat like this—because humor reveals the deeper issues, problems, concerns, values, worries, and anxieties of (a) people. But humor between parent and child is also a good tool for reducing anxiety and stress. It moderates negative moods, lifts spirits, readjusts the frame of mind, and can, as Henri Bergson said, "serve as a corrective function."[6] Things can be said in jest and accepted that could not be said in regular discourse. Emil Draitser called it "playful aggression."[7] In conflicted and problematic relationships, one of the first things that disappears is the sense of humor. I can always tell when a parent-child relationship is rebounding because I will see smiles, jokes, contradictions, prodding, silliness, and just plain fun. It is also important to note whether the humor is reciprocal, meaning either parent or child can initiate a joke or wisecrack. *Humor can also signal recognition.* There are children who try to maintain a stoic attitude only to break out in a smile or laugh when a parent recalls a funny family incident.

15. Capacity to Refocus

It is a normal childhood condition to get off task or lose concentration. This can happen in regard to learning, playing, eating, or just having a conversation. Teaching the child to come back to center and retarget the conversation or activity is a special skill that parents often exercise. They help the child to return to the heart of the matter by spotlighting what they were talking about or doing. *This focus ability is one of the most important personal and social skills a child can develop for later life.* Without it, they are likely to have trouble in school, work, and life in general. Our society requires that you be able to zero in on important elements in our environment. In fact, one of the most common characteristics of ADHD kids is the inability to focus for certain lengths of time. Helping children to push past a point of

5. Sigmund Freud, Jokes and Their Relation to the Unconscious (1960—English).

6. Henri Bergson, trans. C. Brereton & F. Rothwell, Laughter: An Essay on the Meaning of the Comic (1911/2008).

7. Emil Draitser, Taking Penguins to the Movies: Ethnic Humor in Russia (1998) at 122.

frustration and stay on task starts in their early years. Not long ago I observed a child trying to play with some building blocks in my office. The father got down on the floor and the child seemed to be frustrated and busted up his initial construction. The father step by step, word by word, and action by action, helped the child to rebuild the edifice at which point his dad said, "I'm so proud of you. You not only built this, but you kept doing it even when you were frustrated. You'll need to be able to do that with many things. I'm proud of you." With that, he hugged his son who exhibited the largest smile I think I ever saw. By teaching the child to refocus, a supplemental benefit will be the expansion of the child's attention span and all of what that means in life.

16. Customizing Time Allocation to Each Child

The ability and desire of a parent to allocate time and energy is part of their personal commitment. If they have more than one child, they will need to demonstrate a fair balance of time and energy. This is especially difficult when many children are clamoring for a parent's attention at the same time. Proper division of time is difficult to pull off. However, a parent can also be measured in terms of the "makeup time" that they develop due to one child (a sibling) requiring larger amounts of time because of special needs, an emergency, or some other circumstance. Age differentials of the children will also create a demand for careful allocation of time. A newborn child may require more time in the evening and the morning than a 10-year-old who can attend to their dress and other functions somewhat independently.

17. Child Centered

A child-centered parent is one that revolves a lot of their life around the needs and growth of the child. This includes everything from the toys in an environment to books for children to special time for games to school visitations to sharing physical activities to a work schedule that facilitates some free time to vacation plans to discussion time and more. This can be measured in the office by the content and detail of a discussion with a parent. Some parents come in with outlines of what needs to be done in terms of tutoring, doctor's appointments, educational trips, and other child-related matters. Some parents have communicated with me on virtually a daily basis about issues related to the well-being of the child. Others mention little, plan little, and execute little. A home visit, although many Reunification Therapists do not include them in their protocol, can be very illuminating. From the moment you walk in, you can see the child's pictures hanging (not just on the refrigerator) to the special areas for toys to bookcases with just children's books to special chairs and tables for kids and other visible signs that "a child lives here." Many parents are also extremely safety conscious, so special locks on cabinets, safety plugs in electrical outlets, kitchen utensils all put away, special high-positioned locks on the doors leading to the garage and basement, and many other precautionary measures can be seen throughout the home. Children will frequently want to show the Reunification Therapist their bedroom or other rooms that are special to them. There opportunities provide some of the best conversational content between a child and the Reunification Therapist—it's on their "turf."

18. Social Equality

In our society today, the idea and practice of gender, racial, ethnic, age, and other aspects of equality are extremely important. Children are going to interface in schools, the community, religious centers, and society at large with children and adults of all different backgrounds. How does a parent disseminate this sense of respect for the diversity in America? Do they facilitate peer contact with children from different backgrounds? Does the parent show, within their own home, equal appreciation for son and daughter? Do they use movies and videos as a tool for this type of social education? The fundamental question for the parent is, what are their values in this core area of social life and how do they act on these values? This prepares the child for the world today and makes for better social relationships based on respect.

19. Spontaneity

Being able to do things that are unrehearsed, off the cuff, or extemporaneous are an important and enjoyable aspect of parenting for children. Sometimes, the most unplanned activity becomes the most fun and memorable. When I have asked children over decades of interviewing what they remember most about their childhood, parents, and family, it was often the special and (unplanned) time that they had with each of their parents. This could include taking a walk, the free time during vacations, having a conversation, going shopping, or just "chilling out" together and watching a movie. Unfortunately, with children's busy schedules today, their over utilization of technology, and often both of their parents working, the opportunity for impromptu togetherness has become more limited.

20. Involvement in Extracurricular and Co-Curricular Activities

The degree to which a parent can be and is involved in school, medical, religious, peer group, holiday, volunteer, and other types of activities related to their children is important for a number of reasons. First of all, it accelerates the frequency of interaction with the child. In the second place, they can share direct knowledge with the child about activities that are important to both of them. Being at the sports game, the bake sale, the scout meeting, the play, the school trip, and more all add to the social and emotional bonding.

21. Planning for Eventualities

Planning skills are important in all aspects of life from family to community to business to education and professional settings. Parents who plan and explain what and how they did it are providing an important role modeling function. Explaining how they plan to take time off for the school trip is both instructive and caring. Coordinating all of the functions of a family really requires a lot of executive functioning (planning) skills. Children who can plan are much more likely to be successful in school and later life. They need to plan their homework, their sports team practice, their social time, household tasks and chores, Internet use, and, of course, time allocated for the family.

A conversation with a mother on this topic was instructive. She explained her average week of chauffeuring the children, attending all of their extracurricular activities, getting the children to doctors' appointments, making sure they got to religious education, monitoring their homework, limiting Internet usage, food shopping and preparation, working part time from home, planning all holidays and vacations, and making time for her marriage. She asked what I thought about all of this. My response was, "You should write a book on time management." I added, "Please be sure to tell the kids how you do this."

22. Creates a General Sense of Adjustment and Comfort

Healthy parenting involves creating an environment that signals support and solace for the child(ren). Children report "feeling good," "cozy," "content," and "untroubled." In fact, one of the first questions children often ask clinicians when they hear there is going to be a divorce is whether they will they be able to live in their present home or if they will "lose their room"? *The home is a real and symbolic setting for a special sense of comfort from the outside world as well as a zone of safety.*

One father who was going through a divorce was advised to sell the marital home as a leverage tool in the divorce negotiations. He refused, saying, "The children are there more than with me. I will never take that away from them." This is when the mother was simultaneously working against his desired contact with the children.

23. Receptive to the Child's Right and Need to Love the Other Parent

This aspect of parenting involves demonstrating, directly and indirectly, a support, acceptance, and understanding of the child's relationship with their other parent. This is one of the major indicators as to whether various custodial arrangements will work effectively and be healthy for the child. This can be measured in many ways, including the number and type of questions a parent asks, from a positive framework, about their enjoyment with the child's other parent. Saying things like, "I want you to have a good time at mom's" or "I'm glad to hear that dad was able to spend some special time with you because you know he loves you very much." This kind of language (of connectivity) as well as demonstrated respect for the other parent (in front of the child) is key to their social and emotional health. It is the very opposite of alienation attitudes and behaviors.

24. Diversity of Activities

Effective parenting includes providing a wide range of active and passive activities. Active activities include swimming, sports, shopping, and outdoor activities, whereas passive activities include reading, dining together, conversations, and educational games. It is important for a parent to provide the opportunities for these, but also to be selectively involved with some of them with the child. The stimulation, fun, and learning that comes from these activities unifies social bonds. Parental and child hobbies are also part of the diversity of activities and can also be a good educational experience.

Has the Case Reached the "Point of No Return"?

A frequently asked question by judges, attorneys, and other professionals is whether a case is even worthy of initiating or reinitiating Reunification Therapy. In other words, "Is it a lost cause" before it even gets started? There are clearly some metrics that need to be considered seriously but are not necessarily determinative. These include the following:

1. Suicidal History and/or Threats

There may be an identified history of suicidal ideation and/or attempted self-harm behaviors. Some children have been treated individually or institutionally for this mental health issue. It is recommended that if a case does begin under this condition, that a psychiatric consult be employed (throughout the course of reunification). At times, a child will raise this in a session when it has not been raised before. Statements such as, "If I have to see my mom/dad, I'll kill myself." Of course, no such verbalization is taken casually and this is why a forensic psychiatric support system should often be in place.

2. Threats to Run Away

Children and/or a parent might assert that if reunification is attempted, the child will run away (or may have already tried to). Of course, this can present some imminent dangers if, in fact, the child performs this behavior. Stricter monitoring of the child's whereabouts is indicated. However, children cannot be monitored 24/7 as they have "escape" opportunities in going to and from school or disappearing on a weekend. Some children who have threatened this end up at a friend's or relative's house. There are cases where a parent has taken a child to a restaurant as part of their reunification contact plan and the child has disappeared after claiming to go to the restroom. (They frequently call the other parent to pick them up or simply hide out until the time is up.)

3. Threats to Harm a Parent

Some children have physically attacked a parent (or their paramour or new spouse) with and without a weapon in hand. Obviously, threats to do bodily harm and/or "kill" the parent are quite serious. Reunification Therapy should not be dismissive of such threats, as there are (isolated) cases where a child has followed through. One case in point is a child who grabbed a kitchen knife and threatened his father if he did not immediately take him back to his mother's house. Obviously, in these kinds of scenarios, the reunifying parent will need to have some verbal and physical backup plans should this take place. Reunification Therapy may need to be put on hold until such threats and/or actions are addressed and eliminated.

4. Multiple Attempts with Escalating Negative Behaviors

Many cases involve serial scenarios where a child and parent have been through multiple attempts to reunify. It is important to identify if, upon each attempt, the hostility and aggression increased. If it has, it means by the time the next Reunification Therapist gets the case, they will be dealing with a higher peak experience. It doesn't mean that the new intervention cannot succeed, but this escalating history is extremely relevant to where and how the new professional sessions begin. I have had many children assert that, "You will fail. It's been tried many times and they all failed." The problem with these kinds of assertions is that children who make them (or a parent) will often perform negative behaviors to assist the prophecy in coming true. If there is not adequate progress, these same parties will often say, "I told you it wouldn't work and you were wasting your time."

5. A Parent Undermines the Reunification Therapy Process

There are parents who are so committed to keeping a child from a healthy and functional relationship with their other parent that they will work upfront and behind the scenes to undermine the process, content, and possible progress. Creating scenes in an office; making false allegations against the therapist; coaching the child with negative dialogue; using the Internet to gain visibility for their views and create pressure, distort, or lie about what transpired in the therapist's office; coming late and missing appointments; showing disrespect for the spirit and detail of the judge's order; causing confrontations in the office with the other parent; claiming that all past therapists and judges have been "bought off"; asserting "we already have a family and don't need this"; asserting claims of abuse (which may have already been adjudicated and/or dismissed by the police, social agencies, and/or the court); and bombarding the professional with (massive) e-mails, texts, and the like are all ways to undermine the process. Often the communications they send are full of distortions, misrepresentations, or lies.

6. Past and Present Therapies Employed the Wrong Modalities

This means that families entered into a therapeutic process that was ill equipped to service the particular needs of that case. In applying inappropriate theories, plan, and interventions, they left the case with two problems. The first was the original set of issues in the case and the second was the complications, confusions, and problems they may have caused by what they executed. Therefore, the next Reunification Therapist who is hopefully prepared to apply appropriate interventions is (severely) handicapped.

In previous research on children who have experienced alienation, it was estimated that about five percent reach the point of no return, meaning they could not be helped or disengaged from a negative orientation. "These children generally lived with an 'embittered and chaotic' parent who made their *raison d'etra* the campaign against the target parent."[8] This percentage number could now be higher as cases are becoming elongated and treated many times by different professionals.

8. Clawar & Rivlin, *supra* note 2, at 396. This phrase was also used by Wallerstein and Kelly in JUDITH WALLERSTEIN & JOAN B. KELLY, SURVIVING THE BREAKUP HOW CHILDREN AND PARENTS COPE WITH DIVORCE (1980).

7. A Parent Has Reached Their Limit

At times, a parent may have been through lengthy (years) of litigation, mediation, therapy, and co-parenting efforts only to have them all fail to reconcile them with their child. They may run out of energy, money, and/or hope. Some parents opt out as they believe the process may hurt the child whom they believe is "caught in a vice" between the parents and needs relief. These parents may simply "call it quits."

Differential Child Behavior with Each Parent—The Split Screen Phenomenon

One of the more fascinating and important observations that has been made by many researchers and clinicians is that children can present themselves as though they are two different people to each of their parents. Next is an example of what I now called "The Split Screen." On the left-hand side of the split screen is a child who exhibits all of the stated qualities when in the presence of the mother's home. Basically, it is a list of high levels of social and emotional dysfunctionality. On the right-hand side is a characterization of the same child within the father's home. Virtually all of the metrics show a child who is stable and well balanced on the social-emotional spectrum when at her father's residence. These "two child" presentations are not uncommon in high conflict parental relationships.

The Two Georgias: A Split Screen

Georgia at Her Mother's Home	Georgia at Her Father's Home
1. (Overly) Dependent	1. Independent
2. Unstable	2. Stable
3. Needs Dr. Jones (Therapist)	3. Operates well without professionals
4. Claimed separation anxiety	4. Goes on her own even when she wants to stay with dad
5. Medical problems	5. Healthy profile
6. Eats poorly/erratically/irregularly	6. Eats well/diversity of foods/regularly
7. Sleep problems	7. Sleeps well
8. Claims she doesn't do well due to contact with father	8. Happy on visits
9. Problems in school/dance classes	9. Happy at school/dance
10. Cannot be left alone	10. Independent (rides horses alone)
11. Shows signs of regression in social functions	11. Shows no signs of social regression

Georgia at Her Mother's Home	Georgia at Her Father's Home
12. Emergency room visits	12. No emergency room visits
13. Anxious/fearful	13. Swims/not anxious or fearful
14. Receives restrictive or exclusionary messages in regard to her father. Her freedom to love and reach out to people is controlled.	14. Receives open messages. Is able to love all important people in her life.
15. Inappropriate social boundaries (sleeps with mother & stepfather)	15. Appropriate social boundaries (sleeps in her own bed/room)
16. Restricted from reaching out to paternal family members	16. Free to reach out to all family members (and did so)

The scenario in this split screen was one where the mother (on the left-hand side) was continuously hostile to the father and his lifestyle. In other words, the child lived in a world of tension, anxiety, and negativity while residing with her mother. Her mother presented herself as a victim of the divorce, "the other woman," and just, in general, "having been dealt a bad hand." The father presented himself as having moved on with his life, being respectful and positive toward the mother, and, in general, providing a very upbeat social-emotional environment. Of course, this is a case example and the child's behaviors could be reversed at each parent's home (positive at mother's and negative at father's).

Unfortunately, split screens like this are often correlated with a sense of resentment and hostility between the parents because they cannot agree on which child they are talking about. *Eventually, because of the child's desire to please both parents, they may find it easier for social-psychological efficiency to gravitate toward one home or the other.* Due to the idea of "identification with the aggressor," the child in this case could end up leaning more toward the negative environment of the mother, which would mean they need reunification with their father (who has a more positive environment). In a parallel sense, the child could also end up gravitating toward the extremely positive paternal environment and necessitate Reunification Therapy with the mother (who may believe the child needs her mother even more because of all of the problems she sees the child as having).

Of course, this kind of information can be extremely helpful in reunification because the clinician and the legal professionals (also including the judge) can see that it is *possible for a child to have developed two independent types of social behaviors and characterizations* as a result of being in the environment of one parent or the other. In regard to this conundrum, judges have often asked, "Which is the real child?" The answer is, both. *This contradiction in patterned behaviors can be the result of alienation, but it can develop for other reasons, too.* One simple reason is that children reflect off of the expectations and desires of a particular parent and so this develops a synchrony of attitudes and behaviors that coordinate with the particular parental expectations and environment. Obviously, it would be good if the child could develop a unified presentation of self, but as long as parents remain bifurcated in their views of the other parent and subsequent expectations of their child, unification of the child's behaviors is problematic, at best.

For the Reunification Therapist, the question arises as to which side of the split screen they see or should work with. This dilemma often results in the need for social counseling for the parents, as much as, or more than is needed with the child.

Abuse Cases

Abuse accusations are, unfortunately, quite common in high-conflict divorce and custody cases. There is a relatively high frequency of these accusations resulting in either "false" or "unfounded" conclusions. However, some parents who support the filing and investigations do not want to let go of the accusation or their belief that there has been inappropriate behavior on the part of the other parent. Often the police, Children and Youth Services (CYS), and, at times, the court itself have set aside the accusation as not meaningful or groomed for the custody deliberations. Even this does not necessarily result in one of the parents insisting that "abuse" is or was absent. They may share this belief and associated feelings with the child(ren). They may also work with therapists who either helped in the filing or now support it. In other words, the issue cannot be put to rest and comes to possibly contaminate the reunification process. Of course, there are legitimate scenarios where abuse has occurred and the therapist is asked to rebuild the bonds as best they can under this problematic condition. This latter scenario may require a special treatment plan.

The term abuse is now so widely used that the professionals involved (including lawyers, GALs, and others) need to make sure that there are some specific references that can be identified. Because a (step)father pushed a child one time, is that "abuse"? Because a parent tended to holler a lot (when homework wasn't done), is that "abuse"? A parent broke up a verbal and physical fight between two siblings and resulted in the parent having to hold one child against a wall in order to prevent further escalation. Is that "abuse"? Is waking a child up early in the morning to finish their homework when the child didn't do it the night before "abuse"? Is "abuse" removing all technology from a child for a couple of days because they were not following parental rules in the house? Is it considered "abusive" when parents fight in front of the child?

The term has come to be applied to such a multitude and intensities of behaviors that it may have lost some of its original definition of seriousness and negative impact. Also, accusations of abuse are often missing part of the story. So, for example, did the child and his father who reported a stepparent pushing the boy leave out the part of the story that the boy himself was aggressive and threatening prior to alleged push? Is a reported parent-child confrontation over profanity missing the fact that the child was excessively profane over a period of months and given many warnings to cease the behavior? Children themselves are increasingly coming into therapist's offices and clinics with their own application of the term abuse. As a case in point, one boy asserted to me that his father was "abusive." When asked what that meant, his response was, "He's always on my case." He further explained that his father pressured him to do his homework, practice his music, be respectful to his mother, get up for school on time, and other generally (positive) parental behaviors. Obviously, a parent who believes in boundaries, limits, and discipline can and does end up with the label "abusive." Reunification Therapists have an obligation to make sure it is clear that the term has specific references to actual problematic behaviors. Children especially will sometimes leave out their own contributions to instigation, manipulation, arrogance, and other precipitous actions. A good example of this is a confrontation that developed between a father and his 16-year-old son who had already grabbed the keys to the family car. When the father started to inquire as to where he was going, with whom he would be spending the evening, and other legitimate parental questions, the son became indignant and told the father he didn't have to answer those questions since he doesn't ask his father those questions when he is going out with his friends. At this point, the father grabbed for the keys as he told his son, "I know the kid you're going with and he has the reputation of being one of the drug dealers at the local high school." This resulted in a scuffle at the front door, at which point the father gained physical ascendency until the boy calmed down; the boy was released unharmed. The son then called the police, who came and filed a report. An investigation was made and the incident ended up being used in the custodial conflict between the parents. The father received the label "abusive" as a result of this and the son's culpability disappeared over time. It took a while in the Reunification Therapy to get the story out in its entirety.

Of course, there are cases where domestic violence and child abuse (physical, sexual, or emotional) have occurred. See Appendix K on page 279 for a checklist of qualities in an abusive relationship. In a case that mirrors many others, a women experienced extreme forms of social, physical, and emotional control by her husband. This resulted in her finally seeking help from a Domestic Violence Center. Additionally, the young child overheard the father's berating of his mother over many years and he himself was the recipient of verbal and physical aggression. This is a more complicated type of case, as the father alleged that no such abuse had occurred (even though he himself had actually written letters apologizing for his excessive behaviors). The complication here is that the mother and child knew and believed that abuse was part of their background history. The father continued to deny that it ever occurred and sought reunification with his son. The Reunification Therapist was then faced with a clinical and ethical dilemma as to how (and if) they should proceed with the court-ordered mandate of re-bonding child and father. This type of case is a perfect example of the necessity of a risk assessment. If a child, who was abused, is forced to reengage with the abuser, there are possible short-term and long-term consequences. It could be further complicated by a history of multiple attempts to reunify the child and parent, as was such in this case. Previous attempts to reunify father and son resulted in the child decompensating at even the thought of having to see his father or even anything reminding him of his father. The child became re-traumatized due to flashbacks at the thought, sight, or sound of his father. This was even noticed by school teachers and professionals who became concerned about the child's well-being manifested in his school performance and behaviors.

In some cases, it could be the children who begin to articulate abuse during the reunification forum. Following is an example of accusations the children made concerning their mother. The accusations were vigorously denied by the mother; she claimed that the father was a master of alienation and had brainwashed the children to say and believe these negative things within the short span of a month. One of the children happened to be in a separate therapy session and shared some similar and more extreme accusations. That medical doctor, as a mandatory reporter, filed a report with Children and Youth Services that ended up being investigated by the police. More and more information began to come out about many forms of abuse, including sexual abuse. The point being made here is that real or fabricated abuse allegations can come out in all different ways from all different sources. This requires an extremely thoughtful, ethical, and objective professional. Ultimately, there will be a somewhat subjective call as to what to do with the information revealed. It is easier if it has already been adjudicated and set aside. However, even in this situation, the professional will still have to deal with the social and emotional fallout that may have occurred. This is a case where children were eventually separated from their mother and temporary custody was allocated to the father. The children were in need of reparative therapies and the mother was excluded from contact. So, what started out as a reunification focus became a child protection case. Eventually, CPS and law enforcement became involved and moved the case from a civil matter to a federal criminal proceeding. There is real abuse. Reunification Therapists need to be sensitive to the differences between accusations that are grounded and those that may be otherwise.

Figure 9.3 is a diagram from a sample case where the children were progressively exposed to more and more scenarios of abusive experiences and problematic parental behaviors. The clustering of these experiences took on a geometric impact pattern for the children.

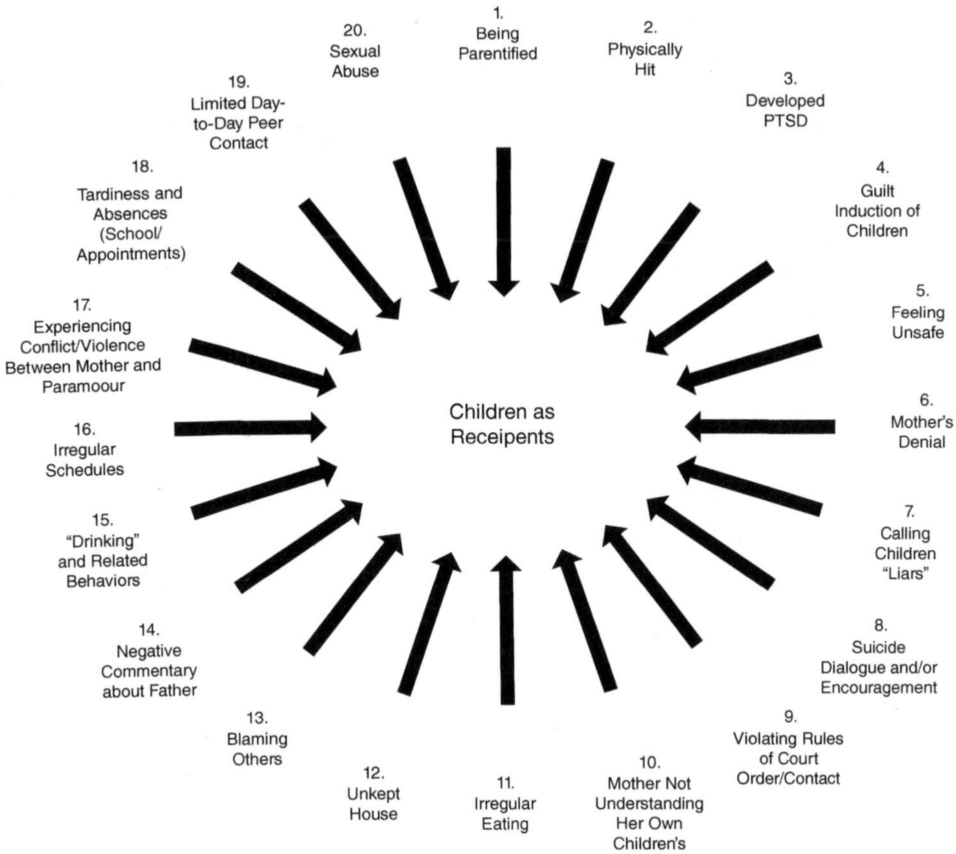

Figure 9.3 Accusations and Impact of Children and Other Parties Concerning a Mother's Behaviors and/or Conditions Relating to Her Child Care

Chapter 10

Guidelines for Attorneys

"Knowing the professional practice and perspectives of the (forensic) experts makes for better client representation."

— Stanley S. Clawar

Attorneys in family matters related to reunification quickly find out that they are likely to play more roles than they ever played in law school or elsewhere. Obviously, the first and key function is to represent the needs, interests, concerns, and goals of their client. Once they have established this dimension of representing the client, they often have to ask themselves many questions, including, do I have enough information and evidence to develop a case strategy?

Case Strategy

Creating a case plan or case strategy is often the second stage of client representation. Judges prefer that cases be presented in an organized, coherent, and systematic fashion. They do not like rambling, 20 character witnesses, and skipping around from story to story. Case preparation is best done around as few coherent, but meaningful, themes as possible. Are the key themes in your case educational, medical, supervision, mental health issues, compliance issues, neglect, safety, losses to the child, parental histories, parental access, alienation, or some other theme that is relevant to the "best interests of the child"?

Supporting Evidence

Strong supporting evidence, including letters, texts, e-mails, school records, medical reports, custody evaluation(s), mental health reports, professional witnesses, videos, and the like, provide a base for "objective" materials that do substantiate the themes of the case. Attorneys need to fully prepare, even if they think "it might settle." Judges can tell (and don't appreciate it) if attorneys are inadequately prepared. One of judges' favorite phrases is "they are wasting the court's time."

Client Management

The term counselor developed over time for a reason. Attorneys are supposed to counsel their clients on the law, evidence, strategies, demeanor, and likely outcomes, including risk assessments of certain types of presentations before the court. Herein lies a potential difficulty for many attorneys. Even if they do a good job in being the counselor, they may find that their client disagrees with one or all of these attorney functions. This leads us into the issue of client management. Many clients can finally come to see the wisdom of their counselor, but others may remain resistant to the point of potentially damaging their own case. This could present attorneys with an ethical issue of impasse with their own client (which down the road can turn into either being defamed on social media or even worse, being sued). Attorneys need to keep proper documentation of all of the advisory functions they provide to their clients, as these records will become important when and if an attorney seeks to withdraw from a case or needs materials to supply to their liability insurer. Consult documentation is also important to help the client be refreshed as to what was shared between them in previous meetings. Some attorneys (incorrectly) keep scant documentation. Ironically, this may increase with years of experience.

Difficult Clients

Difficult clients need to be differentiated from clients with difficulties.[1] A difficult client is one who is generally oppositional, noncompliant, and operates against the guidance and directives of their own attorney. A client with difficulties is one who can more likely be educated to be part of the legal team, on their own behalf. When attorneys explain the what, when, where, how, and why to clients with difficulties, they often find that those difficulties are put to rest. The educative foundation of attorneys is key in satisfying the client with difficulties.

1. For more on this, see the ABA publication entitled "You and Your Clients" by Stanley S. Clawar. Clawar, S. S. (1996). *You & your clients: A guide to client management skills for a more successful practice* (2nd ed.). Chicago, IL: General Practice Section, American Bar Association.

Use of Experts

Use of experts is a common, but not infrequently, double-edged sword. Picking experts who are ethical, experienced, professional, and state their findings and opinions within the scientific framework of their discipline can be most helpful. On the other hand, the "hired gun"[2] can actually damage a case in many ways. They can state things for which they have no scientific or ethical bases. For example, they might give an opinion on custodial arrangement without having seen all relevant parties. This is common in alienation cases. These types of experts may make derogatory findings about a parent on limited or no direct contact (or information) with them. They may also make recommendations and conclusions that do not follow from their findings or the findings of others. Judges often find these experts who take the time and energy of the court as wasteful. However, they may be allowed to testify on the basis of allowing an attorney to "make a record."

Details of the Process and Experience

Attorneys who are requesting reunification need (and should present) a strong rationale, especially if it has been attempted previously. They should present the reasons; the type of professional needed to do the job; the conditions surrounding the counseling or therapy that will heighten its success (see the chart in Chapter 6 titled "Impeding versus Facilitative Factors of the Reunification Process" on page 106); the obligations of all relevant parties; if and when a GAL is to be involved; and exact dimensions of time, money, and reporting back to the court. These are just some of the delineated factors that a judge should hear so that he or she understands that the recommendation is highly detailed, and therefore more likely to result in success. The qualifications of the expert to be chosen should also be articulated; as noted elsewhere, the disciplinary background does not matter as much as their forensic experience, knowledge, success, track record, and ethical reputation. Demonstrate the need for this area of expertise.

Questions to Anticipate

Many judges have asked if there are conditions under which reunification counseling either doesn't work or should not be recommended. All lawyers

2. See the article entitled "Spotting the Hired Gun" in the Family Advocate by Stanley S. Clawar. Clawar, S. S. (fall 2014). Spotting the Hired Gun. *Family Advocate, 37*(2), 6.

and experts should be prepared for this question and be able to provide an honest and objective answer. Other questions to be prepared for may include the following:

- First and foremost, why do we need a Reunification Therapist? Can't a regular therapist do?
- If we've had previous failure, why should we do it again?
- Are there options other than more "therapy"?
- How will we handle the child who is (or already was) oppositional?
- What do we need in the court order to heighten the compliance of the parent(s) who has (or have) already been identified as problematic?
- Are there different types of reunification therapies? Which one matches this case best?
- If this attempt does not work, the court will be interested in what the attorneys' proposals will be as a next step.
- I understand there is something called a risk assessment and I would want to see that performed prior to actually immersing the child in (yet another) reunification activity.
- The court has heard evidence presented on two different theories. One was a "phase-in" theory that we need to proceed slowly and cautiously. The other was a "radical immersion" theory that suggested that quick and significant contact should be instituted between the parent and child. Of course, the court is aware of a third possibility of doing nothing and leaving the status quo. I would like to hear arguments for or against any of these position.

Client's Guide

Following is a listing of things to guide your client, should they be ordered to or agree to Reunification Therapy:

Attorney's Guide for Their Clients

- Make sure your client is clear on the court order.
- Advise on appropriate conduct.
- Explain noncompliance.
- Reinforce what Reunification Therapy is and is not.
- Frame when your client should contact you (their attorney).
- Emphasize compliance with the Reunification Therapist's guidelines and procedures.
- Your client's behavior both in and out of the office is equally important.

- Under no conditions is your client to be aggressive with the Reunification Therapist.
- Understand that Reunification Therapy can ask for involvement of various parties.
- The better the cooperation, the more it helps your client's case (and the children).
- Your client has a responsibility to make it work whether you are the parent in need of re-bonding or not.
- Be aware that the Reunification Therapist will issue opinions on your client's compliance.

Updates and Possible Testimony

Attorneys can ask for updated conferences and information, unless otherwise prohibited. They can (and should) represent their client's interest, but arguing excessively with opposing counsel in front of the Reunification Therapist will not be productive. The goal of these meetings is, in part, to extract information to help your client help the process. Remember, the Reunification Therapist can also report on the attorney's cooperation. The Reunification Therapist is not on the witness stand at these update conferences (even if they end up there at a later time). It is important for the attorneys to clarify if the Reunification Therapist can and will testify if required or requested.

Most Reunification Therapists know that testimony is an important component that is part of the job. Attorneys sometimes receive emergency calls from their clients and/or the Reunification Therapist when special problems arise. They need to be prepared for this possibility. The first things to do is listen to the Reunification Therapist without interruption, as they usually have some serious issues to share—often needing support for client compliance. Once the Reunification Therapist is done with their explanations, questions are appropriate. The following section provides such a scenario.

Progress and Mutual Communication Obligations

A Reunification Therapist set a conference call with both attorneys to apprise them of the progress on the case. The attorney for one of the clients listened and asked, "So, what's the bottom line? You cite some progress and some sticking points." The Reunification Therapist queried, "You both set an agreement for Reunification Therapy; it's not a court order so my influence is somewhat limited." The same attorney said, "If you gave a directive, what would it be?" The answer given was, "The children should be told by both parents to go with the father in his car to the sessions. He has done nothing I can find that is unsafe or inappropriate." Both attorneys said, "Done! We will make it happen."

Attorneys have a right and obligation to see to it that the Reunification Therapist is within the court's guidelines or the agreement as set. These are called professional boundary issues. Most Reunification Therapists know how to do this; others however do not.

Reunification Therapists need to be careful by always copying (all) relevant parties in communications. If they make missteps, an attorney can remind them who is "in the loop." Attorneys have the same obligation, though I have seen slip ups on this. A one-off error is not cataclysmic nor does it necessarily imply bias.

Sample Questions for Attorneys to Ask Reunification Professionals

- What is their training and background related to the case and its issues?
- Will they share and articulate a treatment plan?
- What are their metrics for success/progress?
- What releases do you require of my client?
- What is your understanding of the court order or agreement of the parents?
- When and how do you provide feedback to the attorneys, GAL, or others related to the case?
- What is your confidentiality policy in reunification cases?
- What is your understanding about possible testimony?
- How much notice do you need for testimony?
- Do you have an average timeframe for cases like this?
- Is there anything, generally or specifically, the attorneys can do to assist the process?
- Do you issue progress reports?
    - o How frequently?
    - o In what form?
        - E-mail
        - Full report/summary type report
        - Telephone
        - In session conferences
        - Skype/FaceTime
- Are the fee arrangements clear?
    - o What is your understanding of them in terms of:

- Who pays what and when?
- What services are exactly billed for?
    - Office
    - Progress reports
    - Preparation for testimony
    - Other
- How do you interface with the child advocate, GAL, or mediator/arbitrator?
- What documents do you usually need to proceed?
- If there is an ongoing or ordered custody evaluation, how do you interface, if at all, with the evaluator?
    - o Does this hamper your work (when an evaluation is ongoing)?
- Does ongoing litigation impact your work?
    - o If so, how?
- Do you initiate contact and/or can I?
- If I have information that is relevant to your work, can I share it?
    - o In what form?
    - o When?
- Is there anything else about your process or role that I should know?
- Will you contact me if there are any specific issues related to my client?
- Thank you (addressed to the Reunification Therapist) and I will try to be as helpful as I can in the reunification process.

Attorneys can function better if they have knowledge of the process, methods, and goals. They can be of service to their clients and execute their jobs as officers of the court.

Examining Reunification Experts in Court

Following are questions to help examine a reunification professional in court:

- Did you review the relevant court order?
- What was the judge's directive?
- What parties were ordered to cooperate?
- Did you find the parties so ordered to be cooperative? Could you please gives some details as to how the parties were or were not cooperative?
- Could you tell the court what metrics you used to measure progress, or lack thereof?
- Experience in Reunification Therapy

- Training attended?
- Number of cases?
- Publications in the field?
- Talks/presentations?
- Number of years practicing reunification?

- Do you have a specific treatment plan for this case?
  - (If it is absent, this becomes a whole other line of questioning.)
  - Isn't it professional protocol to design a treatment plan for all mental health services? (The answer should be yes.)
  - If there is one, you may need to critique or support:
    - Its detail
    - Its relevance to the case
    - Its measures of success
    - Its procedures
    - Projected outcomes
    - Timelines
    - Causes of the weakened parent-child connection (see list of Causal Considerations on page 25).
- Procedures
  - Joint session with parent and child?
  - What parties were involved?
- Progress to date
  - If negative or none, why?
  - If positive, how so?
  - Is more time needed for (further) progress?
  - Are different procedures needed?
  - Would other assistance from the court be helpful at this time? If yes, what form of assistance?
- "Point of No Return" Questions[3]
  - How long and intensive has the period of time been during which the child experienced programming and brainwashing?
    - The longer and more intensive, the more difficult the reunification process.
  - How many programmers and brainwashers or alienators have there been?
    - The more numerous, the more difficult the reunification process is.
  - How long has the child been isolated or restricted from the target parent?
  - Does the target parent have adequate communication skills to help in the rebuilding process?

3. Caution must be exercised here, as some impossible looking scenarios can show progress or even reversal.

- o How extensive have the socio-legal violations been of the alienating parent?
- o How many previous attempts have there been with little or no success?
    - The more of these, the lower the probability of success at the present time.
- o How many different alienation techniques have been applied to a particular child?
    - The more of these, the lower the rate of success.
- o Can the alienating parent be controlled, limited, or at least channeled in the re-bonding process.

- Cooperation
    - o If you, as the attorney, have assisted with cooperation in regard to the order, have the expert say so.
- Alienation
    - o If alienation is not the casual issue, what is?
    - o If alienation is an issue:
        - Who is the perpetrator?
        - Has it gotten better, worse, or stayed the same?
        - What is the damage impact to parent-child bonds?
        - What type of alienation?
        - To what extent?
        - What are some examples or measures of its existence?
        - What is to be done from here?

Tone of Witness Examination

Be careful in examining a court appointed or agreed-upon expert. Respect is key. Should you need to challenge them, do so with a factual base. Summarize any weaknesses they demonstrate, if it doesn't serve your client's goals. Remember, the judge is listening to whether your client's goals and behaviors are "in the best interest of the child." A parent who looks oppositional out of impulse, hatred, revenge, and/or anger will do poorly in getting the ear of the court.

Reunification Therapy Weaknesses

If there are misgivings about the credentials, procedures, bias, treatment plan, risk assessment, or conclusions/recommendations, address them in a thoughtful manner. Judges do not like witness badgering or intimidation.

The judge will hear the professional's weakness(es) (if present) when surfaced gingerly. Don't let tone damage the facts—as it can do.

Changing a Reunification Therapist should be recommended and done by not only showing the weaknesses of the present expert but by proposing a more positive alternative in selecting a professional, a better plan, clearer metrics, improved timing of contacts, and the like.

Format of a Reunification Report

There are different formats of reports, starting from a simple bullet point memo identifying the court order, parties involved, treatment plan, compliance measures, and metrics explaining the progress or lack thereof. The more detailed format or fuller report includes the all of these items, but provides more depth and may include opinions, commentary, summaries, conclusions, and, if appropriate, recommendations. All formats should make suggestions for moving forward in terms of the parties, the number and types of meetings, control of interfering parties, extra GAL assistance, auxiliary professional input, or even just staying the course. Any change in the treatment plan should be presented as part of any reporting format.

A Lawyer's Dream, or Was It a Nightmare?

"Guten Morgen" said the counselor to his new client
She said, "I hear in family law that you're the giant";

"Well, I don't know about that, what's your family matter?"
"I need to get the children, keep all the family monies, and move out west where the land the flatter;"

"My boyfriend's probation is almost done, he promises to stop drinking and disengage from the mob
And even said he would pursue a job";

"Sounds like a tough case to me
Which I hope you can see";

"What do the children say?"
"Pretty much what I tell them each and every day";

"So you can't help?
Gee you are highly rated on yelp";

"Yes, but the court has its limits
And doesn't tolerate any gimmicks";

"I think I'll be a good witness
I even took an improv course for mental fitness";

"Not sure how much I can do"
"Okay, thanks, I'll look for someone new."

Chapter 11

Guidelines for Judges (and Masters[1])

"The better educated we are, the better we can do our job."

— Family Court Judge

"Don't sell me, educate me."

— Family Court Judge

"I'll decide on the facts of the case, precedent law, and the credibility of the witnesses."

— Family Court Judge

"It's about parenting, then it's parenting, and finally, it's parenting."

— Family Court Master

Judges can be confronted with parent-child relational separations anywhere in the entire process of a family coming before their court. Knowing the causative factors in Chapter 3 "Causal Considerations—Broken Bonds—How Did It Happen?" can be helpful. As already stated, the general assumption in separation and divorce cases is that alienation is usually the culprit. As previously stated, this is not necessarily the case and really needs to be determined by a custody evaluation with an alienation study component as part of the assessment or some other forensic professional (possibly including the Reunification Therapist). Judges sometimes order a separate alienation study, without a custody evaluation. They also can order an evaluation to see if reunification is appropriate. This is a new concept (by your author) that may be helpful in cases of higher conflict and

1. In many municipalities, masters, conciliators, arbitrators, co-parenting counselors, and mediators have the authority to order/recommend parental guidelines.

parent-child separation of long-standing. A brief, focused study to even determine if Reunification Therapy is in order can save time, energy, monies, and possible duress. It can also help to set a framework for forward movement, should it be recommended. Most knowledgeable Reunification Therapists will use their first few sessions for such a determination anyhow. Specifying it as a separate function may be helpful to the court. Let's call it a *Reunification Assessment.* It can be a brief, focused, and delineated operation with low cost.

Some parent-child social bonding problems may be part of a larger constellation of other issues—social/personality differences, childhood grievances carried over into the parental separation/divorce, contamination from poor professional services, and sibling influence—to name a few possibilities. In any event, no matter the cause, the dilemma still exists. Once the judge determines that there is a need for Reunification Therapy, some *clarification of guidelines can increase the probability of a more successful outcome.*

In my previous book, *Children Held Hostage: Identifying Brainwashed Children, Presenting a Case, and Crafting Solutions,* I articulated guidelines for judges dealing with alienation cases. The guidelines for alienation and reunification endeavors have a lot of overlap, but will be further elaborated upon later.

Judges can assist in heightening the potential success of a reunification order by considering the following.

Issue a Timely Ruling

Not letting a ruling languish too long from the time of litigation to the actual issuing of the order is helpful. One of the reasons for doing this is that *the longer the time gap that parent and child have in their contact, the more accelerated the re-bonding problems.* Clients and attorneys have often used the phrase "the judge is on it and cares" when a timely order is, in fact, issued. *Time gaps are an enemy* in the reconciliation between parent and child.

Setting Specific Time Limits

Setting specific time limits on the professional intervention is functional. By the court indicating that they want feedback on the success, or lack thereof, by preset dates, it can reinforce the exigency of the matter to all parties. This guideline can be expedited by appointing a GAL or some other court-related functionary, if possible, to assist in gathering this information on behalf of the court.

Keeping the Focus on Reunification

By emphasizing in the court order that reunification means actual communication, contact, involvement, and interaction between a parent and child, the court can help in the clarity of the goal setting for any and all professional involvement. This prevents various therapies (not oriented toward reunification) from being carried on ad nauseam. *The bulk of existing therapies do not work to facilitate re-bonding* (as most were not designed to do so).

Explain the Court Order to Both Parents

Many judges are aware of the importance of doing this. If the court order is decided and written while the parties are before the court, it is an easy process. However, a judge may wish to do this by Skype or FaceTime with the attorneys and their clients if the order is written after a hearing (which is often the case). Conflicting parents are less likely to misinterpret the judge's intent when it is explained directly to them by the Judge. Obviously, other court-related functionaries can also provide this guidance if the judge deems it appropriate. So, co-parenting experts, GALs, court mediators and arbitrators, and others can perform this function. At the end of such an explanation, the parents should be asked to explain, in their own terms, what they understood the order to be and its meaning especially in terms of their own specific behaviors (this is called the *Feedback Function*). In about half of the cases, at least one of the parents will state a misunderstanding and/or incorrect behavioral follow-up that is expected of them. At this juncture, the court order should be reviewed again with a summary question for the parent or parents to restate their understanding and their behavioral follow-ups. This feedback process needs to continue until all parties understand the same thing at the same time, resulting in the expected adult behaviors.

Many Reunification Therapists are faced with a parent who starts a session with their understanding of the court order that is not in line with the intent of the judge or the Reunification Therapist. It then takes time to realign their understanding. Some Reunification Therapists will then involve both attorneys to try to create client alignment with the court order. Even at this juncture, it is possible for an attorney to disagree on the meaning of the order. For example, in a recent case, a mother and her daughter believed that they were to attend three to four sessions and at the end of those sessions, the reunification process would be considered over. This was not the intent of the court, nor the understanding of the Reunification Therapist. Actually, three or four sessions were provided for getting to know the child and gathering relevant history. At that juncture, the real reunification between parent and child (in terms of actual contact) was to begin. Because of this confusion, the attorneys and their clients had to return to the court for the judge's reaffirmation of the actual process. Some of this confusion or possible manipulation could have been eliminated by the judge or their designate had they stated all conditions up front and directly to the attorneys and their clients. As noted, the author would estimate that in about half of all reunification cases, there is some intentional or unintentional misinterpretation of the court's directives. Unfortunately, this can get the reunification process off to a disjointed start—as all parties are not on the same page at the same time. No Reunification Therapist should attempt to begin the process until the same understanding is shared by all. I have seen children come in with an understanding that reunification does not involve actual contact with the other parent. Obviously, somebody has shared with them an inaccurate view of what this kind of intervention entails. I have heard children say, "You mean I have to talk to my father?," "I hope you don't expect me to sit in the same room with my mother," "I'll come and see you, but that's about as much as I'll do," or "Nobody told me that I have to spend time with Jim" (children who have been alienated and/or estranged will often call the alienated parent by their first name in order to distance their real biological and/or social connections to them). Of course, some children can develop their own (mis)understandings without adult input.

Explaining the Court Order to the Child(ren)

Sometimes it can be very helpful for a judge to take a few moments to indicate the court's expectations, including the cooperation of the child(ren). By doing this, the court removes the burden of a particular parent, attorney, or professional being blamed for what is about to transpire. Judges who do this will often tell the child(ren) that it is the court's opinion that having both of their parents in their life is important and even further explaining why this is the case. Sometimes judges will even let child(ren) know that they are aware (if it's true) that the child may have some of their own oppositions or concerns. Even with this, it is the judge's opinion that parent-child re-bonding is a good thing to do and that the court will be receiving reports back on everybody's cooperation. Asking the children to repeat back their understanding can also be helpful. I have had a number of children say, "Unless a judge tells me, I ain't doing it." So, as many judges have said, "There is a time and place for my role and authority." For some children, a court order frees them up from looking like they are taking sides between their conflicted parents. A boy recently said to his mother, "What can I do? The judge said I have to do it." He privately revealed to me, "I was relieved. I don't have to feel guilty about seeing my dad."

Identifying Measures of Compliance

By putting in the court order what the judge considers to be measures of cooperation and success the court can expedite the process. Also, by offering things like attendance at specified dates, coming on time, following the guidelines of the Reunification Therapist, sharing information with the GAL, progressively improving parent-child communication, sharing school and other information with the parent seeking the re-bonding, and a whole host of other specific measures the order can be better articulated. *The more conflicted the case, the more specifics are suggested to be put into the court order.* This gives the court objective metrics by which to assess not only compliance but also progress. This articulation of exact judicial expectations should be refined as much as possible. They may even include statements of possible interference and how interference will be viewed by the court.

If the judge wants the mother to have school pickups, it should be said, rather than "the parents will cooperate over school matters." Or say both. Parents are good at taking general directives and poking holes in them. So, if parents are told to jointly pick a therapist, they may fail to come to agreement. But, a more specific directive may be to give them a two-week timeframe to jointly pick a therapist, or the GAL will pick one for them.

Protecting the Professionals

Professionals can be insulted, intimidated, harassed, and/or (threatened to be) sued by oppositional parents. When the court indicates that the professionals involved will be protected by various forms of immunity, they go a long way to providing a comfort base for the professional executing their designated services. This is especially important where parents have previously been successful in driving respected and ethical professionals out of the case. *Some parents have a history of intimidating professionals* who seem not to agree with their anti-re-bonding goals. Some judges have issued absolute immunity and others have provided limited immunity related to established case law in their state. Many professionals have their own protective releases. By the judge ordering the parties to also sign them, they assist the professional and the case in moving forward.

Be Cautious about Using Terms Such as "Consult"

Some parents will take this to mean that they have a wide range of discretion in regard to what, when, and how they share information with the other parent. Oppositional parents may send medical information to the other parent after they have already made the decision for actual care, but claim they have "consulted" with them. If the judge wants a true collaborative process on major life issues, they should so specify this. Many children who are medically and/or socially-psychologically compromised may need the approval of both parents prior to any (serious) professional intervention unless otherwise ordered by the court. In crisis situations, the court may allocate decision making power to a GAL—such as the need for a serious (crisis) medical intervention. *Parents with oppositional histories will interpret any terms that are vague to their advantage* in order to continue their interference with a re-bonding or sharing process. For these types of parents, the less latitude here, the better.

Inform All Parties of the Potential Penalties for Noncompliance

Especially in cases of progressive opposition, *it's important for a parent to know that the court is serious about mending the broken bonds and that if full compliance is not performed, that there will be sanctions.* These sanctions can include financial penalties, payment of legal fees, payment of professional fees, payment of court costs, or modification of physical and/or legal custody, to name a few consequences for noncompliance. Oppositional parents often try to get a "read" on the judge in their case. By the judge indicating that he/she would hope to not have to be in a position of activating sanctions, but have readily available possibilities should they need to be employed, the judge affirms the possible reality to problematic parents. This kind of dialogue is more likely to be necessitated in cases that have a patterned history of oppositional behaviors, which take many forms. Some judges like to give examples of parental behaviors that would lead to sanction(s). This can be issued in an informational tone with the underpinning of "make no mistake that the court is serious about the goal of this parent and this child(ren) reconnecting in a healthy relationship. The court will accept nothing less than full support for this goal."

Identifying Others Who May Interfere with the Re-bonding Process

Throughout the course of family law cases, it often appears that there may be other players who are negatively impacting on a parent-child relationship.

Paramours, grandparents, cohabitants, stepparents, and even some professionals may have played a role in creating and/or supporting the segregation of a parent and child. Some judges like to issue meaningful warnings about and to any and all of these "players." In one case, after the judge had listened to a comprehensive list of witnesses, he decided that one of the key sources of obstructionism was the stepfather. He asked the stepfather to rise in the court and told him that he was convinced of his culpability in trying to damage the relationship between the young children and their father. He warned the stepfather, in very clear terms, that if the court heard any further stories about his negative commentary about the father and other forms of obstructionism, that the court would hold him in contempt and that he would be most unhappy with the court's actions at that point. After asking if the stepfather clearly understood what he was saying, he told him that he "may be seated." In following the course of that case, it appeared that was enough to create a real cease and desist situation for this stepparent who, among other deeds in the past, told the children, "Your father doesn't love you."

Specifying the Credentials of the Reunification Therapist

Indicating in a court order that the "therapist" or "counselor" should have forensic experience in cases that match the conditions and problems of this case will go a long way toward preventing professional-client mismatch. In a recent case (representing many others) a therapist was appointed who was practiced in the areas of general psychotherapy and had de minimis knowledge and experience in forensic matters. This therapist commenced to not only fail to solve the re-bonding problem but also expanded the family issues in very broad and damaging ways. It is crucial that therapists or counselors be vetted by their forensic knowledge, experience, track record, research, publications, teachings, and ethical reputation. Judges can inquire, "Are you sure the credentials match the case focus of re-bonding this parent and child as the court wishes? How so?" The attorney's answer should match the skills mentioned in Chapter 8 of this text, "Skill Sets and Qualities to Look for in Selecting Reunification Experts," on page 149.

Case Oversight

Given the caseload of the average family court judge, they do not have the time to monitor each court order. Rather than depending on emergency or contempt citations from the attorneys (which may be necessitated at certain times), they might do well to appoint a GAL or similar functionary to gather information and report to the court. Elsewhere I have recommended a somewhat new career option called a *court monitor*, and various municipalities have moved in the direction of using established court personnel (parenting evaluators, mediator/conciliators, and others) to assist in this process. Also, the dockets can be so full that important information does not get before the court for three, six, or more months. In reunification work, as already noted, *time is of the essence*. As a side but related note, many lay and professional people adhere to the idea that "eventually children come around." This means that if a child is disengaged from a parent at age 14, that waiting until they are 16 or 18 may be a good idea because they may "see the light." As stated before, I know of no research that substantially supports this idea, nor does my 40 years in the field validate it, in the least.

Expectations of Case Conduct

Most lawyers have what they consider to be the "book" on different judges in terms of their likes and dislikes, the way they process cases, their history of judicial rulings, their issuance of sanctions, and other dimensions of their judgeship. Conversely, judges have their own "books" on attorneys. It expedites cases if judges are willing to reaffirm in the beginning of the case the type of information and style of presentation that gets "the ear of the court." In other words, trying to waste time with a dozen character witnesses could be contraindicated. Having clarity on appropriate courtroom conduct and what that means could also be helpful. Many judges have expressed shock by the lack of knowledge some attorneys have about courtroom decorum.[2] Many judges are also shocked by the lack of knowledge of proper case presentation and challenge. I have seen judges chastise attorneys for lack of proper forms of address to and in the court. Judges have even had to inform all present that any use of cell phones will not be tolerated. So, the manners, ethics, content, and style desired by a particular judge can be very helpful to issue up front—especially for attorneys who have not been before them in previous cases. Even reminding attorneys who have been before a particular judge of judicial expectations can still be helpful. I have even had some judges inform attorneys, in the beginning of a case, how experts and other witnesses are to be treated by the attorneys and what is important to the court. It used to be assumed that these dimensions of professionalism were known (and properly performed) before entering the courtroom; unfortunately, this is no longer universally the case.

2. Many law schools are now offering new courses on courtroom procedures and etiquette.

I have experienced some judges taking the time at the beginning of the case to explain the phrase "in the best interests of the child." Interestingly, it has often helped attorneys channel their efforts on behalf of their clients in a more focused fashion. Connected to this idea, some judges have even stopped a line of questioning and said, "Could you tell the court what this has to do with the children?" or "I'm not getting the connection between this witness, your line of questioning, and the parenting concerns held by the court." In other words, *the central foci of all family cases are the children's well-being and how parenting, in its various forms, is related to the children.* Any other matters may be tangential unless the connection is clearly made by the attorney. Sometimes, attorneys think they are making the connection only to accidentally reveal a weakness in their own case. For example, in one case an attorney was trying to demonstrate (as noted elsewhere in this text) that a father was "abusive" by his parenting behaviors. By the time he was done, it became clear that the father was disciplinary, boundary setting, willing to issue sanctions if the children did not meet expectations, and related behaviors to this type of parenting. The judge was left with more of a conundrum than a conclusion. Even an expert brought into the case raised the question that was already on the judge's mind as to what the difference was between a "strict" parent and an "abusive" parent. In effect, the line of questioning used by the mother's attorney backfired and actually helped to diminish the argument that the father was "abusive." The judge concluded, "Frankly, I think we need more parents who set boundaries to disobedient children."

Clearly State the Type and Number of Witnesses/Experts that the Court Will Hear

Many judges like to issue, up front, a declaration of the scope and number of witnesses that will be permitted. Some judges have set limits on character witnesses (one or two for each side), number of "experts," and other related procedural guidelines. Many judges have even articulated the amount of time that may be allocated to an expert. In one case, an attorney wanted an entire day for an expert (who was famous for going on and on and also being known as a "hired gun") and the judge indicated that "an hour or two will be allocated, so get your salient points in as efficiently as you can. Of course, I will allocate a similar timeframe to opposing counsel, if so requested." By channeling the various dimensions of the trial, a judge also guarantees a more realistic point of conclusion to the case. This is especially important in cases where a parent has manipulated the system by elongated trials so that there is no conclusion or an extended conclusion and another hearing must be held—often many months or more away. These delays also delay the start of any potential reunification, if a judge is to so indicate. This can become important for some other latent reasons. *For example, if a child is not presently unified with one of the parents, it is also commonly found that they are disengaged from that parent's extended family.* So loss of contact with a mother or father can translate into a loss of contact with aunts, uncles, cousins, grandparents, and others. *Usually a parent is not a "stand-alone" issue in terms of what is going on between them and a child.* This means that the longer a child is not reunified (if conditions indicate they should be), the longer their "ancestral" loss will occur. There are cases where grandparents died without ever seeing their grandchildren again. The losses to the child are obvious. I've actually gone to graveside with some children to help them say "goodbye."

When Is an Expert an Expert?

The question always arises as to when is an expert an expert? In general, there are three criteria.

- The person must be qualified in an area of scientific, technical, or other specialized knowledge.
- The specialized knowledge must assist the trier of facts to understand the evidence or to determine a fact in issue.
- The expert's testimony must be limited to matters within the scope of his or her specialized knowledge.

There may be exceptions to this criteria, such as in Nevada. The Nevada court has ruled that there can be four nonexclusive factors to determine a person as an expert.

- Formal schooling and academic degrees
- Licensure
- Employment experience
- Practical experience and specialized knowledge

Furthermore, a witness can also answer questions to demonstrate to the court that they have training and/or practical experience to qualify as an expert in lieu of formal training (*Higgs v. Nevada*[3]). Nevada goes a bit further in noting that being qualified as an expert is not enough; they must "assist" the trier of facts. Nevada further refines the term "assistance" by noting that two factors should be present.

- "Relevancy" refers to evidence that "must make the existence of any fact that is of consequence to the determination of the action more

3. Higgs v. State, 222 P.3d 648, No. 49883 (Nev. 2010).

or less probable." However, this could be outweighed by evidence of prejudice.

- The evidence presented should be a product of reliable methodology. This includes being recognized as an expert in the field, evidence being open to be testable, having published and peer-reviewed materials (but not all materials need to be peer reviewed), generally accepted in the scientific community, and the evidence presented is based more on facts than on assumptions, generalizations, conjectures, or opinions.

All of these dimensions can and should be assessed by the local trier of facts—with a fairly wide range of discretion. This definitional perspective provides the judge with the capacity to make decisions, within a given a range, of what will "assist" them to utilize information and even to determine when an expert is an expert.

How to Determine If a Witness Is Biased or Skewed

There are a number of warning signs that a witness may have different types and degrees of bias. Following is a list of some of the signs to look for. Even some known experts may present some of these characteristics.

- Pro or anti female/male patterns (sex bias)
- Slanted on custodial arrangements (always favors joint custody)
- Knowledge of genders is limited (gender bias)
- Not up to date on research and therefore holds outdated views
- Locked into one school of thought (cognitive behavioral therapy, for example)
- All reports read the same—except for name changes
- Volume versus quality—"the more the better" approach
- Lets one party (i.e., the children) run the case
- Focus versus scattered on major case element(s)
- Hired hand reputation
- Professional position not relevant to parties/issues at hand
- Violates professional, communal, or legal ethics (ex parte behaviors)

Possible Indicators of Problematic Experts

- Outdated credentials
- Research and/or subject matter weaknesses
- Main occupation is trial presentation

- Mostly adversarial work
- They always find what one attorney wants
- Ethical challenges exist in their professional history
- Doesn't admit areas of weak argument/facts
- Sticks to a standard script
- "Know it all" style
- Travels the "circuit"
- Often gathers information quickly for a "packaged report"
- Data may not be comprehensive
- Conclusions do not match facts, descriptions, or methods

Judicial Case Interview

Following is an interview by a judge and a 14-year-old southwestern girl (who was heavily enmeshed into the mother's disdain of her father). This was another case where a boundary-setting parent received the "abuse" label.

Judge: So, Allie, what do you want to tell me about your family?

Allie: My "family" is my mom and me.

Judge: And your father? How does he fit in?

Allie: He doesn't.

Judge: Could you explain that to me?

Allie: Well, he's never really been there, so I don't get the pressure now to be with him.

Judge: You don't understand why he is trying to see you?

Allie: It's just to make trouble for mom and me.

Judge: Any other reasons you can think of?

Allie: I guess because he's a control freak.

Judge: Is there anything else?

Allie: Well, he doesn't really do anything for the family or me. He never did. Whenever he wants something, he always tries to get his way too.

Judge: If you're asked to do or not do something, who do you listen to?

Allie: Only my mom. Even my last therapist said I don't have to listen to him.

Judge: Do you know why your therapist told you that you don't have to listen to him?

Allie: Yeah, he's abusive! Dr. Smith said so, too.

Judge: What made him be labeled as abusive?

Allie: He always has to control everything in our lives and I'm sick and tired of it.

Sample Court Order

The following are examples of items that can be considered in a court order regarding the appointment and duties of a Reunification Therapist, the appointment and duties of a GAL, as well as expected guidelines for parents. Obviously, items can be added, deleted, or changed based on case specifics, such as the arrangement of fees. Possible sanctions can also be articulated within the order as well as other items as the judge and GAL, if appointed, deems necessary.

AND NOW, this ___ (Day) ___ day of ___ (Month) ___ ___(Year) ___, it is hereby ORDERED and DECREED:
[Appointing a Reunification Therapist:]

1. ___(Therapist Name)___, is hereby appointed as the Reunification Therapist to conduct Reunification Therapy with ___(Parent to Reunify)___ and ___(Child)___. The duties of the Reunification Therapist are as follows:
   a. Obtain appropriate signed releases from the parents;
   b. Design a clear treatment plan with goals, techniques, and timelines utilizing specific metrics;
   c. Articulate a detailed Risk Assessment as well as preventative and reactive measures for each item where applicable;
   d. Seek guidance, advice, and/or input from third party professionals, as needed;
   e. Issue written and/or verbal progress reports to the GAL, the Court, or Counsel every four to six weeks including, but not limited to, the current progress and compliance of all parties or lack thereof;
2. ___(Therapist Name)___ shall be granted Common Law Immunity as established by ___(State)___ case law.

[Appointing a GAL:]

1. ___(GAL Name)___, is hereby appointed as Guardian Ad Litem, (GAL) for ____(Child)____. As part of the general statutory powers and duties set forth in ___(GAL State Law Statute)___, and for the purposes of facilitating Reunification Therapy between ___(Parent to Reunify)___ and ___(Child)___, the GAL in this case shall perform the following specific tasks in addition to those required by state law:
   a. Meet with and/or have access to all of the relevant parties at the discretion of the GAL;
   b. Coordinate the necessary information, parties, and professionals in order to execute the terms of this Order;
   c. Receive regular progress reports, written or verbal, from the Reunification Counselor/Therapist once every four to six weeks;
   d. Oversee and participate, as needed or requested, in any considerations related to the Risk Assessment phase of Reunification Therapy;
   e. Monitor the reunification process and, if deemed necessary, with the consultation of the Judge, issue an interruption or cease and desist of the reunification should it be deemed harmful or problematic to the child (or other parties);
   f. Receive and/or initiate contact with the Judge at their own discretion, but no less than once every four to six weeks;
   g. Issue a written status report to the Court and counsel once every six to eight weeks including but not limited to the progress of reunification, the wellbeing of the child, the compliance, or lack thereof, of all parties, as well as possible sanctions for any act(s) of noncompliance.

[Guidelines for Parents:]

1. Both Mother and Father shall fully cooperate with the Reunification Therapist and GAL and do the following:
   a. Cooperate fully with all requests made by the Reunification Therapist and/or GAL;
   b. Sign any and all releases within seven (7) days of receiving the releases, including an Indemnification of the Reunification Therapist, conditions of confidentiality, fee agreements, and/or other releases as requested;
   c. Parents will sign releases for school records, access to any and all therapists, medical doctors, or others as deemed necessary by the Reunification Therapist;
   d. Pay the costs of the Reunification Therapist and GAL on an equal (50/50) basis and in a timely manner either when requested or in conformance with any fee agreements;
   e. Accept and acknowledge that the traditional confidentiality is not the same as the confidentiality of Reunification Therapy and that the Reunification Therapist may share information with

the GAL, Court, Counsel, and/or other professionals as deemed necessary by the Therapist;

f. Accept and acknowledge that compliance will be monitored by the GAL and the Court and any noncompliance may be met with recommended sanctions including but not limited to custodial arrangements, monetary fines, and more;

g. Participate respectfully and civilly in the process both during and outside of the professional sessions and setting;

h. Follow recommendations made by the Reunification Therapist and/or GAL as to behaviors, attitudes, speech, and/or interventions between each other (Mother and Father) as well as the child;

i. Refrain from threatening, intimidating, accusing, and/or interfering with the Reunification Therapist and/or GAL in regard to the performance of their duties as designated by the Court as well as cautioning family members and/or third parties from doing the same.

[Other Considerations:]

1. The Reunification Therapist and GAL are considered to be neutral independent professionals. As such, counsel shall not initiate any contact with the professionals in any manner including, but not limited to, letters, emails, text messages, and telephone calls. In the event the Reunification Therapist and/or GAL believes that contact with counsel is necessary, the contact shall be initiated by the professional including both counsel for Mother and Father. Any exception to this can be approved by the GAL, if necessary.
2. Should testimony be necessary by either the Reunification Therapist and/or GAL, the costs will be borne by both Mother and Father on an equal (50/50) basis. It shall be paid at least 2 weeks prior to court dates as per the designated fees set in the fee agreement issued by the Reunification Therapist.

The Judge: A Prudent Guide

Judges are there to decide
Not just to be present for the ride;

Precedent law is the key
But, that doesn't reduce the attorney's fee;

(*continued*)

Who did what to whom?
This question brings on a veil of gloom;

Experts are there to opine
But the final decision is still all mine;

Contempt filings point the finger
Even if the blame long does not linger;

I must digest the facts before the court
And make sure all do properly comport;

With all this in mind I have to be a beacon of light
And keep to the best interest of the children while parents do fight;

If the parents only knew
What their combat will ultimately do.

Signs that Reunification Therapy May Be Indicated

- A parent with a positive history has not seen a child for a significant amount of time.
- Serial accusations have been filed and disbanded with by agencies, the court, and/or professionals.
- There is forensic evidence of alienation. (See the Parent-Child Estrangement Inventory in Chapter 4 on page 81.)
- There have been varied mechanisms to delay contact between a parent and child.
    - o Contempt citations
    - o Medical excuses
    - o Professional and/or Parent assertions the child "is not ready"
    - o Other
- A parent still has some degree of legal custody but has been preempted from effective decision making and is "cut off" by the other parent.
- A parent has tried mediation, counseling, personal pleas, and other attempts to see/be with a child, which have all largely failed.
- A child is in trouble in school, with peers, with the law, or in other ways and a parent has not had effective contact or guidance capabilities.

- There have been attempts to malign the reputation of a parent with no grounding in social reality.
- Reunification Therapy has been done, but with no treatment plan or risk assessment.
- It has been done, but not by one with the correct skill sets.
- It has been done, but was truncated due to an obstructionist parent.
- One part is recommending a radical intervention, but more moderate means have not (all) been attempted.

The Judge: A Prudent Guide con't

"So counselor, I caution you to up the pace
As you continue your case";

"Your honor, I like to call the court appointed expert to the stand.
Who will likely, with all logic, disband?"

"Very well, but limit the scope
Remember, this court is no dope";

"Yes your honor, I now call the nation's expert on alienation
And I'm sure he will further the case's obfuscation";

"Doctor, let's cut to the chase,
As his honor is concerned about the pace";

"Do you have an opinion on the matter?"
"Yes, I do, so let me perform some psycho-blather";

"The mother is likely the culprit
But, the father lectures as if on pulpit";

"So, I say
It's likely a toss either way";

"And with that, I'm living up to my reputation
To cause further case consternation";

(continued)

> "Counselors, please come to sidebar
> I don't think we have gotten very far";
>
> "So, I'd like to get you to settle the matter
> As my docket is getting much fatter";
>
> "If your clients can't agree, I'm likely to order a seven by seven
> And that's a better deal than they will get, even in heaven."

Figure 11.1 details some of the factors that impact on judicial decisions—lawyers, therapists, GALs, and others can benefit from reviewing them. Of course, judges are usually keenly aware of them and either try to consider or regulate them as best as possible in order to facilitate a healthy case resolution

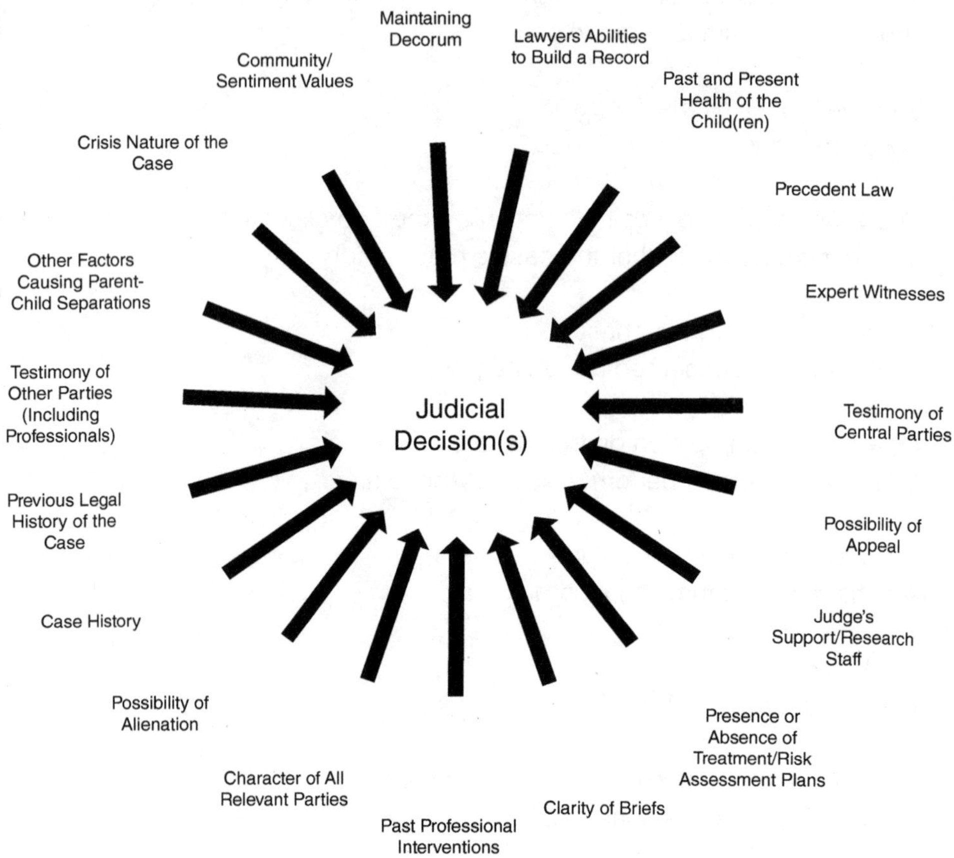

Figure 11.1 Nineteen Factors Impacting on Judicial Decisions

Ten Takeaways for Judges

Following are some key factors to consider and possibly employ when listening to various experts (opine).

- **The grounded factor**. Quick tools to evaluate grounded information versus ungrounded information/opinions of "experts." That is, there is a firm, objective basis for their process, methods, and conclusions.
- **The research factor.** Problems in method/procedures that may impact on or damage professional conclusions/opinions.
- **The tracking factor.** Is the expert following the judge's court order, case focus, and central issues?
- **The power factor.** Do some experts usurp the judge's domain? Some have histories of being chastised on the record in previous cases.
- **The boundary factor.** When do experts overstep their actual areas of expertise?
- **Science changes.** Are all disciplines culturally, historically, and research-wise constrained? Do they recognize this?
- **Objectivity.** Do they have anything positive to say about both parents?
- **Are They Defensive?** Or are they educable? Explaining in content and style.
- **Focus.** Do they stay on point (of the case) or wander every which way?
- **Respect.** Can they understand there may be alternative views even if they don't abide by them?

Chapter 12

How GALs Can Help in the Reunification Process

"I'm a guardian who sheds light. I have to keep reminding everyone of those two key functions a court-appointed GAL—guarding and shedding light."

— A GAL from the Northeast

More and more cases across the country involve the services of a guardian ad litem (GAL). Guardians come in all different varieties. Some are attorneys, some are social workers, and some may have other professional backgrounds. Their charges in cases can vary greatly, depending on the directives of a judge, mediator, or arbitrator. At times, they may also interface with Children and Youth Services or Child Protective Services on behalf of (overseeing) the well-being of a child.

There are many ways in which they can be helpful, but some basic skills are necessary for all of their services. These include:

- Legal knowledge
- Ability to execute a court order
- Ability to interface with clinicians
- Ability to maintain good relationships with social agencies and other professionals
- Willing and capable of making decisions in crisis situations
- Fairness and objectivity while gathering information from all relevant parties
- Ability to testify and report to the court when necessary
- Empathic skills
- Likes and gets along with children of all ages and backgrounds
- Ability to draft clear and focused memos and reports

Assuming these skills are in place, it would also be helpful if they have a track record of working on a wide range and intensity of family law cases. So, now we are ready to look at the various ways they can help the reunification process.

1. Monitoring the Process

This is a crucial function. Having someone to oversee the therapeutic and related activities surrounding the children and parents can be very helpful to the courts. Having an objective set of eyes can keep everyone on track with the goals, objectives, and methods of the reunification process.

2. Assist with and Approve Therapeutic Guidelines

GALs are able to assist with both the therapeutic guidelines and post-therapeutic guidelines. By letting therapists know what the socio-legal interests are of a guardian, the therapist can better design their methods and content in forensic (and clinical) terms.

3. Running Interference When Needed

Running interference when needed with different parties is as much a messenger function of different perspectives as it is "interference." However, if something is going in a direction that is not good for the child, the GAL can so apprise the relevant parties. If an overnight parent-child contact recommendation by the therapist is deemed precipitous, it can be slowed down or eliminated by the GAL (or they can accelerate the contact, too). Translating the therapist's approach to a problematic parent is part of this function.

4. Support or Challenge Therapeutic Recommendations

This item is related to the preceding item of running interference. GALs can either support or challenge recommendations that are made by a clinician through verbal means or in report form. This can result in a creative process where a new understanding would arise due to the different perspectives. On the other hand, if the GAL feels strongly that certain recommendations should even be executed, they can so indicate this.

5. Provide "Push Back" on Parental Problems

GALs often push back on parental problems. In virtually all cases, one or both parents may have problems or issues that may impact on the ultimate goal(s) of reunification. Insightful GALs can separate out the parental (and marital) problems from the goal of reconnecting a parent and child. They can do this either through the therapists or by speaking directly with the parents themselves.

6. Crisis Intervention as Needed

A social, medical, educational, family, or other crisis can arise during the bridge-building process. GALs have their ears out for such occurrences and can assist by accessing additional resources, by extricating the child if necessary, or helping the reunification counselor moderate the crisis.

7. Keep the Child(ren) on Target

Children can get sidetracked for a number of reasons (including historical family ones). Keeping all parties focused on the goal of building or rebuilding a parent-child relationship is extremely helpful. I have seen good GALs do this by asking simple questions, such as "What does this (issue, topic, or piece of history) have to do with why we are here?" or "Are we getting off track here? This sounds like a divorce issue, so let's not contaminate our present goal."

8. Represent the Children's Needs and Answer Questions for Them

A GAL is to be able to represent the child(ren) on specific issues related to the case and answer questions (also in court). Judges often trust the judgment and research of their GALs. In fact, they may even perceive them as the only objective force before them. Judges may have many questions, such as "Were the parents in compliance with the order?," "Is the therapist making progress?," or "Do we need to do anything different from here?" This activity of being a "voice for the child(ren)" can help to shed light on important aspects of the case. The "voice" doesn't (usually or necessarily) mean the full empowerment of the child. Instead it means the child is heard and the input is then able to be utilized in the re-bonding process.

9. Communicate with the Court Both In and Outside Regular Hearings

GALs should be able to communicate with the court outside of the regular hearings. Many GALs are permitted to send messages to the judge, if they deem it significant in terms of their socio-legal charge. This is especially the case if there is a crisis and they need the direction and approval of the judge for some special action on behalf of the child.

10. Push and Keep to All Timelines

Pushing and keeping to the timelines that have been set by the court and/or the therapist are both within the GAL's power. All treatment plans should have timelines even if they are approximate. This helps to provide a reasonable understanding by which specific things should be accomplished. Timeframes can include an initial meeting without the child(ren), leading to various frequencies and types of contact between parent and child(ren) to recommending parent-child contacts outside of the office setting to facilitating various types of communication (text, phone, Skype, FaceTime, in person, etc.). If timelines are not met, GALs will often ask for reasons and help to set a corrective process to get back on track. Of course, some cases have up and down patterns in progress and can be tolerated, to a degree.

11. Reinforce Protection of the Therapist

The reunification process can be made more wholesome by the GAL reinforcing the protection of the therapist. This means that the parents are clear that the therapist is respected and that the court will support their plan and approach. This is important, especially in the highest level of conflicted cases, as one parent may seek a weak link in the reunification process. These types of parents will then attack that weak link. If the weak link (read unprotected) therapist is so identified, they may increasingly become targeted with accusations, threats, professional character assassinations, and other hostile or disruptive behaviors. A GAL can reinforce to that type of parent that "they will have none of that" and that their negative behaviors are to cease and desist. If those inappropriate, assaultive behaviors continue, the GAL may consider that this necessitates function number six, crisis intervention, as well as the ninth function, communicating back with the court outside of the regular hearings.

12. Get Needed Data

Many GALs are a composite of information from all the various sources—therapist, mediator, co-parenting expert, the parents, attorneys, the school, the child(ren), and any others who might have information relevant to the goal of reunification. They can gather this data in person, by memo, by video, by reports, and by many other means. They employ discretion in deciding how it is to be utilized and what the diversity of information means for the re-bonding process. This integration function is one of the most important and difficult to perform.

13. Reinforce Court Orders and Goals

By knowing the legal dimensions, they can often translate these into clear expectations and behaviors for the parties involved. These parties include the parents, extended family, the therapist, and any others who have a need to know (NTK) and/or getting clarification on the orders and goals of the court. By performing this function properly, they can help all parties to move in the proper direction and successfully accomplish the re-bonding result.

14. Obtain and Review Progress Assessments

Ultimately, GALs need to offer an opinion on how close or far away the process is from the predefined goal(s). Sharing their views on this, with some regularity, is very beneficial as the GAL serves as a reality anchor. Of course, this assessment is made within the context of the original treatment plan (which may have continued to evolve since its initial conception). This function also helps to realign the process and methods, if needed. A GAL-based progress report to the court is common in these cases. Progress includes identifying any possible impediments—both human and circumstantial.

15. Makes Sure Risk Assessments Are Done and Considered

Identifying the social, emotional, and physical (e.g., medical) problems, issues, and/or dangers is very important to all treatment plans, but it rarely appears. If a child has a history of asthma attacks exacerbated by stress, is it so considered? If a child has threatened to run away, what is the risk and back-up strategy? Sending a child away to an alienation center that requires exclusion from their primary parent is fraught with different potential problems. The risks and plans to support the child must be explicated.

16. Follows Guidelines Outlined by State Law and the Particular Judge

Most, if not all states, have predetermined a GALs responsibilities within the state law. It is imperative that a GAL follows these guidelines. It's also important for the Reunification Therapist to be knowledgeable about the law, especially their duties and obligations. For example, in Pennsylvania state law, Title 23 § 5334(b) outlines their powers and duties.

> **§ 5334. Guardian Ad Litem for child.**
>
> **(b) Powers and duties.**—The Guardian Ad Litem shall be charged with representation of the legal interests and the best interests of the child during the proceedings and shall do all of the following:
>
> (1) If appropriate to the child's age and maturity, meet with the child as soon as possible following the appointment and on a regular basis thereafter.
>
> (2) On a timely basis, be given access to relevant court records, reports of examination of the parents or other custodian of the child and medical, psychological and school records.
>
> (3) Participate in all proceedings.
>
> (4) Conduct such further investigation necessary to ascertain relevant facts for presentation to the court.

(5) Interview potential witnesses, including the child's parents and caretakers, if any. The Guardian Ad Litem may examine and cross-examine witnesses and present witnesses and evidence necessary to protect the best interests of the child.

(6) Make specific recommendations in a written report to the court relating to the best interests of the child, including any services necessary to address the child's needs and safety. The court shall make the written report part of the record so that it may be reviewed by the parties. The parties may file with the court written comments regarding the contents of the report. The comments filed by the parties shall also become part of the record.

(7) Explain the proceedings to the child to the extent appropriate given the child's age, mental condition and emotional condition.

(8) Advise the court of the child's wishes to the extent that they can be ascertained and present to the court whatever evidence exists to support the child's wishes. When appropriate because of the age or mental and emotional condition of the child, determine to the fullest extent possible the wishes of the child and communicate this information to the court. A difference between the child's wishes under this paragraph and the recommendations under paragraph (6) shall not be considered a conflict of interest for the Guardian Ad Litem.

These guidelines articulated in the state laws may vary, but (should) generally have the same principals.

When a judge appoints a GAL, they can, and many do, also articulate specific guidelines for a GAL to follow above and beyond the state statutes. Some examples are:

- Coordinate all the necessary information, parties, and professionals in order to effectuate the terms of this order.
- Receive regular progress reports from the Reunification Therapist once every ___ weeks.
- Meet with and/or have access to all relevant parties at the discretion of the GAL.
- Oversee and participate as needed and/or requested in any risk assessment considerations on a regular basis.
- Monitor and, with consultation of the judge, issue an interruption and/or cease/desist of Reunification Therapy if it is deemed hurtful to the child as part of the risk assessment.
- Receive contact from and/or contact the judge as each party deems necessary, including telephone communication, but no less than every ___ weeks.

- Issue a written report to the court and counsel once every ___ weeks. This includes recommendations as well as the status of areas of success, concern, and/or failure.

In summary, GALs have a crucial role, when functioning effectively. The preceding areas of GAL activity can, of course, be supplemented by themselves, the court, suggestions from the Reunification Therapist, and/or the parties involved. Ultimately, it is the judge and GAL who decide the functions. Attorneys certainly have, and often do exercise, an opportunity to review how the GAL functions on behalf of their clients.

GAL: A Call to Action

I'm supposed to shed the light
But first I need to know what's right;

Each constituent tries to pull my chain
Until they find out it's in vain;

So the children I do guard
And at times, the professionals I have to retard;

Travel here and there, guidance for all, reports to write
For children's interests and needs I do fight;

All in all, it's a rewarding task
Even though not much glory in which to bask;

But onward I hastily go
Happy the judge believes I really do know;

Each child is precious in their own way
And I work to encourage their say;

What's good for my young charge's life
Involves removing the embedded strife;

Wish me well in the noble mission of my choice
I have to go now—I hear a child's voice.

Appendices

A. Child Inventory of Parent's Characteristics

This checklist can be used in an interviewer or a parent and child can fill it out separately. Seeing both the agreement and differences can provide insights into the reunification process. The parent can check it off by what they think their child will say.

Father/Mother Does for Child

- ❑ 1. Loves me
- ❑ 2. Cares for me
- ❑ 3. Protects me throughout my life
- ❑ 4. Teaches me values
- ❑ 5. Teaches me life experiences
- ❑ 6. Sends me to the best schools
- ❑ 7. Sends me to camps and visits me
- ❑ 8. Provides (professional) counseling when needed
- ❑ 9. Helps me to set goals
- ❑ 10. Provides me with the best, safest transportation
- ❑ 11. Provides a good home
- ❑ 12. Provides me with food for my health and growth
- ❑ 13. Sets up trips/vacations
- ❑ 14. Has been there for me in hard times
- ❑ 15. Is a confidante (someone I can trust)
- ❑ 16. Is loyal to me
- ❑ 17. Is honest with me
- ❑ 18. Is a good role model
- ❑ 19. Has been planning and saving for the future so I can go to college
- ❑ 20. Takes time out of their day to attend my events
- ❑ 21. Has warned me of danger (peers, drugs, etc.)
- ❑ 22. Has tried to stop/prevent drug use so I'll be healthy
- ❑ 23. Worries about me
- ❑ 24. Has provided the best medical care possible for me

- ❑ 25. Has asked little of me except to be honest, fair, do well in school, and be respectful
- ❑ 26. Provides technology I can use
- ❑ 27. Encourages afterschool activities
- ❑ 28. Is there when I need them
- ❑ 29. Shares entertainment with me
- ❑ 30. Tells me to respect my other parent
- ❑ 31. Other things they do:

B. The Parent-Child Incompatibility Quiz

This quiz is employed to determine the child's attributes that may impede the Reunification process.

1. Do you remember conflicts and misunderstandings back into their childhood?
2. Do you have arguments that go nowhere?
3. Do you feel you had a breakthrough, only to find out things were worse than ever? If you saw small progress you got hopeful, only to have your hopes dashed?
4. Have you said to yourself, "I've tried everything humanly possible, and still no connection"?
5. Does the child seem to have values and behaviors that no one else in the family has?
6. Did you struggle to "show them the light" in their lousy selections of friends?
7. Does s/he never seem to learn from their mistakes?
8. Did s/he appear sincere ("I'm not drinking again") only to find out they lied all along?
9. Did they do things beyond your belief?
   a. Stole money from the family
   b. Had sex in your own house
   c. Stayed out and you didn't know where they were
   d. Got arrested
   e. Found only "friends" who were hardcore losers
10. Did s/he start fights with you for no reason, which resulted in you "losing it" for no reason?
11. Caused rifts within the family?
12. They were so extreme you actually considered or did throw them out?
13. You felt abused by your own child?
14. No therapist could really help?
    a. Some didn't get it.
    b. Others were parent blamers.
    c. Some just couldn't handle it.
15. You wondered where you went wrong.

16. You found letters, alcohol, drugs, sexual paraphernalia, etc., in your own home that they had bought or brought in?
17. When discovered they said, "It's not for me, it's for a friend."
18. They expected everything (food, money, car, help), but gave nothing back?
19. You spent nights thinking about what would magically change them?
20. You believed if you waited long enough, time would make things better?
21. You depended on them when you shouldn't?
22. You sense your personal health and happiness was being damaged?
23. You tried reason, pressure, control, guilt, manipulation, kindness, ignoring, confronting, and everything else—but failed?
24. The older they got, the more difficult it became?
25. They brought embarrassment to you and your family?
26. Your other children were angry with you for "not getting it"?
27. You didn't know how much more you could take?
28. The child accused you of what they were actually doing?
    a. Stealing their money
    b. Not being sensitive
    c. Not listening
    d. Being a control freak
    e. Ruining their lives
    f. Being selfish
    g. Etc.
29. You became convinced they were shortening your life?
30. You said to yourself, "If they weren't flesh and blood, I'd have nothing to do with them"?
31. Your predictions about what would happen were almost always right?
    a. That kid will get you into trouble—you'll get arrested if you . . .
    b. You're school work comes before pleasure—you'll pay a cost.
    c. You're pushing your family away and they may not be there when you need them.
32. They always had the wrong priorities?
    a. Bad peers
    b. Party time
    c. Self-indulgence
    d. Drugs
33. They had "discipline" for what they wanted, but never what you wanted?
34. They always expected a bailout in a crisis?
35. You were always there to pick up the pieces; they were never there when you needed them?
36. They'd disappear (even within the home) for long periods of time?

37. They were jealous of what the other children got, even if they got more?
38. They drained family resources?
    a. Money
    b. Time
    c. Love
    d. Energy
    e. Trust
39. They feed off of and create conflict—peace was not present when they were there?
40. They could not see their own gifts, talents, and capabilities? If you pointed them out they said you were pressuring them to be more like you. If you didn't acknowledge them, they said you didn't care.
41. You never felt like anything you did for them was appreciated or fully grasped?
42. They talked about how other friends or families were better and understood them?
43. You couldn't tell if their "depression" caused the drug problem, or vice versa?
44. They would stare you down or try to shout you down?
45. You felt their behaviors and agendas were ruining the "home" atmosphere you valued?
46. You secretly wished they would be out of your life?
47. You worried a lot about what would become of them?
48. You wandered when they would "get it"?
49. You were anxious when they were at family functions?
50. When they looked like they were on the path to sincerity, they would always do something to screw it up?
51. You felt stupid, weak, or just a failure because you couldn't turn them around?
52. You sensed you were, at times, enabling them but couldn't stop (helping) being there, or just plain caring?
53. You wished, at times, you didn't care so damn much?
54. You hoped it would get better with age and time, but you were wrong. The problems, needs, and demands got bigger and worse? You often felt better when they were gone for periods of time?
55. You wondered when, where, and how it would all end?
56. You tapped into family savings/retirement/loans to bail them out? If you ever challenged them (even nicely) they said, "It's my life," or "you're a control freak"?
57. They never paid you back, even if they promised?
58. You were warned by family, friends, and/or professionals that "they will be the death of you"?

59. Some even said, or you felt, you were "abused"?
60. You wondered what you did to deserve this lot in life?
61. You lost time from your jobs, careers, family, friends, and leisure to go to school, the police station, lawyers, therapists, and courts on their behalf?
62. You sensed you were being disrespectful to yourself by dealing with them (because they showed no respect to you)?
63. They could be nice—when they needed you, money, time, a ride, protection, a "witness," or some other personal need? The rest of their time—"out of their way."
64. You felt you were supporting a "stranger"?
65. You gave many sermons on life, love, friendship, caring, the future, trust, hope. None of it seemed to sink in?
66. Your stress levels were so high that others noticed it and expressed their worry about you?
67. You believed that a parent, with enough love and guidance could make the difference, but you saw that this was wrong?
68. They allowed others (boyfriends, girlfriends) to show disrespect and/or exploit you (eat your food, sleep in your house, etc.)?
69. You worried about your home, car, and personal property when you were not personally present?
70. There are non-blood relationships that you trust more than your child?
71. You were anxious in your own home?
72. There were uncomfortable periods of silence (in the car, etc.) when you couldn't speak?
73. There was usually "tension" in their presence?
74. They seemed happy, or not concerned, that you were upset?
75. If you were honest with them about the situation they always turned it back to you?
76. One of their favorite lines was, "I'm not talking about this anymore"?
77. You felt exploited by your own child?
78. You began to play into their anger (because your "buttons" could be pushed)?
79. You thought things you couldn't believe you were thinking?
80. They would punish you (silence, withdrawal, curing, insults, etc.) if they were caught and challenged?
81. You wished you had done it differently with them sooner?
82. At times, you may have felt they would hurt themselves (they may have even talked of suicide)?
83. They tried to pit people against each other?
    a. Parent and stepparent
    b. Parent and sibling
    c. Parent and therapist

84. They often succeed in their set-ups?
85. They came to value "street smarts" over "book smarts"?
86. They seem to "know it all"?
87. Their social skills (other than manipulation) were notably poor?
88. The good times were few and far between?
89. You couldn't see them clearly for a long time, because you thought the "turn around" was going to happen "this time"?
90. You kept trying to figure out what happened to them and/or what you did that caused this?
91. At times, you thought they were just plain evil?
92. You couldn't understand why they shouldn't get it after crashing and paying the consequences so many times?
93. They put themselves in harm's way (drunken parties, drugs, drinking and driving, deviant friends, out all night, bus hopping) but never made the connection that they chose the situation that then resulted in the chaos?
94. You wondered why they seemed so self-destructive?
95. They treated the "dregs" with respect and the respectful they treated terribly? They always seemed to have life's rules backwards?
96. "Peace" became your mantra? "I just want peace."
97. You swore you wouldn't help again, but you did, many, many times?
98. You felt, or heard, that your child hates you.
99. You loved, supported, saved, and gave time and time again only to have your face stamped on?
100. Eventually, you can envision being "divorced" from your own child (but may have felt guilty over that thought)?
101. They have rewritten history (you weren't there for them, they did so much for everybody, no one cared for them, etc.)?
102. You've thought about what they would think about at your funeral? (Did they get it now?)
103. You never believed children should be enemies, but that's what it feels like?
104. Although they hurt others greatly, they always ended up as victims?

C. Inventory of Child's Assets, Strengths, and Positive Qualities

	Very Poor 0	Poor 1	Fair 2	Good 3	Very Good 4	Excellent 5
Apologetic						
Balance Time Well						
Business Savvy						
Calm under Stress						
Computer Skill						
Creative						
Courteous						
Curious						
Diet and Nutrition						
Energetic						
Family Oriented						
Follows Through						
Frustration Tolerance						
Good Memory						
Good Reader						
Good Vocabulary						
Good with Language						

	Very Poor 0	Poor 1	Fair 2	Good 3	Very Good 4	Excellent 5
Good Writer						
Grades						
Handles Stress Well						
Helps the Underdog						
Helps with Animal Care						
Helps with Household Chores						
Homework						
Interaction with Extended Family						
Kind						
Leader						
Loves Animals						
Loving in General						
Loyal						
Manners						
Mechanical Skills						
Memory						
Methodical						
Musical						
Neat						
Organized						
Participation in Extracurricular Activities						
Patience						
Physical Coordination						
Planner						

	Very Poor 0	Poor 1	Fair 2	Good 3	Very Good 4	Excellent 5
Proactive						
Protective						
Respect for Father						
Respect for Mother						
Respect for Other Family Members						
Respect for Siblings						
Respect for Teachers						
Respectful in General						
Saves Money						
Sense of Direction						
Sensitive						
Sleep Patterns						
Smart Academically (Studies and Performance)						
Smart Socially (Reading People)						
Smart—Street Savvy						
Solution Oriented						
Sports Minded						
Stands Up for His Rights						
Tolerates Frustration						
Truthful						
Work Ethic						
Writes Well						
Other Qualities						

D. Predicting and Reacting to Possible Child Abduction

Legal System Factors

Factor	Brief Description	Presence of Factor			
		None	Low	Medium	High
Temporal—A long, drawn out case.	The longer the case has gone on, the greater the likelihood.				
Multiple filings and cross filings.	These cases often involve a multiplicity of real and falsified issues.				
Escalating and multiple claims against the target parent.	If one set of claims fails, others are filed.				
All filings fail to deter the target parent.	Many target parents persist to try to be with and raise their children.				
Hits upon a judge who sees the case clearly.	Judge identifies the more combative parent. This can trigger the abducting parent.				
Target parent is on the cusp of success or is awarded a change in their behavior.	The target parent is winning contact and influence.				

Attorney Issues

Factor	Brief Description	Presence of Factor			
		None	Low	Medium	High
They have been warned by an attorney to "get it together" or they can lose the child.	At this point, they will often fire their attorneys and if other flight risk factors are evident they could prepare to exit.				

Social-Emotional Factors between Parents and for the Abductor

Factor	Brief Description	Presence of Factor			
		None	Low	Medium	High
Communication between the parents is minimal and/or hostile.	Denying communication even about the child's needs is a way of denying the existence of the other parent. Kidnapping is the ultimate act of negating the need for the target parent.				
Objective reality does not change their negativity.	No judicial or professional input changes their views or behavior.				
Has programmed and brainwashed the child against the target parent.	Creates an "in group" that includes self and child, versus an "out group" that includes the target parent. Regularly denigrates the other parent to all who will listen.				

Expertise

Factor	Brief Description	Presence of Factor			
		None	Low	Medium	High
Threatens and/or litigates against experts.	These parents will often turn against experts, including their own or court-appointed experts.				
Consensus by most of the therapists, conciliators, and judges.	Most professionals are able to identify the problem parent. One of the parents is unchangeable and projects all blame onto the other parent in the face of no or contrary evidence.				

Antisocial Behavior

Factor	Brief Description	Presence of Factor			
		None	Low	Medium	High
Interference with visitation and court orders.	Has a history of interfering with court-ordered visitation, both in actuality and spirit.				
Consults with underground organizations or other social networks.	Contacts made to prepare flight.				
Entrapment and/or illegal activities.	Hires detectives, files frivolous law suits, hires hit men, damages the vehicle or other property of the target parent.				
Attempts to manipulate all legal, therapeutic, educational, and family members.	Presents stories, thoughts, issues, and problems to taint (the professionals') views they hold of the target parent.				

Personal Characteristics

Factor	Brief Description	Presence of Factor			
		None	Low	Medium	High
Parental network.	Joins with other parents who coach them on manipulation.				
Can't separate own needs from child's.	Merges personal needs with the child's needs.				
Doesn't heed warnings.	Doesn't heed warnings from experts or other professionals regarding what's best for the children.				
Stamina.	Successful in wearing down professionals, judges, and others.				
Isolation.	Will isolate child(ren), target parent, and others.				

Exit Activities

Factor	Brief Description	Presence of Factor			
		None	Low	Medium	High
Makes moving arrangements.	Use moving company or friend/relative to transfer or change property.				
Puts financial matters in order.	Liquidation of properties, investments and unusual banking activities are also indicators.				
They hold dual citizenship or have connections out of state or country.	Connects with social support networks in case of abduction.				

What To Do: Judges and Other Professionals

Factor	Brief Description	Presence of Factor			
		None	Low	Medium	High
Programming and brainwashing are always present.	Mental and social kidnapping always predate physical kidnapping.				
Know PKPA, UCCJA, and other laws.	Know these acts.				
Advise about consequences.	Detail consequences if conflict continues.				
Post bond.	Consider this as a way to limit flight risk.				
Retain passports.	Keep these, or give attorney(s) the responsibility.				
Monitored visitation.	Need supervisors who will file reports to the court.				
Counseling.	Should engage in goal-oriented conflict resolution counseling with feedback.				
Monitoring system.	Have some official provide feedback to the court.				
Investigate domestic violence allegations.	Need expert with no preconceived biases to act quickly.				
Educational programs.	Teach parents about the negative impact of conflict and abduction.				

Disengage child.	Get child out of the most dysfunctional relationship.				
Get solid experts.	Need experts who are neutral and who care about the child(ren).				
Don't give second chances.	If a parent is caught, don't give them a second chance.				
Stop dividing families.	Don't tolerate experts who make the problems worse.				
Share slate.	Link with other municipalities.				
Timely decisions.	Delays in issuing a ruling or evaluating a case can exacerbate problems.				
Special help for child(ren).	Special treatment for children—be specific in goals, timelines, and feedback.				
Specific custody orders.	Reduce misunderstandings and delineate consequences of noncompliance.				

E. Activity Checklist for Reunification, Custody, and Alienation Evaluations

It is helpful to know what parents have actually done with a child over time. Here is a sample list of some possible involvements that parents may have had with their children.

	Have Taken Child(ren) to			Participated in with Child(ren)		
Sports	**Never**	**Some**	**Often**	**Never**	**Some**	**Often**
Aerobics						
Baseball						
Basketball						
Boating						
Canoeing						
Catch						
Dance						
Fishing						
Football						
Golf						
Gymnastics						
Hiking						
Horseback Riding						
Hockey						
Hunting						
Ice Skating						
Jogging						
Martial Arts (Judo, Karate)						
Ping-Pong						
Racquetball						
Rugby						
Sailing						

Sports	Have Taken Child(ren) to			Participated in with Child(ren)		
	Never	Some	Often	Never	Some	Often
Sledding						
Skiing (cross-country/downhill)						
Soccer						
Snorkeling/SCUBA						
Swimming/Water Ballet						
Tennis						
Volleyball						
Walking						
Water-skiing						
Other						

Travel	Have Taken Child(ren) to			Participated In with Child(ren)		
	Never	Some	Often	Never	Some	Often
Local Trips						
Trips in the United States						
Foreign Travel						

Educational	Have Taken Child(ren) to			Participated In with Child(ren)		
	Never	Some	Often	Never	Some	Often
Reading						
Helping with Homework						
Tutoring						
PTA						
Homeroom Parent						
Classroom/School Volunteer						
Parent Teacher Conferences						
Computer Activities						
Helping with School Trips/ Parties/Games/Plays						
Music Lessons						
Helping with Music Practice						
Attending Concerts/Plays						

Visits to Museum	Have Taken Child(ren) to			Participated In with Child(ren)		
	Never	Some	Often	Never	Some	Often
Art Museums						
History Museums						
Science Museums						
Railroad/Antique Car Museum						
Aerospace Museums						
Industrial Museums						

Family Activities	Have Taken Child(ren) to			Participated In with Child(ren)		
	Never	Some	Often	Never	Some	Often
Amusement Parks						
Arts and Crafts						
Sporting Events						
Beach						
Birthday Parties						
Car/Bike/Motorcycle/Boat Maintenance						
Carpentry						
Cleaning						
Collecting (Stamps, Insects, Rocks, CDs, Cards, etc.)						
Cooking						
Gardening						
Holiday Celebrations						
Lawn/Yard Work						
Pet Care						
Playing Indoor Games						
Playing Outdoor Games						
Reading Stories						
Sewing						
Visiting Family						
Visits to Zoos or Parks						
Watching Television						
Other (specify)						

F. Research Techniques and Sample Characteristics

This study is a result of 40 years of research covering approximately 1,000 cases of alienation, reunification, and other forensic topics. The sample was obtained as the result of various types of case referrals, including court orders, attorney agreement, GAL initiated, as well as client and other professional referrals. Research methods included the following:

1. Participant observation of children with their parents and other family members
2. Private interviews with children
3. Private interviews with parents
4. Group interventions with children and parents
5. Review and evaluations of court hearing transcripts
6. Participation in the legal process at various phases
7. Selected observations of interactions of clients with their attorneys (and at times opposing counsel)
8. Meeting and evaluating members of the extended family
9. Meeting members of the community and friends/neighbors of the families
10. Observing children in their homes
11. Discussing cases with lawyers from across the United States and abroad
12. Meeting with judges, conciliators, guardians ad litem, parenting coordinators, and other members of the court systems
13. Consultations with social workers, psychologists, psychiatrists, clinical sociologists, mediators, family therapists, and others involved in the process of dealing with families in transition
14. Responding to crisis-intervention requests from therapists, parenting coordinators, lawyers, counselors, parents, and children
15. Meeting with school officials
16. Meetings with members of various religious communities
17. Review and study of diaries by children, parents, and others related to the cases
18. Analysis of counseling, mediation, parenting coordinator, and therapy sessions and reports

19. Participation in various phases of follow-up on all of the preceding
20. Use of structured interviews/schedules for assessment of custodial considerations
21. Contacts with agencies such as Children and Youth Services
22. Evaluation of forensic reports
23. Visits to hospitals to meet children and professionals
24. Contact with police departments, other law enforcement personnel, and DA's offices where applicable
25. Contact with other researchers, clinicians, and authors
26. Assessment of testimony by expect witnesses
27. Referrals and visits to drug rehabilitation facilitates

As a result of this multi-method approach to data collection and study, the research was organized around central themes relevant to reunification issues that became the basis for our chapter headings.

One of the primary motivations in undertaking this study was to be able to delineate the phenomenon that attorneys, judges, parents, counseling professionals, parenting coordinators, mediators, guardians, and others were constantly telling us was one of their overriding concerns, that is, how to re-bond parents and children, why efforts fail, what are the therapies that work, when should Reunification Therapy not be undertaken, is alienation the exclusive cause, what orders work best, and programming/brainwashing. Judges seemed especially concerned with understanding the bases of children's opinions—for example, are they credible? Where do their ideas come from? Did one parent unduly influence them? How much weight should be given to a child's opinion? On what basis were the child's opinions, ideas, or stated observations founded? Attorneys often sought to understand what their clients were or were not doing with their children in order to better advise and assist them in the legal or reunification process. Attorneys wanted more knowledge of the process that may be impacting on their client and the children. Parents were deeply frustrated, either because they were accused of unduly influencing a child or because they were the recipients of the influence that another parent exercised over a child (in other words, they were the "target" parent). Children regularly expressed dismay, anger, hostility, and other social-emotional reactions in regard to being involved in a one-sided or cross-fire situation in which one parent was assaulting another. Children often solicited our guidance in order to extricate themselves from the process. Children were, at times, hostile to re-bonding. Why? What history is relevant? In order to be able to deal with these and other issues, we felt it necessary to thoroughly research the process and be able to categorize the phenomenon.

One of the first tasks of social and behavioral science is to develop typologies. In this sense, our study was initially heavily descriptive, though the years of study also allowed us to make an initial analysis as to the reasons for a parent's involvement in the causal factors and subsequent reunification process. Many of these cases were followed up for a period of years (some for as long as 10 to 25 years) so that some understanding could be obtained of the longitudinal effects of Reunification Therapy and high conflict divorces, as well as to determine where and how the process has changed. However, this study does deal with these latter issues more than the first edition. A future publication will address the issues of the longer-term consequences in even more detail.

G. Divorce Is a Process

Uncoupling Components[1]:

Financial
Residential
Sexual
Familial
Hopes
Dreams
Duties
Children Sharing Duties
Friends
Future (Plans)
Problem Solving
Gestalt
Promises
Possessions

Occurs over Time

Divorce Can Be Caused By:
Financial Factors
Communication Weaknesses
Unrealistic Expectations (Happy)
Problem-Solving Skills (or lack thereof)
Other Attractions
Cultural Misunderstandings
Sexual Issues
In-Law Intrusions
Taking Marriage for Granted
Role Modeling
Low Social Skills

Some Social Correlations with Family and Divorce Phenomena:

Income
Social Class
Religion
Regionality
Ethnicity
Race
Communication Skills
Values
Common Experiences (or lack thereof)
Philosophy of Relationships
Family Cultures
Age
Family History of Divorce

1. Elements that were impacted of divorcing/separating couples

H. Examples of Parental Statements Challenging the Reunification Process

1. He/she doesn't really care about the child.
2. They have no or limited history of child rearing.
3. They never came to any of the child's functions or school meetings (in the past).
4. It's really all about child support.
5. They are just trying to break me (financially and/or emotionally).
6. My child is afraid or anxious.
7. I have doctors who would tell you this is a bad idea.
8. I'm out of this. I won't sit in the same room with him/her.
9. Good luck. This is our ____ (numbered) attempt.
10. I hope you won't hurt __________ (child's name).
11. How do you make the child go if he/she doesn't want to?
12. I have people you should talk to first so you understand what you're getting into.
13. I don't think it's a good idea for them to be alone.
14. I think this will make her medical issues worse.
15. Just telling him/her about it brought on more migraines.
16. He/she is so close to their stepfather/stepmother that they already have another (main) parent bond.
17. They (the other parent) have a bad lifestyle.
18. They (the other parent) has a drug history.
19. They (the other parent) have hyper-sexual interests (e.g., pornography).
20. They (the other parent) are living with the person who broke up our family and the child knows it.
21. The timing isn't right now. The child may come around (in months, years, etc.).
22. The child is so worried that it is impacting on their school work.
23. I simply cannot afford it.
24. This is a form of child abuse.
25. I'm watching you carefully.
26. I insist on taping your sessions.
27. I need to be in the building during the session for her safety.

I. Children Who Refuse to Visit

Reasons Why Children Will Not Visit

1. Loyalty conflicts.
2. Aligning with one parent and simultaneously rejecting the other.
3. The child learns that in order to be loved and accepted, he/she must choose to reside only with the programmer/brainwasher (Threat of Withdrawal of Love Syndrome).
4. Protectiveness of "victimized" parent who may be lonely or sad while the child visits the other parent.
5. The child experiences anxiety or fear related to visiting one parent. Anxiety or fear can be induced by the other parent over a period of time. The child associates fear with the target parent and "refuses" to visit.
6. Many adolescents refuse or resist visitation for some of the following reasons:
   a. To punish the target parent for some perceived misdeed (a punishment, restrictions, curfew, or chores).
   b. The child is jealous of a parent's new relationship, stepparent, or stepsibling(s) or does not have a good relationship with the parent's "new family."
   c. The child is "bored" in comparison to more activities at the other home (or more compatible activities).
   d. The child's peer network is at the other parent's home.
7. The child is acting out his/her own anger or hostilities for the separation or divorce.
8. The child may have been given inappropriate information by a programmer/brainwasher, such as:
   a. "Your father destroyed our family with this divorce."
   b. "He pays no support for you. If he really loved you, he would."
   c. "Your mom wanted an abortion, but I wanted you."
9. Restriction of permission to love the target parent ("Dad says that if I go to live with mom, that I'll never see him again.")

10. The child may have adopted the other parent's negative thoughts, beliefs, opinions, and observations regarding the target who may be thoroughly disliked.
11. The parent-child relationship may have become discordant, hostile, and argumentative due to programming/brainwashing. The target parent, unaware of these dynamics and/or of intervention strategies, witnesses the parent-child relationship becoming seriously damaged.

Remedies

1. Have the court order explained directly to the child by a trained personnel (judge, conciliator, GAL, etc.).
2. Create a follow-up schedule in order to measure compliance on a timely basis. This can be done by the judge, GAL, or other personnel appointed for this purpose.
3. Develop a profile of the problem types in order to be able to better identify the likelihood of a particular child not complying with a court order.
4. Explain the court order to the parents and indicate to them how they are expected to help with the compliance.
5. Develop a list of penalties for noncompliance.
6. Develop a support system to aid in compliance.
7. Insist that the parents participate in custody conflict resolution counseling when indicated. (For example, in order to reduce the loyalty conflict for a child who has been identified as experiencing them.)
8. Get the parent(s) who is the most resistant to reinforce the court order in front of the child.
9. Identify the residential issues that may be facilitating noncompliance. Develop specific suggestions for these issues (such as when a child refuses to go to a home because he/she may be experiencing physical conflict with a stepsibling).
10. Identify particular losses that a child may be experiencing as a result of an increased visitation order (peer group losses, activity loss, etc.). Build a compensatory schema.

J. Recommendations for Alienation-Based Cases

1. Focus on reconciliation, not antagonisms (cut off hostilities if they go on too long).
2. Use past stories to reaffirm the love bond where possible.
3. Help them to understand that the more distant they are, the worse it gets.
4. Reaffirm that nonbonded parent's love is real.
5. Educate why family bonds are important (private with children).
6. Get bonded parent to support reunification (publicly).
7. See each child separately as well as jointly and work with their positive history.
8. Reaffirm why we are here (solution focused).
9. Challenge and rework distortions ("You're ruining my life"). Their lack of acceptance is a factor in creating some problems.
10. A parent is not supposed to disappear. "A new dad." No, this is not correct.
11. Don't look doubtful. Be directional.
12. Don't ask unnecessary empowerment questions ("What can your father do?")
13. Use self-fulfilling prophecies ("Things will get better as we relax and do new behaviors," "All kids know initially that they need the love of both parents.")

K. Predictor Cues of an Abusive Relationship

❑	1. Put downs, character assaults, attacks personal dreams and hopes
❑	2. Frequent (intentional) interruptions
❑	3. Other blamers (profanity develops)—"It's always your fault"
❑	4. Self-absorbed (personal needs come first)
❑	5. Threats (to leave, divorce, etc.)
❑	6. Silent treatment/glaring commonly used
❑	7. Attempts to isolate you from friends/relatives
❑	8. Uses minor incidents as a catalyst for fighting (inability to prioritize)
❑	9. Conflict omnipresent (tensions)
❑	10. False make-ups ("I'll change, I'm sorry"—recycle)/honeymoon period
❑	11. Uses sex as only a form of closeness—controls this
❑	12. Drugs pre-date arguments (alcohol, etc.)
❑	13. Secrecy ("This is our life—no one else should be involved in our affairs")
❑	14. Jealousy, exaggerated suspicions
❑	15. Restricts development/growth (intellectual, social, economic, educational)—"my way"
❑	16. Angry/upset more often than happy/peaceful
❑	17. Negative (more than positive) focus
❑	18. Control is a basic theme (obedience—sets direction, monetary budget, social control)
❑	19. Need to be right (others are stupid, short-sighted, etc.)
❑	20. Creates anxiety ("victim" is upset, don't know why)
❑	21. Instigates shame and self-doubt—confused—losing identity; self-confidence weakens
❑	22. Physical incidents—intimidation (finger-pointing, fear of being hit, etc.)
❑	23. Words/actions disconnected ("I love you" vs. "get out of my life")
❑	24. Makes you pursuer in the relationship—also apologizing for things
❑	25. Takes more than gives
❑	26. Rejects need for help—know-it-all ("counselors are stupid")
❑	27. Has relational problems elsewhere and in the past
❑	28. "Causes scenes"—hollering/screaming—embarrassment
❑	29. Guilt inducer ("After all I've done for you")
❑	30. Assertions of knowing yourself better than you know yourself

L. Risk Assessment Factors: A Brief Inventory of Considerations[1]

Case Name:
Key Parties:

- Adults
- Children

Court Order:

- Specificity of Professionals Duties, Timelines, & Authority
- Goals Set
- Protection of Professionals Articulated
- GAL or Other Monitoring Available
- Reporting Requirements for Professionals
    - o To Whom
    - o Frequency
    - o Form
    - o Done To Date

Length of Case: __________ Months: __________ Years: __________
Litigation History:

- A New Case → Serial Attempts for Resolution

Professional History:

- First Time → Serial Attempts

Past Success vs. Partial Success vs. None:

- Outcomes
- Partial Success
- No Success
- Regression

1. This inventory can be used in conjunction with the items detailed under Risk Assessment starting on page 174.

Levels of Cooperation:

- Parents
  - o Seeking Parent
  - o Bonded Parent
- Child(ren)
- Extended Family Members
- Other Professionals

Past Treatment Plan:

- New Case → None Written → Many Plans
- Are Copies Available?

Problematic Aspects:

- No or Poor Understanding of Reunification Therapy Process, Content, and/or Goals
- Child Socio-Psychological Problems/Issues
- Parent Socio-Psychological Problems/Issues
  - o Seeking Parent
  - o Bonded Parent
- Threats of Self-Harm (child)
  - o Details
  - o Dates
  - o Treatment, if any
- Medication History
  - o Type
  - o Purpose
  - o Treating/Prescribing Doctor(s)
- Peer Problems
- Sibling Conflict(s)
  - o With Whom
  - o Content
- Threats to Seeking Parent (if any)[2]
- Other Threats/Lawsuits
  - o Against Other Parent
  - o Against Professionals
- Cooperation Problems
- Separation Problems for Child and/or Parent
- (Exaggerated) Fearful Claims against Parent Seeking Reunification
  - o What Fears?
  - o Are They Reality Based?

---

2. Threats may need to be taken seriously. For an article that displays an unfortunate outcome to a case, please see Erin McCarthy, *In Radnor Wawa, 30 Seconds of Terror: How a Years-Long Custody Battle Escalated to Murder*, THE PHILADELPHIA INQUIRER (Apr. 6, 2019), https://www.inquirer.com/news/pennsylvania/wawa-shooting-radnor-delaware-county-main-line-20190406.html.

- Past Socio-Legal Issues
  - o Contempt Citations
  - o Drug Use/Abuse
  - o Felonies
  - o Misdemeanors
  - o Threats to Harm
  - o Agency Involvements
- Compliance with Court Ordered and/or Professional Release

Factors Facilitating Reunification Therapy	Factors Impeding Reunification Therapy[3]
1.	
2.	
3.	
4.	
5.	

This tool can be used to overview a potential Reunification Therapy case. The parameters may not only limit the scope, content, and the length of a case but could also set boundaries for some parties possibly not understanding the process at all. It also helps to set starter concerns, conditions, and frameworks.

Risk to all parties are evaluated with a special focus on the child. Physical, social/emotional safety is taken into account. At times, these factors may come to light once the case begins rather than be fully available prior to the initiation of the case.

Conditions of Risk: Concerns and Case Acceptance Factors

Check all that apply. Explain the rationale for each condition.

	Conditions of Risk	Rationale
❑	Concerns about Any Problematic Aspects	
	Of Timing (When to Start)	
	Parties	
	Methods	
	Projected Length	

3. For a comprehensive listing of facilitating and impeding factors, please see Chapter 6, "Impeding and Facilitative Factors."

	Conditions of Risk	Rationale
❑	Concerns about Helpful Supportive Aspects	
	Seeking Parent	
	Bonded Parent	
	Other Family Members	
	Professionals	
	GAL	
	Others	
❑	Can be Undertaken with the Following Guidelines/ Recommendations	
	Need More Legal Clarity	
	Better Parent Collaboration/Support	
	Individual Work with One or Both Parents Prior to Initiation Is Indicated	
	Constraints on Past Negative Behaviors	
	Lawsuit Potentials	
	Threats to Various Parties	
	Inappropriate Challenges	
	Noncompliance with Court Order/Agreement	
	Other	
❑	Do Not Undertake at this Time	
	Defer Case	
	Time and Conditions	

M. Intake Information for Initiating Reunification Services

- Children's Names and Ages
- Special Needs, if Any
- Children's Educational Placement and Grade
- (Ex)Spouse/(Ex)Partner's Name and Age
- Present Relational Statuses for Both Parents
- Residence(s)—Parents and Children
- Contact and Parenting History for Both Parents
- Present Contact Level and Type Between Parents and Children, if Any
- Religious Affiliation for Parents and Children, if Any
    - o Practicing—Yes or No
- Legal History
    - o Filings, Dates, Adjudications, Judge or Master, etc.
- Present Order or Agreement
- Names of Attorneys and Contact Information
- GAL Information, if Any
- Previous Attempts at Reunification Therapy and Results
- Present Therapist, if Any
- Levels and Types of Commitments to Reunification Therapy

Next is a checklist for parents of ways they are willing to help the reunification process.

Ways I Can Help the Reunification Process/Alienation Assessment

Check All That Apply

❑ 1. Get child(ren) to appointments/visits on time.

❑ 2. Support the therapy process.

❑ 3. Support the approaches of the Reunification Therapist, process, and any matters related to alienation.

❑ 4. Learn new ideas.

- ❑ 5. Learn and practice new scripts for communication.
- ❑ 6. Try to improve my communication with the other parent.
- ❑ 7. Get others to be helpful:
    - ❑ a. Sibling(s)
    - ❑ b. Grandparent(s)
    - ❑ c. Old Friends
    - ❑ d. DAs
    - ❑ e. School
    - ❑ f. Other Relatives
    - ❑ g. Others_______________
- ❑ 8. Stop any behavior that might negatively impact on the child(ren) or process.
- ❑ 9. Participate in joint sessions with child(ren).
- ❑ 10. Participate in joint sessions with the other parent.
- ❑ 11. Participate in joint sessions with_________ (child's name).
- ❑ 12. Keep a progress log and share it with the Reunification Therapist.
- ❑ 13. Self-correct if I make mistakes.
- ❑ 14. Keep to the court order or agreement as per its guidelines.
- ❑ 15. Not say anything negative about the other parent, the process, or the professional.
- ❑ 16. Ask questions if something is not clear.
- ❑ 17. Speak up to the Reunification Therapist if I have any concerns or issues in order for them to be addressed.
- ❑ 18. Stay or leave the therapy center as requested.
- ❑ 19. Share ideas that will help the goal.
- ❑ 20. Be open to constructive criticism.

N. Checklist of Possible Releases Noted by the Court and/or by Professionals Related to Reunification Therapy

- ❑ Fee Arrangements and Conditions
- ❑ Confidentiality Conditions
- ❑ Credentials of the Professional
- ❑ The Reunification Therapy Process with Varied Components
- ❑ Exit Conditions for the Professional
- ❑ Testimony—Options and Conditions
- ❑ Permissions to Communicate with Other Parties—Specified
- ❑ Indemnification
- ❑ Pro Se Cases—Do you take or not take these types of cases?
- ❑ Professional's Area(s) of Expertise Identified
- ❑ Reports/Memos—Texts, E-mails, etc.—Types of Communications that Are Accepted
- ❑ Areas of Support that May Be Needed—Psychological, Psychiatric, Sociological, Medical, Educational, Legal, Co-Parenting Expert, GAL, etc.
- ❑ Conferences—Legal and Others
- ❑ Combinations of Meetings—Mixing and Matching Parents and Children (and Others, if Needed)

O. Sample Sources of Referral (Approximate Breakdown)[1]

Referral Source	Number of Cases	Percentage
Court Order[2]	134	62%
GAL Referred	10	5%
Attorney Agreed Upon	30	20%
Self-Referral	16	8%
Previous Client	10	5%
Totals:	**200**	**100%**

1. This is a sample of 200 cases taken out of approximately 1,000 separations/divorces over an approximate 40-year period. Information, patterns, and experiences were drawn from the entire population. Interviews with judges, lawyers, GALs, therapists, co-parenting counselors, (step)parents, teachers, coaches, grandparents, paramours, clergy, mediators, medical doctors, masters, and children from the entire database informed much of the book.

2. These represent different levels of litigation from case beginning before a first trial to many trials or legal conferences. Some involve Reunification Therapy while litigation is ongoing and forensic evaluations are taking place.

Glossary of Reunification-Related Terms

Abuse. Damaging the child's physical, social-psychological, cultural, and affiliation realities and potentials.

Acting in. A behavior in which children turn their social-emotional problems inward as a way of coping with the programming/brainwashing or other negative features of their parent's breakup. Pent-up emotions, blaming self, and states of confusion are some manifestations.

Acting out. A behavior in which the children direct their social-emotional problems onto the external environment—other people, institutions, or objects—as a way of coping with the programming/brainwashing or other negative features of their parent's breakup. Aggression, hostility, drug-taking, blaming, and manipulation are some manifestations.

Alienation. One result of a programming/brainwashing process that often results in the estrangement of the child from the target parent. Historically, this term was originally used by Karl Marx to signify estrangement from work, family, others, and, ultimately, oneself.

Aligned parent. The parent with whom the child is more identified and bonded (at the time of reunification). Also see Connected parent.

Alignment. Process whereby a child begins to side with one parent over another.

Alliance. An affiliation that can either support or hinder a re-bonding process.

Alternative explanations. These are all possible causes of broken bonds (other than or in addition to alienation).

Ambivalence. A technique employed by the programming/brainwashing parent that often confuses the child. Both positive and negative messages are issued in regard to the target parent. Contrasting feelings can develop in the child toward the target parent because the child loved the target parent historically but is under pressure to modify his or her positive feelings and behaviors into negative ones.

Anger directed toward both parents. Children begin to develop negative feelings toward both parents as a result of the programming/brainwashing process or other negative adult behaviors.

Anxiety arousal. A technique employed by programming/brainwashing parents that induces uneasiness, distress, worry, and agitation in the child. It may also be studied in discovering particular fears inculcated into the child by the alienating parent.

Anxiety theory. This is one of 19 different "theories" that children, parents, and/or professionals sometimes posit as excuses to not engage in the reunification process. It refers to the child being upset in dealing with and/or being in the presence of the parent seeking to improve the parent-child bond.

Arbitrator. A professional (legally appointed or agreed upon) who possesses decision-making authority.

Backlash/backfire effect. When a child turns against an alienation program, an alienating parent, and/or the professionals. The child can develop values, attitudes, opinions, and behaviors that are in contrast to those set in motion and desired by others.

Behavioral regression. An impact factor whereby children withdraw as they are forced to close off from the target parent; a return to earlier developmental behaviors may occur—bed-wetting, baby talk, clinging, or the reinstitution of early childhood fears/phobias.

Belief patterns. A constellation of individual beliefs that are often placed under one or more central themes. The themes might have to do with effective parenting, lifestyle issues, who is the better parent, and/or a belief about where the child will be better off in the future. Parents will often try to connect past and present events in a distorted way to create a problematic belief structure that will hinder the child's affiliation with the target parent.

Biased evaluators. Professionals who often start out with a pro-mother, pro-father, or pro-joint/sole custody stance or may have some other underlying bias. Parenting coordinators, therapists, conciliators, and others who are performing family problem-solving functions should have neutral and objective perspectives.

Birthright. The belief that a parent has special rights and influences because of their biological linkage to a child. Some may also use the term to refer to a child's right to love and be loved by their birth parents.

Bonding/social bonding. It is a process of developing close, interpersonal relationships between parents and children. There are different types and intensities of social bonding. It is also used to explain linkages between siblings and extended family members.

Brainwashing. The actual selection and application of particular techniques, procedures, and methods as bases for inculcating a negative program or belief system about the target parent.

Bridge-building techniques. Building or rebuilding relational connections between a target parent and a child. These techniques are not traditional therapeutic techniques, but new social interventions for (re)establishing social bonds with or without alienation present.

Broken bonds. These are the breaches, damages, disintegration, and losses that occur(ed) between a parent and child.

Bubble busting. Refers to challenging elements of a relationship that need to be understood (and sometimes analyzed) in order to reestablish healthy social bonds.

Can't change theory. This is one of the 19 "theories" employed by children, parents, and/or professionals to resist the reunification process. It asserts that an individual hasn't changed up until now, and, therefore, cannot change in the future. (It can also be called a "negative prophecy.")

Character assault. A technique employed by programming/brainwashing parents that attacks the moral, social, spiritual, educational, or other dimensions of the target parent's character, integrity, and image.

Chemistry isn't there theory. This is one of the 19 "theories" employed by children, parents, and/or professionals to resist the reunification process. It suggests that there is an invisible force that links people, which was either never there or has been (significantly) damaged or dissipated.

Child as parent's best friend. A detection factor (also in alienation scenarios) by adults who do not employ parental direction, guidance, and authority; they usually act as a peer to the child. This has the effect of undermining authority or discipline that may be exercised by the target parent who believes he or she should exercise appropriate role prerogatives of a "parent." Being "best friends" draws the child into the relationship with the programming/brainwashing (alienating) parent.

Child centered. A parent who has, as their main focus, the life and well-being of the child, suggesting that the child is their highest priority.

Child cynicism. An attitudinal component developed by children that contains negative perspectives about a parent, professional assistance, past history, or hope for the future.

Child Protective Services (CPS). A social agency that deals with investigations related to allegations of child abuse and neglect, as mandated by individual state laws. Also see Children and Youth Services (CYS).

Child threatens parent. A detection factor evidenced by children who issue challenging or aggressive messages to the target parent. This exists in both alienation and non-alienation related cases. These messages may be in the form of blackmail, control, and/or rejection of the target parent's authority. Some may physically threaten and/or attack the target parent. This is usually transferred aggression from the programming/brainwashing parent with the child as the vehicle.

Children and Youth Services (CYS). A social agency that deals with investigations related to allegations of child abuse and neglect, as mandated by individual state laws. Also see Child Protective Services (CPS).

Choosing the best deal. An (alienating) impact factor whereby children receive overt and covert bribes in order to side with a programming/ brainwashing parent and then must choose what to do. "We did have Disney World planned in June, but. . . ."

Clarity. The degree to which a mental health labels and processes are understandable to professionals, the court, and parents.

Client management. The ability and degree to which a lawyer can guide and direct a case with the support and understanding of their client.

Coaching behavior. A detection tool that is revealed by prodding behavior on the part of programming/brainwashing parents; it is most readily observable when children take statements out of context and, secondarily, use highly sophisticated adult language. "Say what's in your heart, dear."

Coercion of ideas. Forcing a child to have ideas that mirror those of the brainwashing parent and that are often damaging to the child and his/her relationship with the target parent.

Collaborative isolation process. A process whereby a parent and a children join together in what appears to be a unified group against what has been defined as outside forces. A collaborative isolation process is identified by words like we, us, and our family. The isolation component is an attempt to stay separate from the target parent, both physically and/or social-psychologically. Coercive labeling, such as calling the target parent by his/her first name is an example. "You have to go to Bill's house today." This relabeling can result in modifications of social identity. (For example, the belief that the target parent is no longer a real parent.) This process can also be executed towards evaluators and others to "freeze out" the target parent or anyone who does not buy into the distortions of reality. Also see In-group/out-group.

Collusive. The incorporation of the child into the belief patterns, thoughts, and behaviors of the bonded (programming/brainwashing) parent.

Compartmentalization. A social-psychological process where separate categories are set up in the thinking process. Compartments of "good parent" vs. "bad parent," "loving" vs. "unloving," "supportive" vs. "not supportive," "paying support" vs. "not paying support" are identified by the programming/brainwashing parent and reinforced through a repetition process. Eventually, children come to think in these separate (and often dichotomous) categories. Some judges, lawyers, and other professionals have referred to this as "black-and-white thinking." There is often a deep curiosity as to how children come to develop this "black-and-white" view of a parent and their life, when in fact, reality exists in shades of gray or even the reverse of what the child has come to believe.

Compliance. The fourth stage of the programming-and-brainwashing process whereby the child begins to demonstrate that he or she shares the attitudes, beliefs, opinions and, ultimately, the behaviors that the programmer/brainwasher desires.

Conciliator. A private or court related/appointed professional who attempts to mediate socio-legal issues between two or more parties.

Conditional love. Love employed by (programming/brainwashing) parents that is based on the child's acceptance of their ideas, values, opinions, and behaviors concerning the target parent. This also makes children more vulnerable; it predisposes them to greater negative impact from the programming/brainwashing process.

Conditions of noncompliance. The factors that surround a child's behavior when they do not "go along with the program." The more physical/social-psychological contact the child has with the target or seeking parent, the less likely compliance is to take place. Social styles and personality conflicts of the programming/brainwashing parent and the child may also be a factor. Deep historical bonding with the target parent may counterbalance the programming/brainwashing parent's assaults. Also, strong court orders and judicial follow-up can often assist in supporting a child's noncompliance with the target parent. Noncompliance can also refer to reactions to court orders and/or a therapist's suggestions.

Confusion of a birth parent's importance. A detection factor revealed by children who have come to diminish the significance of the biological (or social) parent; they have received subtle or obvious inputs regarding this attitude from the negative (programming/brainwashing) parent. Physical punishment, isolation, bribery, distortion, and other techniques are often used in order to obtain this end. "It's (more) important for you to be with your peers, at your age."

Connected parent. Another term reflecting a higher degree and social and psychological linkage between a parent and child. Also see Aligned parent.

Constructed memory. The ability to create recollections that are exaggerated, distorted, inverted, and/or fabricated. Memories can also be deleted as part of a reconstruction process. Also see Memory creation.

Contempt citation. A legal filing where a parent is alleged to have violated a court order or directive. A judge may adjudicate that a parent is in contempt (they have violated the order) or not in contempt. Hostile (programming/brainwashing) parents usually (repeatedly) violate the (spirit of) the court orders and guidelines. Precision, monitoring, and accountability will lessen their ability to undermine a court order.

Contextual memory. The ability to stimulate recollections, understandings, and/or emotions by placing a subject (child) into a different physical and/or social setting.

Continuances. A legal request by an attorney or client who is pro se (represents themselves) to continue the case at another time. Various reasons can be given for the continuance. Judges may or may not grant continuances. Some negative (programming/brainwashing) parents use this as a tool for keeping the status quo, causing stress, and creating financial pressures, if it is to their advantage.

Continuity and family history. An argument historically more often employed by women, and now by more men than in the past, that states that they have had the majority of contact and upbringing experience with the children, and that, therefore, they should continue in this role; it can also serve as a platform for messages to the child.

Control freak. A popular term to refer to individuals who seek to relegate all or many aspects of life in regard to the child. How frequently they speak on the telephone, the number of minutes that they spend with another parent, and measuring the exact time and place in terms of location are just a few areas of possible control. Attempts to control school and medical records and other aspects of a child's life are also common. Another popular term today is helicopter parents. This refers to parents who hover over their children. This behavior seems to increase for parents who target the other parent in negative terms.

Co-parenting. A process whereby two or more parents work together to assist in raising a child. It involves coordinating schedules; levels of respectability; types of communication; and agreements on medical, educational, social, and other core aspects of a child's life. Co-parenting experts are now developing into a separate professional sphere.

Corrective process. A professional's ability to assist in modifying beliefs, histories, behaviors, and understandings that are (factually) incorrect or distorted.

Court monitor. A person who can be appointed by the court to oversee the execution of a court order. Also see Guardian ad litem.

Court order. A set of guidelines issued by a member of the court or a judge directing a party or parties to perform certain behaviors. Some orders imply or state sanctions for noncompliance.

Covert participation. A behavioral style that (programming/ brainwashing) parents use in which they appear not to be doing anything "upfront," but behind the scenes they are manipulating time, ideas, environments, professionals, and other areas of the child's life. Detection may be difficult because of the clever nature of the discreet behaviors. These parents will often make statements like "I really don't know what you are talking about," after they have carefully orchestrated a vacation that interferes with the time of the other parent.

Credibility. Believability of a person's opinions and statements of fact; the likelihood that the person (child) issued the "facts" of his or her own accord (versus the presence of coercive and manipulative mechanisms).

Crisis intervention. A skill necessitated by reunification experts to assist with social-psychological trauma and threats to self-harm or harming others. In Reunification Therapy, it can also refer to a party's attempt to interfere with a court order and related acts of noncompliance. Verbal, reputational, and other attacks against the therapist can also activate this skill set.

Cross-examination. The interrogation of a witness who has already testified by direct examination. The goal is often to challenge the knowledge, factual basis, ethics, and credibility of the witness's testimony.

Crossover. A social-psychological (and possibly physical) state whereby a child enters into a highly rigid position of negativity in regard to a target or seeking parent. Sometimes they (the child) can be brought back to a place of improved bonding.

Cross-programming. A common process where both parents are performing programming/brainwashing (alienating) behaviors on the same child, often at the same time. This creates high levels of confusion, distortion, anger, and possible self-isolation (in order to avoid both sets of messages) on the child's part. These are the cases where children will often ask if they can live with a grandparent or ask for help in stopping the behavior of both of their parents. This dynamic creates a lack of any safe haven for the child. They tend to placate both parents and can appear as two different children. They may even seek a safe haven with another family.

Custodial involvements. The degree of legal and or physical involvement that a parent has. The legal custodial involvement leads to rights to make decisions in regard to core areas of the child's life (educational, medical, peer group, travel, special needs, etc.) and physical contact specified during a given week and/or holidays. In some cases, custodial contact can set court as ordered supervision; these cases usually involve conditions where the court has become convinced that there is some jeopardy to the child.

Dangling love. An aspect of conditional love whereby programming and brainwashing parents hold out the reward of affection and caring until the child conforms to the negative attitudinal and behavioral characteristics toward the target parent that they desire.

Delusional (Disorder). A new term being employed in the custody literature that relates to the reality distortions discussed in the alienation literature. Reality is modified or reversed. "Mommy never loved me."

Denial-of-existence factor. A series of techniques used to deny or to not acknowledge the social existence of the other (target) parent.

Deprogramming. Treatment procedures and techniques employed in order to correct, neutralize, modify, clarify, terminate, reverse, and/or reduce the impact of programming/brainwashing on the child. It consists of re-labeling, moral assertions, interrupting, contrasting, challenging, re-establishing the relational history, reorienting, re-equilibrating, and accepting (to name a few of the components of the process). Target parents can use these corrective measures also. Therapy centers that isolate the child for periods of time to correct alienation should be evaluated and possibly utilized with caution. Risk assessments are indicated.

Desire to move or leave a geographical area. This can serve as a basis for relational distancing. Economic factors may drive the relocation.

Detection factors for possible alienation. Those factors that may be used in identifying the presence and intensities of programming/brainwashing. They include contradictory statements, inappropriate information, character assault, collusion, children becoming a spy, use of indirect statements, restriction of permission to love and be loved, unchildlike statements, good parent versus bad parent mentality, comparative martyr role, inducing fear of contact with the other parent, anxiety arousal, secret keeping, child appears as mirror image of alienating parent, confusion of a birth parent's importance, manifestations of guilt, scripted views, unmanageability for no apparent reason, radical changes and dysfunctional behavior, nonverbal messages, coaching behaviors, "brain twirling," children threatening their parents, child as parent's best friend, and physical survival messages.

De-unification. This is an unusual situation whereby a child is looking for disengagement from one or both parents. They may seek deeper affiliations with grandparents, another relative, or a family of a friend.

Diagnostic utility. The degree to which a mental health label is useful in understanding the phenomenon of parent-child relationships and developing a treatment plan. Caution should be exercised in regard to the exclusive use of psychological labels, as estrangement, alienation, and bonding problems are fundamentally social processes (even if psychological consequences may result).

Difficult client. A client who has high levels of dissatisfaction with either the lawyer, the case strategy, or the court process. This is differentiated from a "client with problems" or difficulties. Difficult clients continue to find problematic aspects with their lawyer or the case. They not infrequently can sabotage their own case.

Direct examination. The questioning of a witness by the party that has called that witness to provide evidence in order to support the case that is being made. It includes identifying key facts, ideas, and scenarios that are in support of the case being presented.

Distortion. Taking a set of facts or circumstances and reworking their meaning so that they fit a particular thematic focus. Views, attitudes and/or opinions held by a child that are often modifications of reality. "My mother never had anything to do with bringing me up." "My father never pays support." These kinds of statements can often be demonstrated to be contradictory to social reality because there may be evidence that they are incorrect. They are at the core of being able to detect, or at least, research the possibility of programming/ brainwashing. Any so-called deprogramming (or undoing of alienation) process will need to focus on distortions as the key issue. Realigning distortions with past and present realities is a necessary process for re-equilibration of the child's mental health and future social relationships. Extreme vacillations by children from antagonism to a desire to affiliate are at times undergirded by distortions. Some children live with these distortions into adulthood. Also see Delusional.

Dysfunctional families. Families that do not contribute positively to the physical, social, psychological, spiritual, educational, and/or medical well-being and potential of a child.

Early warning system. Ways for professionals, parents, or others being able to read cues at an early stage of the parent-child problems. Seeing clusters of statements, a change of behaviors in the child, unusual language by the child, statements of disengagement, and a host of other attitudinal and behavioral signs can be indications of the presence of relational problems or even alienation. This can help early intervention.

Effective parenting. Parents who execute proper educational, discipline and boundary setting, medical, family, social, social-psychological, social etiquette and manners, peer, religious (where relevant), and extra and co-curricular activity oversight and guidance.

Embittered-chaotic. A term employed by Wallerstein and Kelly (see more in Bibliography) for parents who have intense anger and do not shield the child from (any of) the divorce bitterness and chaos.

Emotional (psychological) bases. The psychological bases for the alienation process (programming/brainwashing), which can include revenge, rejection, survival, confusion, anxiety, control, hostility, fear (of loneliness), and guilt. These have social causes.

Empowerment of the child. An impact factor whereby a parent overtly or covertly assists a child in gaining and expressing inappropriate power for his or her age and status. "I can tell the judge, I have rights too." This is normally associated with alienation, but children may develop empowerment in other ways.

Enmeshed. The degree to which parents become too intensely involved in the life of their child and vice versa. Parent and child identities may blend or merge.

Entrenched. When children become stuck in particular behavioral and attitudinal patterns from which they find it difficult to extricate themselves.

Escalating litigation. Keeping the litigation process active and increasing the tone and severity of the filings/accusations. Even in the face of limited factual materials, filings and counter filings may proliferate. When one litigation is lost, another is filed, often of a more severe nature in terms of accusations/issues.

Escalation pattern. A process whereby one or both parents increase the intensity and severity of content in attacking the integrity of the other parent.

Estrangement. Another term for alienation; it is useful, as it denotes the goal of turning parents into strangers—they may lose their social identity and role functions. Some experts employ the term to suggest unintentional alienation.

Ethically based practice. An attorney or other professional who abides by their professional affiliation guidelines for appropriate conduct with clients, the courts, other professionals, and applying specific protocols.

Evaluation process. The process that a professional would perform to evaluate the presence versus the absence of alienation, bonding problems, and other dimensions of parent-child problems. Courts will often order an evaluative process for custodial problems in general (broader than just focusing on alienation, abuse, or other specific family issues.)

Ex parte. A communication process whereby a party that should have been included is excluded (e.g., an attorney speaking with a Reunification Therapist without the presence of opposing counsel).

Exclusive language. These are words and phrases that are used to refer to the redefinition of the family. Exclusive language emphasizes "in-group" and isolates anybody defined as "out-group." This is specifically used for isolating a target parent as he/she is clearly not part of the "we." As children come to take on an exclusive language, it is evidence of a deeper incorporation into the social bonding problems. "I have my new family so I don't really need to see John (his birth father.)" Alienation can be one result.

Expert witness. A person with special knowledge, experience, training, and/or education relevant to a component of a legal case.

Fabrication. The making up of facts that have no or limited reality basis in reality. Also see Distortion.

Facilitative factor. Any factor that assists in the re-bonding between a parent and child.

Factitious disorder imposed on another. The newer diagnostic term for Munchausen by Proxy. It involves falsifying and/or inducing medical, psychological, and/or physical symptoms, diseases, and/or injuries onto a child. The child experiencing this phenomenon feels legitimately ill, impaired, or injured.

Factual distortions. Changing, eliminating, and/or creating "facts" that support the goal of damaging the child/target parent relationship. "Rewriting family history" is one such technique.

Failed before theory. This is one of the 19 "theories" employed by children, parents, and/or professionals to resist the reunification process. It is an assertion which claims that other professionals have tried to reunify a parent and child and have failed. This is used as a basis for predicting future failure by a parent or child.

Family culture. The values, beliefs, rituals, roles, routines, customs, traditions, and norms of a particular family.

Fear of contact with the other parent. A detection factor that involves a child's expressing fear of being with a parent; the fear is (usually) related to overt and covert messages sent by another adult; therefore, it is induced fear.

Feelings are important theory. This is one of the 19 "theories" employed by children, parents, and/or professionals to resist the reunification process. This is when children or a parent ask the parent seeking reunification to honor the (usually negative) feelings that support social disengagement.

Flight-risk factor. The degree to which a parent is likely to flee a jurisdiction with the child.

Forensic consultant. An expert with different disciplinary (behavioral science) backgrounds who provides advice, information, and/or recommendations. He/she covers areas such as case strategy, assessment/evaluation, testimony, expert critiques, mediation, and research applications.

Forensic evaluation. An evaluation requested by the court, attorneys, clients, or others to assess alienation, child custody, abuse allegations, potential for Reunification Therapy, or other socio-legal issues.

Forensic evaluator. An expert with psychological, social work, sociological, psychiatric, or other disciplinary background who assesses factors relevant to parenting and childhood issues.

Forensic knowledge. The information (and skillsets) possessed by a professional that blends their particular discipline with socio-legal factors.

Forensic. The relationships between social/mental health/family issues and the legal processes/system.

Gatekeeper. A term often employed for someone appointed to oversee the progress and success of a court order or agreement between attorneys and/or clients. This can be a GAL or some other professional.

Globalized negatives. This is about statements, opinions, or attitudes issued against a particular parent whereby most dimensions of their character and behavior are put into negative terms.

Goal-oriented process. A key element in Reunification Therapy whereby specific (behavioral) goals are set and measured.

Goals/objectives. The ends desired or posited by the courts, parents, GAL, and/or child (or any party) to a conflict scenario.

Grooming. A term usually applied to an adult who progressively facilitates trust in a child only to use that for exploitive purposes later on (e.g., sexual or physical abuse). Children can also be "groomed" to develop negativity toward another parent.

Guardian ad litem (GAL). Attorneys and/or other professionals who are appointed by the court to "shed light on" the case and specifically the children's situation. Guardians ad litem have the job of representing to the court what they believe is in the best interest of the children. Guardians ad litem may also represent the children's wishes, should they also be in their own best interest. This may mean making contact with any and all people deemed relevant to the case. The parents will often attempt to influence the guardian ad litem to view the case from their perspectives.

Guilt. A detection factor of parental influence manifested by uncomfortable feelings a child has concerning his/her own feelings, ideas, and behaviors. Guilt may appear whether the child believes or does not believe the parental input. It is heightened by being pressured into active participation against a target parent. Guilt to protect a perpetrating parent can be as strong as guilt from attacking a parent. It can be mild to immobilizing.

Hard to manage child. Children who present attitudinal and behavioral characteristics that make it very difficult to set and keep healthy boundaries. They frequently have low compliance with adult or authoritative requests.

Historical contradictions. Term for the disparity between what occurred in the past and what is taking place in the present. A form of historical contradiction is inversion where the past will actually be the opposite of what is being portrayed in the present. This "flipping" is very common in custody cases. For example, a parent who was having a series of affairs accuses the other parent of, historically, being involved outside the marriage. A parent who filed for divorce may invert this process and indicate that the other parent was the prime mover of the divorce. A parent who is accused of being unloving to a child may actually have been the primary care parent in the past. Also see Rewriting history and Distortions.

Hostage. This is when a child is trapped by their parental conflicts.

"I'm the only one who really loves you" factor. This is a cluster of techniques employed by alienating parents to convince the child that the target parent, or those associated with the target parent, is not sincere in their loving and caring for the child.

I have rights theory. This is one of the 19 "theories" employed by children, parents, and/or professionals to resist the reunification process. These children (or one of their parents) assert that they have legal, ethical, or social rights that need to be honored.

Identification. The process of taking on the qualities of the mother and/or father. As an impact factor on children, the normal, healthy identification may be damaged because children are not able to maintain a sense of balanced identity under the parental pressure. Social identification damage is a common result of children under family duress.

Impeding factors. Any factor that interferes with or undermines the re-bonding between a parent and child.

Inappropriate and unnecessary information. A technique employed by parents whereby they inculcate information into the child concerning areas such as support or past lifestyle, sexual interests, and orientations of the target parent.

Indoctrination process. Another term for inducing beliefs in the child. It involves many steps—isolation, stripping, redefining out-group/in-group, repetition, and reinforcing inferior status (of a target parent). The child then internalizes the values, beliefs, opinions, ideas, and behaviors of a negative parent toward the target parent.

In-group/out-group. One of the most common primary goals of a parent who creates one-sided alliances. This process entails creating a sense of inclusion versus exclusion. The clearest explanatory schema in regards to this process and its results is in the sociological literature (see Sumner, William Graham). The problem in reunification is that some children have lost their in-group identity with one or both parents. Reestablishing this is at the core of reunification work. Also see Wirth, Louis, and Marginality.

Inner world. The world that children often turn to when they are denied the opportunity of sharing their life with the target parent; it may be the only safe environment available. Fantasy, worry, ruminations, and daydreaming can be part of this process. Probing it can result in denial, anger, or emotional release and relief.

Intervention. Any attempt to assist, change, or improve the health of a social behavior or relationship.

Intransigence of the perpetrator. The persistence of programming/brainwashing or anti-reunification parents in regard to accomplishing their goals of indoctrination and parental segregation is strong. This quality can frequently be found in programming/brainwashing/anti-reunification parents. Intransigence can be seen when these parents are ordered by the court or given suggestions by therapists that their behaviors are problematic. A common response to this is to intensify their problematic behaviors and challenge/attack the agent of perceived change.

Jealousy. A social-emotional basis for programming/brainwashing involving envy of some aspect of the target parent's life. Economic success, new purchases, a paramour, travel, or happiness can be a trigger for jealousy.

Judicial interventions. This refers to judges who will issue court orders or recommend other actions that will help to change the process and/or the impact of negatives on a parent-child relationship. Attorneys, being officers of the court, also have a role here. They may experience ethical contradictions because of their need to represent their clients versus what they deem in the best interest of the child. It is the judge who will have to supersede all other parties in regard to the "best interest of the child." A guardian ad litem may also be party to judicial interventions. In many cases, no meaningful changes will occur without significant and sanctioned interventions by the judge.

Judicial response. The reaction of the legal system to the problems between a parent and child.

Kidnapping. A process whereby a child is mentally, socially, and/or physically segregated from one of their parents. Social-psychological (mental) kidnapping can occur while living next door.

Knowledge of the potential risks of implementation and involvement in a deprogramming and/or reunification process. It includes an understanding of any (potential) negative and positive impacts to the child who may undergo these processes.

Lack of culpability. A pattern that anti-reunification parents have that is characterized by blaming the other parent and demonstrating a lack of responsibility. They accept little or no responsibility for any of their actions, problems, or damages. Their own behavior is usually explained away by use of deflection techniques. It also applies to alienating parents.

Learned hatred. The ability to transfer negative feelings/perspectives from a person (usually an adult) to a child.

Learned xenophobia. The ability to accept and develop negative feelings/perspectives about an entire group (e.g., an extended family).

Lexicon of reconnection. A language that facilitates re-bonding. These are social-emotional terms that are connected to positive relationships. Terms of caring, love, support, endearment, and protection are in this framework.

Loss. One of the greatest or most significant impact factor on children involved in a problematic family dissolution process and other-parent child dilemmas; the loss may include love, parental contact, peace, knowledge of family ancestry, values, self-awareness, and future relationship possibilities.

Loyalty conflicts/issues. Parent-induced dilemmas that are often inculcated into the child; these tear children between their feelings of commitment to, love, and desire for affiliation with both parents. The resolution for the child is often only possible by choosing one parent—usually the programming/brainwashing parent.

Manipulating both parents. An impact factor whereby children come to realize that they have power to manipulate their parents; this is often a latent or an unintended consequence of a programming/brainwashing process.

Marginality. A sociological concept used to explain a social position that is confused, weakened, or creates contradicting behavioral demands onto a person. "I'm the father, but have no rights or say." Also see Park, Robert, and Wirth, Louis.

Martyr factor. The behavioral pattern of problematic parents who always position themselves as the victim, the superior one, the all-knowing one, the all-caring one, and in other ways, the excellent, but aggrieved parent.

Master. A figure in the court who, at times, also has (quasi)judicial authority to hear and opine on a case.

Maybe later theory. This is one of the 19 "theories" employed by children, parents, and/or professionals to resist the reunification process. This is a view that reunification, if done at all, should be done at a later time.

Mediator. A court appointed or private professional who tries to bring two or more parties to an agreement over core (family) issues.

Memory creation. The ability to generate ideas, feelings, thoughts, events, and opinions that did not likely exist at all or in the form presently presented. Also see Constructed memory.

Memory. The capacity to recall and/or recognize particular events, emotions, contexts, scenarios, opinions, and social relations that occurred in the recent or distant past.

Metrics. Identifying particular behaviors, interactions, and interventions that can be quantified as part of a progress assessment in Reunification Therapy.

Mirror imaging. A process whereby a child imitates the attitudes, opinions, behaviors, and speech patterns of a parent figure (or others).

Misperceptions. These are inaccurate views of social reality (e.g., "My father/mother doesn't really love me").

Modus operandi (MO). In criminology, this denotes a pattern of operation. Generally, parents perform behavior in regular patterns. Anti-reunification parents will usually attack the same issues of character, manipulate educators in the same way, represent the historical events with similar distortions, and manipulate professionals with the same stories. They are patterned behaviors. This allows for higher rates of predictability and intervention by professionals. Pro reunification parents also have their patterns of supportive behaviors.

Morality factors. Techniques that utilize moral judgments against the target parent concerning his or her values; lifestyle; choice of friends; or success or failure in various aspects of life such as career, financial, relational, or residential choices. The target parent is deemed inferior in these and other realms. Most parents have moral judgments on each other—positive and negative. Their infusion into the child may help or hinder the reunification process.

My life's fine theory. This is one of the 19 "theories" employed by children, parents, and/or professionals to resist the reunification process. An assertion that things (other than their relationship with the parent who wants to reunify) are fine—education, peers, activities, etc. are all presented as positive and not in need of any disruption.

Need to be rescued. An impact factor (on reunification and/or alienation) that some children harbor a secret desire to be rescued from the parental conflicts. "I wish the judge had told my Dad to stop saying these things."

Need to know (NTK). An abbreviation for a situation where anyone has a specific rationale for understanding certain information.

Nobody gets it theory. This is one of the 19 "theories" employed by children, parents, and/or professionals to resist the reunification process. An assertion by a parent or child that the courts, professionals, and others have all missed the mark in understanding why reunification either didn't or shouldn't work.

Nonbonded (or less bonded) parent. This is the parent who is seeking to improve or establish social bonds with a child. Also see Seeking parent and Unbonded parent.

Obfuscating the issue. A technique that is regularly used by conflicted and/or programming/brainwashing parents. Changing the topic, redirecting the issues, other blaming, ignoring requests for involvement, making simple scenarios into complex problems and a host of other approaches are used to blur the issue(s) at hand. The ultimate goal of obfuscation is to limit the physical and social-psychological access of the child to the other (target) parent and deflect from their re-bonding mission and behaviors.

One good parent is enough theory. This is one of the 19 "theories" employed by children, parents, and/or professionals to resist the reunification process. An assertion that a second parent in their life is not necessary because one is fulfilling all of the child's needs.

Oppositional defiant behavior. A pattern of childhood behavior that is manifested by doing the opposite of what is requested such as affiliation, respectful dialogue, perceiving positives, or other requests and directives.

Paramour factor. The real or perceived romantic presence of another man or woman in the life of the other parent. It serves as one of the most powerful motivators for alienating and anti-reunification behaviors.

Parental abandonment. A situation where a parent has physically and/or social-psychologically left a child for a period of time.

Parental discipline. A parent's ability to delineate social boundaries and limits for a child.

Parent-child estrangement inventory. A listing of behaviors, attitudes, and experiences culled from the clinical and research data. These are commonly experienced in clusters by parents who have become the target in alienation or anti-reunification processes.

Parenting coordinator. A professional often appointed by the court to assist with scheduling, communication, and other collaborative aspects of parenting. They have been criticized as, at times, usurping judge's authority—not something most trained experts actually do.

Park, Robert (1864–1944). An urban American sociologist who wrote on the idea of marginality. Also see Marginality.

Pathological alignment. When the child sides with an alienating or anti-reunification parent against the target parent with resulting damage to the child and their relationship with the other parent.

Phase-in plan. The idea that reconnecting with a parent should be done in progressive steps or stages. Some cases may warrant this, but others do not necessitate its implementation. The reunification plan should identify what is to be done at each step or stage.

Phase-in theory. This is one of the 19 "theories" employed by children, parents, and/or professionals to resist the reunification process. The belief that some parents, attorneys, judges, and mental health professionals subscribe to that it is better for a child to make a slow, cautious, careful entrance into a "new" environment. It is often applied to children who haven't seen a parent for a period of time. Little, if any, evidence exists to support this theory versus others. Whether phase-in or radical immersion is employed should be specific with benefits and possible problems identified. Also see Radical immersion theory.

Physical custodial contact schedule. The schedule that delineates physical contact between children and the parents. It may result from an informal schedule, an agreed-upon arrangement, an articulation by a parenting coordinator, a result of a conciliation process and/or a court order. The schedule can vary from minimal contact to a full equal sharing (7 by 7) or a sole physical custodianship for one parent over the other. Children can be induced to believe that the parent seeking reunification represents a negative in their life or even a danger and, therefore, should be with that parent less time.

Ping pong ball. Another term for a "middle-man factor" whereby a child feels that they are bounced between the two parents' attitudes, values, expectations, and conflicts.

"Point of no return." It refers to children who are "beyond repair" and cannot reestablish a (healthy) relationship with the target parent or parent seeking reunification. It is rare for this to be completely reached. Caution must be exercised in making this judgment, as children who look "gone" have actually developed a (full) relationship with the seeking parent, given the right social conditions.

Poison parent. A term used to denote a parent who creates toxic environments for a child.

Popular and professional "theories." This is the listing of the 19 "theories" that are often employed by children, parents, and even professionals who have opposition to reunification.

Post-traumatic stress disorder (PTSD). A cluster of feelings and behaviors that reoccur over time due to the impact of a serious event in the past. It can include reliving the event, depression, feelings of anxiety, and other symptoms. This is relevant to reunification as some children experience a divorce and conflicts between parents as traumatic event(s). Either witnessing or experiencing abuse can also lead to PTSD. The protracted parental conflict elongates this phenomenon.

Power vacuum. This occurs when there is a gap in the decision-making process in the child's life. For example, two parents who are embattled in custody conflicts for years often end up with neither parent being able to make coherent, stable decisions. Under the fear of conflict and lack of direction, children may step into the role of making their own decisions about their social life, parental contact, education, peers, and other aspects of their socialization.

Power. The ability to influence the acts and/or decisions of others (even if they resist for a time). This can be a social-psychological motive for alienating or anti-reunification parents to gain control and establish domination.

Primary caretaker. A term used by many experts and courts to refer to the parent/caretaker who has done the majority of physical, social, medical, psychological, and educational caregiving. Caution should be exercised in applying this term, as parents often provide significant support and input that may not fit under traditional categories of child rearing. At times, this term has been used as a tool to exclude the parent seeking reunification from having significant input in the child's future. Ironically, sometimes the parent is striving to rebuild or enhance their parenting, but because of a "social contract" that they had in the past ("I work, you stay home") the parent can be cut back on the time they are allowed to be with the child, or on some occasions, can be cut out completely.

Principal of recency. This is the concept that people tend to remember what has occurred most recently in their lives.

Pro se. Parents who represent themselves in legal matters. Their lack of knowledge of due process can complicate and elongates the legal situation. Some reunification experts do not take pro se cases.

Problematic expert. This is an expert who presents as unethical, biased, or can be called a "hired gun." The work they do may not follow clinical and/or scientific protocols.

Program. The content material or themes employed as a basis in assaulting a target parent, usually based on ideologies ("Mothers are superior parents," "Fathers must have an equal part"). It includes a set of directions on how to interpret reality ("If your mother cared, she would be home").

Progress assessment. The ability of a professional to identify attitudinal and/or behavioral improvements in the social bonding between a parent and child.

Progress report. A written document that identifies the progress, or lack thereof, in regard to the stated goals by the court, the parents, lawyers, the child, and/or a GAL.

Proprietary parental control. A proprietary parent is one who sees the child as property. He/she will often speak in terms of ownership: "She's my daughter," "I will do with my son what I choose to do and no one will tell me differently."

Protection from abuse (PFA). A civil order that protects one person from harm by another family member, paramour, or another parent.

Pseudo-adult. An unchildlike role that children sometimes adopt as a result of being overly involved with one or both parents who are in conflict; one characteristic of this role is becoming the problem solver for the parents' dilemmas. Another is when the child becomes the parent's confidant.

Psychosomatic illness. The developing of physical ailments in children (headaches, stomach pain) as a way of coping with the parent conflict; it is a form of "acting in." Also see Acting in and Acting out.

Puppet effect. This refers to children behaving in a way that suggests that someone else is "pulling their strings."

Radical immersion theory. This is a process whereby a child who has been disengaged from a parent is made to immediately and more fully reconnect with that parent. This should be assessed on a case by case basis. Also see Phase-in theory.

Reactive alienation. A parent who performs alienating behaviors because they have been the recipient of the experience themselves.

Readiness theory. This is one of the 19 "theories" employed by children, parents, and/or professionals to resist the reunification process. An assertion by a child or parent that the child is emotionally, socially, and/or medically not prepared to engage in the reunification process (at the time).

Reaffiliation language. This is a particular series of words and phrases that is employed in enhancing the linkage between a parent and child ("Joe" becomes "dad," "Mom's house" becomes "my other home").

Reality anchor. Reality anchors (such as a GAL) help to keep the reunification process in line with the stated goals and timelines. They also assist in keeping all parties focused on the core issues and protocol rather than (historical) distractions.

Re-bonding. Another term for parent and child who are reconnecting. Often they had an effective and caring bond in the past that got damaged for various reasons.

Reconciliation/Reaffiliation. The reconciliation or reconnection of a child who has been physically and or social-psychologically separated from a (target) parent. Some counselors and therapists may not be specifically trained or experienced to deal with a reaffiliation process and could cause additional problems. Reaffiliation is often possible even when there is opposition from the child. A clear plan with goals, interventions, metrics, and coaching is indicated.

Reentry. This refers to parents who have been out of contact with a child due to incarceration. They are reentering society, but also the lives of their children. Children who have been institutionalized also go through a reentry process.

Reflective/reflexive anxiety. When a child becomes anxious as a result of being around a parent and/or parents who are (highly) anxious. Therapists may confuse reflective anxiety with anxiety that is self-generated. Another term for this is "mirror imaging." Also see Mirror imaging.

Reframing social relations. This is a process of helping children to delete or modify distortions or inaccuracies. It also refers to accepting legitimate problems that may have occurred between the parent and child and reframes them so that improvement and forgiveness can take place.

Reintegration. This is reestablishing the interrelationship between a parent and child. It is about enhancing their connectivity.

Relocation. This is when a parent or child physically moves to another geographical setting. Sometimes this in itself could be the cause of a damaged social bond.

Reunification (process). A new term for (re)building the social-emotional bonds between a child and a seeking parent who may have been separated for short or long time periods. Regular psychotherapy may be contraindicated in this process as it was not designed for these types of relational repairs.

Reunification assessment. This is an early phase of professional activity where an evaluation is made as to whether the parties are appropriate candidates for going through the reunification protocol.

Reunification therapy. The term applied to the entire process from assessment, to evaluation, to metrics, to planning, to goal setting, to actual interventions, to progress assessment, to report writing, and finally to case termination with conclusions and recommendations.

Reunification/treatment plan. An articulated statement of the goals, phases, metrics, and interventions that are relevant to particular cases. It may necessitate some modifications as the case progresses.

Rewriting history. A brainwashing technique involving getting children to distort their views and opinions of the past; the process whereby the alienating or anti-reunification parent changes certain facts and/or interpretations in order to restructure the beliefs and opinions of the child.

Risk assessment. The professional skill utilized to evaluate potential problems, difficulties, or dangers in undertaking a reunification protocol. It should also include countermeasures of supportive activities and resources as well as possible crisis intervention. Positive outcomes are also indicated.

Role assessment. The degree to which someone can understand and articulate behaviors related to a social position. Both parent and child are statuses (positions) that have roles (expected behaviors) attached to them. Realignment of roles is a key element of reunification.

Role change. The type and degree of change in expectations and behaviors tied to a particular (parent-child) position. Reciprocated roles are an important concept in reunification work.

Safe haven. A place where children can physically and/or mentally go in order to feel protected, comfortable, and cared for. Reestablishing this between the child and the seeking parent is a component of reunification assistance.

Scared theory. This is one of the 19 "theories" employed by children, parents, and/or professionals to resist the reunification process. This refers to a child or a parent who asserts that fear is a primary element for the child in regard to one or both of their parental relationships. It also suggests that the process not be undertaken or continued because of this emotional status.

School-related problems. A possible result of alienation and/or parental conflict; acting-out, social withdrawal, grade fluctuations, insubordination, hyper-studying, and truancy may be a result or be accentuated. Some parents create alliances at school to "freeze out" the other (target) parent.

Scripted views. A detection tool; revealed by children who doubt their own perceptions because of scripts that have been inculcated by a negative parent. "Daddy doesn't pay support to us." "I'm better off without Mom in my life; she's not a good person."

Secret keeping. The sense of private communications is often held between a parent and child if one or both of them are opposed to reunification. The parent seeking to renew or develop stronger bonds is generally out of this loop of communication.

Seeking parent. This is the parent who wants an improved relationship and performs behaviors that "seek" the improved affiliation. Also see Nonbonded parent and Unbonded parent.

Self-fulfilling prophecy. A phenomenon whereby the outcome is facilitated and/or made to occur by behaviors and attitudes that shape the result. This term was developed by the sociologist Robert K. Merton. A parent posits that a child can't bond fully with the other parent. They hinder the bonding, which leads to weak bonding, and then conclude "I told you so."

Separate therapy theory. This is one of the 19 "theories" employed by children, parents, and/or professionals to resist the reunification process. A parent and/or a child who does not want to undertake the reunification often asserts that they are already or have been in their own separate therapy, and therefore Reunification Therapy is not necessary.

Shut-down messages. It involves an understanding of messages that the negative parent implants in order to prevent deprogramming or positive change. Therapists and target parents will refer to "hitting a wall" with the child. The child will usually repeat patterned scripts when this point is reached in a conversation. "I just don't want her at my games."

Social contract. This refers to formal or informal arrangements between two parties. People can form social understandings and agreements that either hinder or help reunification. It can be important to find out if such "contracts" exist.

Social death. The relational, affection, and cultural loss of a parent-child relationship. This can be the goal of a severely negative parent.

Social factors impeding the success of programming/brainwashing/alienation/anti-reunification efforts. Factors that retard, hinder, or terminate the anti-reunification attempts. The single most important one is positive contact with the target parent or seeking parent. Other factors include the type of contact with the contact parent, characteristics of siblings, external confirmation of the good qualities of the seeking parent, having only one adult engaged in the negative communication process, having a seeking parent who is open to discussions, a strong and monitored court ruling, keen social-perception capacities of the child, and having a professional or legal person who continually clarifies the process.

Social identity. This refers to who a person is in terms of their group memberships—family, sports teams, religion, neighborhood, occupation, peer groups, social class, and more. Certain social identities mesh well with each other and some do not interface as well. Knowledge of this can be useful for judging reunification potential and possible interventions.

Social personality types. These are social characteristics of parents and children that can operate in a coordinated fashion or clash with each other. Educating parents and children on the differences can actually help communication.

Social reality. The social facts that really exist(ed). Parental love, involvement, and interest existed before being distorted by the parental negativity or conflicts.

Socio-historical process. Acquiring information on the (complete) detailed social aspects in regard to the history of the family and individuals within it. It also includes any factors that would impact on the social relationships between parent and child as well as the other members of the family. The legal history is also important in this process. Also see Splitting.

Sociopath. These people generally exhibit antisocial attitudes and behaviors with an associated lack of conscience or empathy. Their low empathic qualities can create a poor platform for Reunification Therapy.

Split screen. A visual technique for demonstrating splitting, noted next.

Splitting. When the child exhibits different behaviors and attitudes in the two parental environments in order to adapt to parental expectations or pressures. They may even appear to be two different children; this is an adaptive mechanism to cope with divergent parental perspectives.

Spy. A child who is covertly or overtly instigated by one parent to retrieve information about the target or seeking parent; this information will eventually be used against the target or seeking parent. Children who have been used as spies may elicit high levels of confusion, anxiety, guilt, and anger. Also see in-group/out-group.

Sumner, William Graham (1840–1910). An American sociologist who coined the phrases in-group and out-group. Also see In-group/out-group.

Surrogates. The other individuals incorporated into the parental alienation or anti-reunification. Surrogates can be neighbors, teachers, religious figures, other family members, siblings (often the eldest is enlisted to help control the younger ones), and even, at times, professionals. Surrogates can also apply to parties who are operating against the reunification process in various ways, even if they are not involved in alienation.

Target parent. The parent who is defined as the lesser parent, enemy, evil one, and/or outsider. There may also be target lawyers, judges, siblings, grandparents, therapists, and others who are perceived and defined as the "enemy." It is used in alienation cases but is broader in its application.

Technique of silence. An approach used by some Reunification Therapists that provides a basis for "creative tensions" that may lead to improved understanding and dialogue.

Temporal distortions. Specific distortions that refer to the rearrangement of time sequences and facts that took place. Parental commitments that took place (or are alleged to have not taken place) during an earlier time of child development. Allegations that a mother never attended to the needs of the child or that a father never spent time with the children. Actual attendance at sporting events and school performances may also be distorted.

Therapeutic alliance. A situation where a client or patient tries to form a relationship with the therapist—sometimes against the other party. A therapeutic alliance can also be used constructively to enhance understandings between the therapist and client/patient. Therapists can use this relational dimension to build linkages between (conflicting) parties.

They don't listen to me theory. This is one of the 19 "theories" employed by children, parents, and/or professionals to resist the reunification process. This is a presentation by a parent or child that they are not "heard." Often they use the term "finding my voice" to express this concern.

They're abusive theory. This is one of the 19 "theories" employed by children, parents, and/or professionals to resist the reunification process. This is an assertion that a child has been harmed in some way by their past relationship with one of their parents. This needs to be understood for its historical meaning as there may be elements of truth in the assertion—or there may not be. Definitional problems (of abuse) may be at the root of these assertions.

Threat-of-withdrawal-of-love factor. A cluster of techniques revolving around the fear of rejection or loss of love from a parent if a child expresses love or desire to be with the target parent.

Timeframe/timeline. The amount of time that will be allocated for the reunification process. This can be from very brief interventions to ones that require longer periods of time. Often this cannot be determined until some initial meetings take place.

Timely ruling. Whether a judge, conciliator, guardian ad litem, therapist, and/or parenting coordinator issue guidelines and recommendations in a timely fashion or not. This is crucial for the stability of the children. Decisions and/or recommendations can drag on; this provides a lack of clarity in regard to the social definitions of the situation for the children. Anti-reunification parents have a vested interest in seeing that (and will work toward the goal) of decisions not being made in a timely fashion.

Toxic parent. A parent who created damaging messages, interferes with parent-child contact, and in other ways damages relational opportunities with the target or seeking parent.

Treatment plan. Another term for reunification plan. Also see Reunification plan.

Treatment. The application of (intervention) methods for reduction and/or termination of broken bonds. Relational access, historical distortions, and possible sanctions of the opposing parent may need to be part of any effective treatment (in more severe cases). Improving the social bonds remains the primary goal of reunification efforts.

Unbonded parent. This is the parent who is experiencing less of a connection with their child and wishes to improve those bonds. There are degrees of this from no connection to a connection that they simply wish to enhance. Also see Nonbonded parent and Seeking parent.

Unchildlike statements. A detection tool for alienation and anti-reunification parents that has two primary characteristics, consistency and over-rigidity, on the part of the child. Children make statements that are not in line with their maturity level. They possess knowledge that is clearly in the adult realm. "You haven't paid child support for eight weeks" (seven-year-old).

Unconditional loved. Love issued by a parent that is not based on expectations of certain negative behaviors or hostility to a target or seeking parent. The child is loved even if he or she loves the other parent. This is an invulnerability characteristic whereby a child knows that at least one of the parents will accept him or her no matter what the life circumstances may be. It is easier to turn against an unconditional love parent as there are often no consequences.

Unification. This refers to the situation where there may have been virtually no connection between parent and child. An entire social (re)building process is likely necessary.

Unintentional process. When the parent (and/or child) is not aware of (his/her own) motives, goals, objectives, and/or techniques to damage a parent-child relationship.

Value affirmations. This occurs anytime an individual, professional or court functionary states a strongly held value or cluster of values. The value of shared parenting, the right of the child to have access to both parents, obedience to the court's directives, belief in whether the therapeutic process can be helpful, or any other strongly held beliefs can be important to know for reunification efforts. The problem arises when the parents hold an individual or set of values that are in conflict. At times, parents will appear to have the same general values, such as the "best interest of the child." However, further forensic research will often demonstrate that there are other values that undergird these values, which are determinant of their actual behaviors. For example, the belief that a child can only have one full-time parent may be a more deeply held value underneath the assertions of the "best interest of the child." The other parent may offer shared parenting as being in the "best interest of the child." Value research is central to custodial and other conflicts. This concept also refers to the statements that judges make in regard to legal and communal values related to family life.

Victim role. This is one of the favorite roles played by alienating and anti-reunification parents. It can be related to inversion of reality. In fact, they may be the perpetrators in terms of victimizing the target parent (and the children). However, they will often take on the position of the aggrieved parent. This can be complicated because there may be periods where they have had legitimate problems and issues which were historically perpetrated by the target parent. Objectivity is key in this realm of assessment and interventions.

Voluntary selection. This refers to clients/patients who send themselves in for a reunification protocol versus those cases that are court mandated or attorney agreed upon. It may just be a case of a parent wishing to improve their bonds with a child (without the active participation of the other parent).

We never got along theory. This is one of the nineteen "theories" employed by children, parents, and/or professionals to resist the reunification process. This is a reference made by a child or a parent to a claimed historical situation of poor relational integration. This may or may not have actually been the case—some parents and children are capable of rewriting history (but not all).

Wirth, Louis (1897–1952). American sociologist who wrote about the concept of marginality. Also see Marginality.

You didn't live my life theory. This is one of the 19 "theories" employed by children, parents, and/or professionals to resist the reunification process. This is an assertion that the professional may not understand the reality context of a child's life. Showing understanding can create some valuable communication around this assertion.

You don't really know them theory. This is one of the 19 "theories" employed by children, parents, and/or professionals to resist the reunification process. This is an assertion by a parent or child that the seeking parent is not really the person that they present themselves to be. It implies that they are manipulative, deceptive, or just plain clever.

Bibliography[1]

Adams, K. (2009). The parentectomy: A memoir, a perspective on rising above parental alienation, a novel. United States: Xlibris.

Amato, P. R. (1994). Life-span adjustment of children to their parents divorce. *The Future of Children, 4*(1), 143–64.

Andritsky, W., & Andritsky, W. (2006). The role of medical reports in the development of parental alienation syndrome. In *The international handbook of parental alienation syndrome: Conceptual, clinical, and legal considerations* (pp. 195–208). Springfield, IL: Charles C. Thomas.

Atwood, B. (2019). Religious Arbitration of Family Disputes. *Family Advocate, 42*(2), 24–29.

Baer, E. (2016, June 28). Can the parent-child bond be restored after alienation? Retrieved from https://njfamilylaw.foxrothschild.com/2016/06/articles/custody/can-the-parent-child-bond-be-restored-after-alienation/.

Beck, C. J. (July 2009). Collaboration between judges and social science researchers in family law. *Family Court Review, 47*(3), 451–67.

Benedek, E. P., & Schetky, D. H. (1985). Allegations of sexual abuse in child custody and visitation disputes. In *Emerging Issues in Child Psychiatry and the Law* (pp. 145–56). New York, NY: Brunner-Routledge.

Bergson, H. (1906). Le rire: Essai sur la signification du comique. Paris: Félix Alcan.

Bergson, H., Brereton, C., & Rothwell, F. (2008). *Laughter: An essay on the meaning of the comic*. Rockville, MD: Arc Manor.

Bernet, W. (1993). False statements and the differential diagnosis of abuse allegations. *Journal of the American Academy of Child & Adolescent Psychiatry, 32*(5), 903–10.

Bernet, W. (1997). Case study: Allegations of abuse created in a single interview. *Journal of the American Academy of Child & Adolescent Psychiatry, 36*(7), 966–70.

Bogatay Family Law. (2017, September 1). Birth parent rights after an adoption. Retrieved from https://www.pittsburghfamilylawfirm.com/birth-parent-rights-adoption/.

Bouchard, T. J. (1976). Unobtrusive measures: An inventory of uses. *Sociological Methods & Research, 4*(3), 267–300.

Brewin, C. R. (1996). Scientific status of recovered memories. *British Journal of Psychiatry, 169*(2), 131–34.

1. This list of articles and books is for review as resources. They represent a diversity of methods, content, opinions, and conclusions. They do not represent intellectual, research, and/or clinical support by the author of *Broken Bonds—Mended Ways: Reunification—Bridge Building for Damaged Parent-Child Relationships*.

Brinig, M. F. (2019). Religion, Child Custody, and Visitation. *Family Advocate, 42*(2), 16–19.

Brooks-Aguilar, S. (2016). Successful stages in reunification: A guide for professionals helping children and parents rebuild after divorce. CreateSpace Independent Publishing Platform.

Brown, J. A. (1963). Techniques of persuasion: *From propaganda to brainwashing.* Gloucester, MA: Penguin Books.

Bruck, M., & Ceci, S. (1999). The suggestibility of children's memory. *Annual Review of Psychology, 50*(1), 419–39.

Campbell, T. W. (1992). False allegations of sexual abuse and their apparent credibility. *American Journal of Forensic Psychology, 10*(4), 21.

Campbell, T. W. (1992). Psychotherapy with children of divorce: The pitfalls of triangulated relationships. *Psychotherapy: Theory, research, practice, training, 29*(4), 646v52.

Ceci, S. J., & Bruck, M. (1993). Suggestibility of the child witness: A historical review and synthesis. *Psychological Bulletin, 113*(3), 403–39.

Ceci, S. J., Huffman, M. L., Smith, E., & Loftus, E. F. (1994). Repeatedly thinking about a non-event: Source misattributions among preschoolers. *Consciousness and Cognition, 3*(3–4), 388–407.

Ceci, S. J., & Bruck, M. (2006). Childrens suggestibility: Characteristics and mechanisms. *Advances in Child Development and Behavior Advances in Child Development and Behavior Volume 34, 34*, 247–81.

Child Sexual Abuse and Divorce. (2016, July 20). Retrieved from https://www.divorcesource.com/blog/child-sexual-abuse-and-divorce/

Clawar, S. S. (1981, October). Improving communication with young patients. *Colloquy: Journal of the Physician-Patient Communications,* 9–11.

Clawar, S. S. (1982, November). Children who must serve as parents. *Pediatrics for Parents, 46.*

Clawar, S. S. (1982). One house, two cars, three kids. *Family Advocate.*

Clawar, S. S. (1982). *Popular and professional misconceptions about joint custody.* Lecture presented at Pennsylvania Bar Institute, Harrisburg, PA. In *Custody update: The new shared custody act and custody rules* (pp. 79–105).

Clawar, S. S. (1983). Questions to raise before accepting children's opinions. *Children's Legal Rights Journal, 4*(5,6).

Clawar, S. S. (1983). Why children say what they say. *Family Advocate, 6*(2), 25–26.

Clawar, S. S. (1983). Children as ping pong balls. *Pediatrics for Parents, 49.*

Clawar, S. S. (1985). A view from beyond: Helping step-children adjust. *Family Advocate.*

Clawar, S. S. (1985). Introducing forensic sociology as an area of sociological practice. *Clinical Sociology Newsletter, 7(3).*

Clawar, S. S. (1985, August). Sure turnoffs to good physician-patient communications. *Resident Advisor: Journal of Physician-Patient Communications, 2*(3).

Clawar, S. S. (1987). Parents as family therapists. *The Single Parent,* 19–21.

Clawar, S. S. (Summer 1988). Firm Advice. *The Compleat Lawyer, 5*(3), 36–37, 39.

Clawar, S. S., & Rivlin, B. V. (1987, May). *Parental programming of children.* Lecture presented at Association of Family and Conciliation Courts 24th Annual Conference, Honolulu, HI.

Clawar, S. S. (1992, February 17). *Programming-and-brainwashing of children in child custody cases, sexual abuse allegations, how to determine if a family report is scientific and developing more successful law practices through behavioral management.* Lecture presented at Lynchburg Virginia Bar Association Family Law Section, Lynchburg, VA.

Clawar, S. S. (1996). *You & your clients: A guide to client management skills for a more successful practice* (2nd ed.). Chicago, IL: General Practice Section, American Bar Association.

Clawar, S. S., & Rivlin, B. V. (2001, July 27). *Parent alienation: Not in the best interest of the children.* Lecture presented at Lorman Educational Services from Alabama State Bar Summer Convention.

Clawar, S. S. (2004). Predicting the abduction of children: The flight risk factors and what can be done. *Family Advocate, 26*(4), 42–47.

Clawar, S. S. (2005). What judges want seven "hot tips" on structuring your courtroom presentations. *Family Advocate, 28*(1), 41–42.

Clawar, S. S. (2005). What judges want—Part II more "hot tips" on structuring your courtroom presentations. *Family Advocate, 28*(2), 46.

Clawar, S. S. (2008, September 15). Clinical sociology. In *The Blackwell Encyclopedia of Sociology*. Wiley-Blackwell. Retrieved from https://onlinelibrary.wiley.com/doi/10.1002/9781405165518.wbeosc207.

Clawar, S. S. (Fall 2014). Spotting the Hired Gun. *Family Advocate, 37*(2), 6.

Clawar, S. S., & Rivlin, B. V. (2013). *Children held hostage: Identifying brainwashed children, presenting a case, and crafting solutions* (2nd ed.). Chicago: American Bar Association.

Concannon, D. M. (2015). *Kidnapping: An investigator's guide to profiling.* USA: Academic Press.

Copertino, "Hague convention on the civil aspects of international child abduction: An analysis of its efficacy," 6 Conn. J. Int'l L. 715 (1991).

Cordero, A. E. (2004). When family reunification works: Data-mining foster care records. *Families in Society: The Journal of Contemporary Social Services, 85*(4), 571–80.

Coser, L. A. (1964). *The functions of social conflict.* New York, NY: Free Press.

Crosby, J. F. (1989). *When one wants out and the other doesn't: Doing therapy with polarized couples.* New York, NY: Routledge.

Custody case. (1999). *Family Advocate, 21*(3), 26–32.

Dallam, S., & Silberg, J. L. (2016, July). Recommended treatments for "parental alienation syndrome" (PAS) may cause children foreseeable and lasting psychological harm. *Journal of Child Custody, 13*(2), 3rd ser., 134–43.

Dalton, C., Drozd, L., & Wong, F. Q. (2006). *Navigating custody & visitation evaluations in cases with domestic violence: A judges guide.* Reno, NV: National Council of Juvenile and Family Court Judges.

Darnall, D. (1998). *Divorce casualties: Protecting your children from parental alienation.* Dallas, TX: Taylor Publishing.

Darnall, D. (2008). *Divorce casualties: Understanding parental alienation.* Lanham, MD: Taylor Pub.

Darnall, D. (2010). *Beyond divorce casualties: Reunifying the alienated family.* Lanham, MD: Taylor Trade Pub.

DePanfilis, D., & Dubowitz, H. (2000). *Handbook for child protection practice.* Thousand Oaks, CA: SAGE Publications.

Dershowitz, A. M. (2019, March 21). I want to be investigated by the FBI. *Wall Street Journal*. Retrieved from https://www.wsj.com/articles/i-want-to-be-investigated-by-the-fbi-11553209347.

Deters, J. A. (2003). Parenting coordination services: A forensic intervention for high conflict child custody cases when parental alienation syndrome is present (Doctoral dissertation, Spalding University).

Deutsch, R., Sullivan, M., & Ward, P. (2008). Breaking barriers: An innovative program for alienated and estranged children. *Association of Family and Conciliation Courts Newsletter*.

Downing, M. D. (2012). Barriers to reunification for incarcerated parents—A judicial perspective. *Family Court Review, 50*(1), 71–76.

Draitser, E. A. (1998). *Taking penguins to the movies: Ethnic humor in Russia*. Detroit: Wayne State University Press.

Drozd, L. M., & Olesen, N. W. (2004). Is it abuse, alienation, and/or estrangement? A Decision Tree. *Journal of Child Custody, 1*(3), 65–106.

Drozd, L., Saini, M., & Olesen, N. (2016). *Parenting plan evaluations: Applied research for the family court*. Oxford: Oxford University Press.

Editorial Staff (Ed.). (2016, July 20). Child sexual abuse and divorce. Retrieved from https://www.divorcesource.com/blog/child-sexual-abuse-and-divorce/.

Ekman, P., Ekman, M. A., & Ekman, T. (1991). *Why kids lie: How parents can encourage truthfulness*. New York: Penguin.

Ellis, E. M. (2005). Help for the alienated parent. *The American Journal of Family Therapy, 33*(5), 415–26.

Ellis, E. M., & Boyan, S. (2010, April). Intervention strategies for parent coordinators in parental alienation cases. *The American Journal of Family Therapy, 38*(3), 218–36.

Elovitz, R. (2018, November 9). False allegations of child abuse in custody litigation (part 2). Retrieved from https://familylawyermagazine.com/articles/false-allegations-of-child-abuse-in-custody-litigation-2/.

Engber, A. (2010). *The complete single mother: Reassuring answers to your most challenging concerns*. Cincinnati, OH: F W Media.

Erickson, B. M. (1998). *Longing for dad: Father loss and its impact*. Deerfield Beach, FL: Health Communications.

Etzioni, A. (1968, December). Basic human needs, alienation and inauthenticity. *American Sociological Review, 33*(6), 870–85.

Falk, G. J. (1959, September). The role of social class differences and horizontal mobility in the etiology of aggression. *Journal of Educational Sociology, 33*(1), 1–10.

Farber, I. E., Harlow, H. F., & West, L. J. (1957, December). Brainwashing, conditioning, and DDD (debility, dependency, and dread). *Sociometry, 20*(4), 271–85.

Faust, J. (2017). Reunification family therapy: A treatment manual. *Family Court Review, 57*(1), 118–20.

Fein, E., & Staff, I. (1993). Last best chance: Findings from a reunification services program. *Child Welfare: Journal of Policy, Practice, and Program, 72*(1), 25–40.

Fernandez, E. (2013). *Accomplishing permanency: Reunification pathways and outcomes for foster children*. Dordrecht: Springer.

Festinger, L., & Carlsmith, J. M. (1959). Cognitive consequences of forced compliance. *The Journal of Abnormal and Social Psychology, 58*(2), 203–10.

Fidler, B. J., & Bala, N. (2010, January). Children resisting postseparation contact with a parent: Concepts, controversies, and conundrums. *Family Court Review, 48*(1), 10–47.

Fineklstein, C. (2003) The heart of an abducted and alienated child. Sarah or Cecile: The identity issue. In: *Das Parental Alienation Syndrom: Eine interdisziplinäre Herausforderung für scheidungsbegleitende Berufe*, Frankfurt, Germany Eds. Wilfrid von Boch-Galhau et al., pp. 175–85 Berlin: Verlag für Wissenschaft und Bildung.

Folberg, J. (1991). *Joint custody and shared parenting*. New York, NY: Guilford Press.

Franco, F., Fogel, A., Messinger, D. S., & Frazier, C. A. (1996). Cultural differences in physical contact between Hispanic and Anglo mother–infant dyads living in the United States. *Early Development and Parenting, 5*(3), 119–27.

Fricker, D. (1986, January 22). Father gets unlimited rights to visit kids taken by mother. *The Morning Call*. Retrieved from https://www.mcall.com/news/mc-xpm-1986-01-22-2515611-story.html.

Friedlander, S. & Walters, M.G. (2010). "When a child rejects a parent: Tailoring the intervention to fit the problem." *Family Court Review*, 48(1), 98–111.

Friedman, D., Bradshadow Schmidt, C., King, H. L., Warshak, R., & Webb, B. L. (2014, June 12–13). *A systematic approach to reunification therapy*. Retrieved from http://www.texascounseling.org/articles/ASystematicApproachtoReunificationTherapy.pdf, Dallas/Adison, Texas.

Gambino, M. (2010, April 20). Greg Miller on "making memories." *Smithsonian*. Retrieved from https://www.smithsonianmag.com/science-nature/greg-miller-on-making-memories-21601824/.

Garbarino, J. W., Guttmann, E., & Seeley, J. W. (1986). *The psychologically battered child*. San Francisco, CA: Jossey-Bass.

Garber, B. D. (2004). Therapist alienation: Foreseeing and forestalling third-party dynamics undermining psychotherapy with children of conflicted caregivers. *Professional Psychology: Research and Practice, 35*(4), 357–63.

Garber, B. D. (2004). Parental alienation in light of attachment theory: Consideration of the broader implications for child development, clinical practice, and forensic process. *Journal of Child Custody, 1*(4), 49–76.

Garber, B. D. (2007). Conceptualizing visitation resistance and refusal in the context of parental conflict, separation, and divorce. *Family Court Review, 45*(4), 588–99.

Garber, B. D. (2012, July). Security by association? Mapping attachment theory onto family law practice. *Family Court Review, 50*(3), 467–70.

Garber, B. D. (2015, January). Cognitive-behavioral methods in high-conflict divorce: Systematic desensitization adapted to parent-child reunification interventions. *Family Court Review, 53*(1), 96–112.

Gardner, R. A. (1990). *Sex abuse hysteria: Salem witch trials revisited*. Cresskill, NJ: Creative Therapeutics.

Gardner, R. A. (1992). *True and false allegations of child sex abuse*. Creskill, NJ: Creative Therapeutics.

Gardner, R. A. (1994) The detrimental effects on women of the misguided gender egalitarianism of the child-custody resolution guidelines. *Academy Forum*, 38(1/2), 10–13.

Gardner, R. A. (1998). Recommendations for dealing with parents who induce a parental alienation syndrome in their children. *Journal of Divorce & Remarriage, 28*(3–4), 1–23.

Gardner, R. A. (1999). Differentiating between parental alienation syndrome and bona fide abuse-neglect. *The American Journal of Family Therapy, 27*(2), 97–107.

Gardner, R. A. (2001). *Therapeutic interventions for children with parental alienation syndrome*. Cresskill, NJ: Creative Therapeutics.

Gardner, R. A. (2001). The recent gender shift in PAS indoctrinators. *News for Women in Psychiatry, 19(4)*, 11–13.

Gardner, R. A. (2002). The empowerment of children in the development of parental alienation syndrome. *American Journal of Forensic Psychology, 20*(2), 5–30.

Gardner, R. A. (2004). The relationship between the parental alienation syndrome (PAS) and the false memory syndrome (FMS). *The American Journal of Family Therapy, 32*(2), 79–99.

Gardner, R. A., Sauber, S. R., & Lorandos, D. (2006). *The international handbook of parental alienation syndrome: Conceptual, clinical and legal considerations*. Springfield, IL: Charles C. Thomas.

Gingerich, W. J., Kim, J. S., Stams, G. J., & Macdonald, A. J. (2011). Solution-focused brief therapy outcome research. *Solution-Focused Brief Therapy*, 95-111.

Glover, M. (Spring 2010). Evidentiary privileges for cohabiting parents: Protecting children inside and outside of marriage. *Louisiana Law Review*, (251), 70.

Goldman, M., Haberlein, B. J., & Feder, G. J. (1965, June). Conformity and resistance to group pressure. *Sociometry, 28*(2), 220–26.

Gould, J. W., Gould-Saltman, D., Greenberg, L. R., & Stahl, P. M. (Summer 2003). Is the child's therapist part of the problem? What judges, attorneys, and mental health professionals need to know about court-related treatment for children. *Family Law Quarterly, 37*(2), 241–71.

Grady, A. (2004). Female-on-male domestic violence: Uncommon or ignored? In *New Visions of Crime Victims* (pp. 71–96). Portland, OR: Hard Publishing.

Greely, K. (2019, June 18). High time to talk to teens. *The Philadelphia Inquirer*, p. 18.

Green, A. H. (1986). True and false allegations of sexual abuse in child custody disputes. *Journal of the American Academy of Child Psychiatry, 25*(4), 449–56.

Greenberg, L., Gould, J., Gould-Saltman, D., & Stahl, P. (2003). Is the child's therapist part of the problem? What judges, attorneys, and mental health professionals need to know about court-related treatment for children. *Family Law Quarterly, 37*(2), 241–71.

Guerriero, A., & Blank, C. A. (2018). Music therapy in a parent-child reunification program. *Voices: A World Forum for Music Therapy, 18*(4), 1–8.

Guidelines for parenting coordination. (2006, January). *Family Court Review, 44*(1), 164–81.

Guidelines for court-involved therapy. (n.d.). Retrieved from https://www.afccnet.org/Portals/0/PublicDocuments/CEFCP/Guidelines for Court Involved Therapy AFCC.pdf.

Hagen, M. A. (1998). *Whores of the court: The fraud of psychiatric testimony and the rape of American justice*. New York, NY: HarperCollins.

Hart, H. (1930, January). The transmutation of motivation. *American Journal of Sociology, 35*(4), 588–600.

Heard, S., & Wheeler, J. (2019). *Family law attorneys and parenting evaluators: improving professional collaboration*. Chicago: American Bar Association.

Heidler, M. (2014). Honest liars. *Scientific American Mind, 25*(2), 40–44. Retrieved from https://www.jstor.org.ezproxy.neumann.edu/stable/24946069.

Heinig, M. (n.d.). Rights of birth parents and grandparents after adoption. Retrieved from https://www.lawyers.com/legal-info/family-law/adoptions/rights-of-birth-parents-and-grandparents-after-adoption.html.

Hoffer, E. (1951). *The true believer*. New York, NY: Mentor Books.

Holtzworth-Munroe, A. (2009, July). For the sake of the children: Collaborations between law and social science to advance the field of family dispute resolution. *Family Court Review, 47*(3), 360–62.

Hoppe, C. F. (1997). Perpetually battling parents. In *The handbook of infant, child, and adolescent psychotherapy: New directions in integrative treatment* (Vol. 2). Northvale, NJ: Jason Aronson.

Hopson, J. (2013). Bad mix for the teen brain. *Scientific American Mind, 24*(3), 68–71.

Hynan, D. J. (2012, July). Young children, attachment security, and parenting schedules. *Family Court Review, 50*(3), 471–80.

Jaffe, P. G., Ashbourne, D., & Mamo, A. A. (2010, January). Early identification and prevention of parent-child alienation: A framework for balancing risks and benefits of intervention. *Family Court Review, 48*(1), 136–52.

Johnston, J. R. (1993). Children of divorce who refuse visitation. In *Nonresidential Parenting: New Vistas in Family Living* (pp. 109–35). Thousand Oaks, CA: SAGE Publications.

Johnston, J. R. (2003). Parental alignments and rejection: An empirical study of alienation in children of divorce. *Journal of the American Academy of Psychiatry and the Law, 31*(2), 158–70.

Johnston, J. R., Walters, M. G., & Olesen, N. W. (2005). The psychological functioning of alienated children in custody disputing families: An exploratory study. *American Journal of Forensic Psychology, 23*(2), 39–64.

Johnston, J. (2005). Children of divorce who reject a parent and refuse visitation: Recent research and social policy implications for the alienated child. *Family Law Quarterly, 38*(4), 757–75.

Johnston, J. R., & Girdner, L. K. (2001). Family abductors: Descriptive profiles and preventive interventions. *Juvenile Justice Bulletin, 1*, 1–7.

Johnston, J. R., Walters, M. G., & Olesen, N. W. (2005). Is it alienating parenting, role reversal or child abuse? A study of children's rejection of a parent in child custody disputes. *Journal of Emotional Abuse, 5*(4), 191–218.

Judge, A. M., Bailey, R., Behrman-Lippert, J., Bailey, E., Psaila, C., & Dickel, J. (2016). The transitioning families therapeutic reunification model in nonfamilial abductions. *Family Court Review, 54*(2), 232–49.

Katz, A. (Fall 2003). Junk science v. novel scientific evidence: Parental alienation syndrome, getting it wrong in custody cases. *Pace Law Review, 24*(1), 239–43.

Katz, D. (1960). The functional approach to the study of attitudes. *Public Opinion Quarterly, 24*(2, Special Issue: Attitude Change), 163–204.

Kelly, J. B., & Johnston, J. R. (2001, July). The Alienated Child: A Reformulation of Parental Alienation Syndrome. *Family Court Review, 39*(3), 249–60.

Kemper, T. D. (1991, December). Predicting emotions from social relations. *Social Psychology Quarterly, 54*(4), 330–42.

Kenan, J., & Bernet, W. (2015). Parental alienation. In *Wiley Encyclopedia of Forensic Science*. Indianapolis, IN: Wiley & Sons.

Kerns, R. W. (2016). Crying wolf: The use of false accusations of abuse to influence child custodianship and a proposal to protect the innocent. *SSRN Electronic Journal*.

Klass, J. L., & Klass, J. V. (2005). Threatened mother syndrome (TMS): A diverging concept of parental alienation syndrome (PAS). *American Journal of Family Law, 18*(4), 189–91.

Kleinman, T. (2017). Family court ordered "reunification therapy:" Junk science in the guise of helping parent/child relationships? *Journal of Child Custody, 14*(4), 295–300.

Knox, D., & Leggett, K. (2000). *The divorced dad's survival book: How to stay connected with your kids*. Reading, MA: Perseus Books.

Kraus, L., Galatzer-Levy, R. M., & Galatzer-Levy, J. (2010). *The scientific basis of child custody decisions*. New York, NY: Wiley.

Kruk, E. (2013, May 9). Parent-child reunification after alienation. Retrieved from https://www.psychologytoday.com/us/blog/co-parenting-after-divorce/201305/parent-child-reunification-after-alienation.

Lamb, M. E. (1987). *The father's role: Cross-cultural perspectives*. Hillsdale, NJ: Lawrence Erlbaum Associates.

Lamb, M. E. (2012, July). A wasted opportunity to engage with the literature on the implications of attachment research for family court professionals. *Family Court Review, 50*(3), 481–85.

Lampel, A. K. (1996). Children's alignment with parents in highly conflicted custody cases. *Family and Conciliation Courts Review, 40*(2), 232–35.

Lansford, J. E., Chang, L., Dodge, K. A., Malone, P. S., Oburu, P., Palmérus, K., ... Quinn, N. (2005). Physical discipline and children's adjustment: Cultural normativeness as a moderator. *Child Development, 76*(6), 1234–1246.

Lateef, A. (2019, June 16). Life after prison "reentry" can't begin to describe the challenges of returning to the outside world. *The Philadelphia Inquirer*, pp. C1–C3.

Laver, M. (2017, November 16). Family time/visitation: The road to safe reunification. Retrieved from http://www.opd.wa.gov/documents/00416-2016_FamilyTime.pdf.

Ledebuhr, M. N. (2018). Parentage and the Modern Family. *Family Advocate, 40*(4), 12–15.

Levy, D. M. (1943). *Maternal overprotection*. New York, NY: Columbia University Press.

Lindahl, M. W., & Hunt, L. A. (2016). Reunification in intrafamilial child abuse cases: A model for intervention. *Family Court Review, 54*(2), 288–99.

Loeb, L. (1986). Fathers and sons: Some effects of prolonged custody litigation. *Bulletin of the American Academy of Psychiatry and the Law, 14(2)*, 177–83.

Loftus, E. F., & Palmer, J. C. (1974). Reconstruction of auto-mobile destruction. *Journal of Verbal Learning and Verbal Behavior, 13*, 585–89.

Lorandos, D., Bernet, W., & Sauber, S. R. (2013). *Parental alienation: The handbook for mental health and legal professionals*. Springfield, IL, U.S.A.: Charles C. Thomas, Publisher.

Lucey, C., Reder, P., & Duncan, S. (2003). *Studies in the assessment of parenting*. New York, NY: Routledge.

Ludolph, P. S. (2012, July). The special issue on attachment: Overreaching theory and data. *Family Court Review, 50*(3), 486–95.

MacDonald, J. (2017, June 14). False allegations of domestic violence: More common than you think. Retrieved from https://www.aggressivelegalservices.com/false-allegations-of-domestic-violence/.

Maldonado, S. (Summer 2008). The best interests of the child: Cultivating forgiveness: reducing conflict and hostility after divorce. *Wake Forest Law Review, 43*, 441–504.

Mart, E. G. (2007). *Issue focused forensic child custody assessment.* Sarasota, FL: Professional Resource Press.

Mazzoni, G., & Memon, A. (2003). Imagination can create false autobiographical memories. *Psychological Science, 14*(2), 186–88.

McCarthy, E. (2019, April 6). In Radnor Wawa, 30 seconds of terror: How a years-long custody battle escalated to murder. *The Philadelphia Inquirer.* Retrieved from https://www.inquirer.com/news/pennsylvania/wawa-shooting-radnor-delaware-county-main-line-20190406.html.

McIntosh, J. E. (2012, July). Reviewing the opportunities: Guest editor's reply to comments. *Family Court Review, 50*(3), 496–501.

Meadow, R. (1993). False allegations of abuse and Munchausen syndrome by proxy. *Archives of Disease in Childhood, 68*(4), 444–47.

Meerloo, J. A. (1956). *Rape of the mind: The psychology of thought control, menticide, and brainwashing.* New York, NY: World Pub.

Merton, R. K. (Summer 1948). The self-fulfilling prophecy. *The Antioch Review, 8*(2), 193–210.

Miller, K. A., Fisher, P. A., Fetrow, B., & Jordan, K. (2006). Trouble on the journey home: Reunification failures in foster care. *Children and Youth Services Review, 28*(3), 260–74.

Multnomah County Family Court Services. (2013). Second chances: A guidebook for parents wishing to reunite with their children. Retrieved from https://multco.us/sites/default/files/dcj/documents/second_chances_master012510.pdf.

NFPN. (n.d.). NFPN's reunification model. Retrieved from https://nfpn.org/reunification/reunification-model.

Nguyen, V., Witte, R., Rutanashoodech, A., Villareal, M., & Horn, M. (2018, November 5). No oversight for reunification programs. Retrieved from https://www.nbcbayarea.com/investigations/No-Oversight-for-Programs-Advertising-They-Reconnect-Children-with-Alienated-Parents-499412851.html.

Noonan, P. (2019, May 09). Opinion | the missing order in American politics. Retrieved from https://www.wsj.com/articles/the-missing-order-in-american-politics-11557443675.

Nugent, W. R., Carpenter, D., & Parks, J. (1993). A statewide evaluation of family preservation and family reunification services. *Research on Social Work Practice, 3*(1), 40–65.

O'Bryan, R. (1987, January 14). Montco judge angrily agrees to jury trial in custody case. *The Morning Call.* Retrieved from https://www.mcall.com/news/mc-xpm-1987-01-14-2568195-story.html.

Palmer, T. L. (2018). How Many Parents? *Family Advocate, 40*(4), 36–39.

Parent-child reunification. (2016, May 10). Retrieved from https://www.divorcesource.com/blog/parent-child-reunification/.

Pearce, T. (2009, March 24). The family Pandora's box: Some victims of parental alienation don't realize until adulthood that one parent turned them against the other. *Https://www.theglobeandmail.com/.* Retrieved from https://www.theglobeandmail.com/life/the-family-pandoras-box/article1150316//.

Pearl, P. S. (1994). Emotional abuse. In *Child maltreatment: A clinical guide and reference* (pp. 259–82). St. Louis, MO: G W Medical.

Racusin, R. J., Copans, S. A., & Mills, P. (1994). Characteristics of families of children who refuse post-divorce visits. *Journal of Clinical Psychology, 50*(5), 792–801.

Rand, D. C., & Rand, R. (2006). Factors affecting reconciliation between the child and target parent. In *The international handbook of parental alienation syndrome: Conceptual, clinical, and legal considerations* (pp. 163–76). Springfield, IL: Charles C. Thomas.

Raso, C. (2004). If the bread goes stale, it's my dad's fault: The parental alienation syndrome (Doctoral dissertation, Concordia University).

Rajaraman, J. (2018, January 9). Planning a successful reunification event. Retrieved from https://www.americanbar.org/groups/child_law/resources/child_law_practiceonline/child_law_practice/vol_31/may_2012/planning_a_successfulreunificationevent/.

Raeburn, P. (2015). *Do fathers matter?: What science is telling us about the parent we've overlooked.* New York: Scientific American/Farrar, Straus and Giroux.

Reasonable efforts to preserve or reunify families and achieve permanency for children. (n.d.). Retrieved from https://www.childwelfare.gov/topics/systemwide/laws-policies/statutes/reunify/.

Rebach, H. M., & Bruhn, J. G. (2001). *Handbook of clinical sociology.* New York, NY: Kluwer Academic.

Reiss, Y. (2019). Issues in Jewish Divorce. *Family Advocate, 42*(2), 30–32.

Reunification assessment. (n.d.). Retrieved from http://emanuals.jfs.ohio.gov/FamChild/CPSWM/Policy/Reunification-Assessment.stm.

Reunification therapy popularity in court orders: A deep dive into RT. (n.d.). Retrieved from https://www.lepageassociates.com/a-deep-dive-into-rt/.

Richardson, P. (2006). A kidnapped mind. Toronto: Dundurn Press.

Rivlin, B. V. (2005). Manipulative techniques of children in the transitional family. *Family Court Review, 23*(1), 21–26.

Rubinstein, L. (2013). A descriptive analysis of custody disputing divorced families with an alienated child (Doctoral dissertation, Massachusetts School of Professional Psychology). (UMI No. 3643895)

Sapolsky, R. M. (2017). *Behave: The biology of humans at our best and worst.* New York, NY: Penguin Press.

Sauber, S. R. (2007). Review of "adult children of parental alienation syndrome." *American Journal of Family Therapy, 35*(4), 385–86.

Schacht, T. E. (1999). Prevention strategies to protect professionals and families involved in high-conflict divorce. *University of Arkansas at Little Rock Law Review, 22*(3), 565–92.

Schein, E. H. (1960, June). Interpersonal communication, group solidarity, and social influence. *Sociometry, 23*(2), 148–61.

Schulefand, K. B. (2017, June 27). Do "family reunification" camps really help fight alienation? Retrieved from https://www.schulefandlawoffice.com/blog/2017/06/do-family-reunification-camps-really-help-fight-alienation.shtml.

Slabach, C., Guillory, D., Walters, M. G., Grilli, H. A., Friedlander, S., & Kretzmer, M. J. (2016, February 19). *The view from the bench and bar: How legal professionals can help when a child resists contact with a parent*. Lecture presented at AFCC-CA Pre-Conference Institute in California.

Slesnick, N., & Prestopnik, J. L. (2004). Office versus home-based family therapy for runaway, Alcohol Abusing Adolescents. *Alcoholism Treatment Quarterly, 22*(2), 3–19.

Smith, L. S. (2016). Family-based therapy for parent-child reunification. *Journal of Clinical Psychology, 72*(5), 498–512.

Snow, D. A., & Machalek, R. (1984). The sociology of conversion. *Annual Review of Sociology, 10*(1), 167–90.

Spector, S. I. (November 1962). A study of firm and permissive home discipline. *Journal of Educational Sociology, 36*(3), 115–23.

Stahl, P. S. (2014). *Forensic psychology consultation in child custody litigation: A handbook for work product review, case preparation, and expert testimony*. American Bar Association.

Stahl, P. M. (2003). Understanding and evaluating alienation in high-conflict . . . Retrieved from https://parentingafterdivorce.com/devsite22016/wp-content/uploads/2016/02/AlienationArticleForWJFL11.pdf.

Steinberger, C. (2006). Father? What father? Parental alienation and its effect on children: part II. *Family Law Review, 38*(2), 9–14.

Sullivan, M. J. (2019). Reunification family therapy: A treatment manual, by Jan Faust, Hogrefe Publishing (2017). *Family Court Review, 57*(1), 118–20.

Tabachnick, C. (2017, May 11). They were taken from their mom to rebond with their dad. It didn't go well. Retrieved from https://www.washingtonpost.com/lifestyle/magazine/a-divorced-father-his-estranged-kids-and-a-controversial-program-to-bring-them-together/2017/05/09/b50ac6f6-204c-11e7-ad74-3a742a6e93a7_story.html.

Templer, K., Matthewson, M., Haines, J., & Cox, G. (2016). Recommendations for best practice in response to parental alienation: Findings from a systematic review. *Journal of Family Therapy, 39*(1), 103–22.

Thomas, W. I. (1901). The gaming instinct. *American Journal of Sociology, 6*(6), 750–63.

Thomas, W. I. (1961). The four wishes and the definition of the situation. In *Theories of society: Foundations of modern sociological theory* (pp. 741–44). New York, NY: The Free Press.

Thurber, J. (1959, February 21). The last clock: A fable for the time, such as it is, of man. *The New Yorker, 35*(1), 28.

Turkat, I. D. (1994). Child visitation interference in divorce. *Clinical Psychology Review,14*(8), 737–42.

Vesell, H. (October 2017). Parental alienation and reconciliation therapy: Moving toward healthy families. *Pennsylvania Bar Quarterly,* 185–96.

Vestal, A. (2005). Mediation and parental alienation syndrome. *Family Court Review, 37*(4), 487–503.

Walker, A. J. (2006). The extreme consequence of parental alienation syndrome—The Richard Lohstroh case of a child driven to kill his father—Will courts move toward allowing children to use parental alienation syndrome as a defense to the crime of murder of their own parent? *Women's Rights Law Reporter, 27*(3), 153–64.

Wallerstein, J. S. (1983). Children of divorce: The psychological tasks of the child. *American Journal of Orthopsychiatry, 53*(2), 230–43.

Wallerstein, J. S., & Kelly, J. B. (1976). The effects of parental divorce: Experiences of the child in later latency. *American Journal of Orthopsychiatry, 46*, 256–69.

Wallerstein, J. S., & Kelly, J. B. (1980). *Surviving the breakup how children and parents cope with divorce*. New York, NY: Basic Books.

Walsh, T. J. (2019). Religion and Marriage: The Implications for Today's State family Codes. *Family Advocate, 42*(2), 6–10.

Walters, M. G., & Friedlander, S. (2016). When a child rejects a parent: Working with the intractable resist/refuse dynamic. *Family Court Review, 54*(3), 424–45.

Warshak, R. A. (1992). *The custody revolution: The father factor and the motherhood mystique*. New York, NY: Poseidon Press.

Warshak, R. A. (2000). Remarriage as a trigger of parental alienation syndrome. *The American Journal of Family Therapy, 28*(3), 229–41.

Warshak, R. A. (2003). Bringing sense to parental alienation: A look at the disputes and evidence. *Family Law Quarterly, 37*(2), 273–301.

Warshak, R. A. (2009). *Divorce poison: Protecting the parent-child bond from a vindictive ex*. New York, NY: ReganBooks.

Warshak, R. A. (2010). Family bridges: Using insights from social science to reconnect parents and alienated children*. *Family Court Review, 48*(1), 48–80.

Warshak, R. A., & Otis, M. R. (2010). Helping alienated children with family bridges: Practice, research, and the pursuit of "humbition." *Family Court Review, 48*(1), 91–97.

Warshak, R. A. (2010). Alienating audiences from innovation: The perils of polemics, ideology, and innuendo. *Family Court Review, 48*(1), 153–63.

Warshak, R. A. (2015). Ten parental alienation fallacies that compromise decisions in court and in therapy. *Professional Psychology: Research and Practice, 46*(4), 235–49.

Webb, S. G., & Ousky, R. D. (2007). *The collaborative way to divorce: The revolutionary method that results in less stress, lower costs, and happier kids, without going to court*. New York, NY: Plume Book.

Weir, K., & Sturge, C. (2006). Clinical advice to courts on children's contact with their parents following parental separation. *Child and Adolescent Mental Health, 11*(1), 40–46.

Weitzman, J. (2004). Use of the one-way mirror in child custody reunification cases. *Journal of Child Custody, 1*(4), 27–48.

Wulczyn, F. (2004). Family reunification. *The Future of Children, 14*(1), 95–113.

Yinger, J. M. (March 1963). Research implications of a field view of personality. *American Journal of Sociology, 68*(5), 580–92.

Zafran, R. (2010). Children's rights as relational rights: The case of relocation. *American University Journal of Gender, Social Policy & the Law, 18*(2), 163–217.

Ziv, A. (2009). The social function of humor in interpersonal relationships. *Society, 47*(1), 11–18.

Following are some resources that present information on reunification and associated topics:

- *Journal of Divorce*
- *Journal of Marriage & Family*
- *Journal of Clinical Psychology*
- *Journal of Family Psychology*
- *Journal of Family Law Review*
- *Family Advocate*
- *Mediation Quarterly*
- *Journal of Health and Social Behavior*
- *Family Law Quarterly*
- *Family Court Review: An Interdisciplinary Journal*
- *Journal of Family Issues*
- *Journal of Child and Family Studies*

Index